Deliberative Politics

PRACTICAL AND PROFESSIONAL ETHICS SERIES

Published in conjunction with the Association for Practical and Professional Ethics

Series Editor
Alan P. Wertheimer, University of Vermont

Editorial Board
Sissela Bok, Harvard University
Daniel Callahan, The Hastings Center
Deni Elliott, University of Montana
Robert Fullenwider, University of Maryland
Amy Gutmann, Princeton University
Stephen E. Kalish, University of Nebraska–Lincoln
Thomas H. Murray, Case Western Reserve University
Michael Pritchard, Western Michigan University
Henry Shue, Cornell University
David H. Smith, Indiana University
Dennis F. Thompson, Harvard University
Vivian Weil, Illinois Institute of Technology

Brian Schrag, Executive Secretary of the Association for Practical and Professional Ethics

Practical Ethics
A Collection of Addresses and Essays
Henry Sidgwick
With an Introduction by Sissela Bok

Thinking like an Engineer
Studies in the Ethics of a Profession
Michael Davis

Deliberative Politics
Essays on Deliberative Democracy
Edited by Stephen Macedo

Deliberative Politics

Essays on *Democracy and Disagreement*

EDITED BY
STEPHEN MACEDO

New York   Oxford
Oxford University Press
1999

Oxford University Press

Oxford   New York

Athens   Auckland   Bangkok   Bogotá   Buenos Aires   Calcutta
Cape Town   Chennai   Dar es Salaam   Delhi   Florence   Hong Kong   Istanbul
Karachi   Kuala Lumpur   Madrid   Melbourne   Mexico City   Mumbai
Nairobi   Paris   São Paulo   Singapore   Taipei   Tokyo   Toronto   Warsaw

and associated companies in
Berlin   Ibadan

Published by Oxford University Press, Inc.
198 Madison Avenue, New York, New York 10016

Oxford is a registered trademark of Oxford University Press

Library of Congress Cataloging-in-Publication Data
Deliberative politics : essays on democracy and disagreement /
edited by Stephen Macedo.
p. cm.—(Practical and professional ethics series)
Includes bibliographical references.
ISBN 0-19-513191-6; ISBN 0-19-513199-1 (pbk.)
1. Democracy.   2. Representative government and representation.
3. Compromise (Ethics)   4. Political ethics.   5. Forums (Discussion
and debate)   I. Macedo, Stephen, 1957– .   II. Series.
JC423.D4344   1999
321.8—DC21   98-50040

1 3 5 7 9 8 6 4 2

Printed in the United States of America
on acid-free paper

Preface

*T*his collection was not difficult to assemble. Within months of its publication, Amy Gutmann and Dennis Thompson's *Democracy and Disagreement* received a most unusual level of scholarly attention.

Symposia on the book were organized at a number of scholarly meetings, including the annual conventions of the American Political Science Association, the Association for Practical and Professional Ethics, and the Pacific Division of the American Philosophical Association. An impressive roster of leading scholars in political theory and ethics confronted the arguments of *Democracy and Disagreement.* Gutmann and Thompson benefited from the questions and comments of scholars at seminars and symposia at many Universities, including the Universities of Capetown, Rome, and Siena, U.C.L.A., the University of Chicago, the University of Virginia, the College of William and Mary, and Rice University.

The idea of a volume of critical essays on the themes of *Democracy and Disagreement* suggested itself readily, and this volume was soon brought to fruition. Most of the essays collected here originated as critical responses at the professional meetings mentioned above. Others originated in the many review essays or scholarly articles that have addressed *Democracy and Disagreement.* This volume could easily have been much longer.

My thanks to series editor Alan Wertheimer for his receptivity to the idea for this volume and for support along the way. Thanks also to Peter Ohlin and Catherine A. Carlin of Oxford University Press for their genuine cooperativeness and expedition. I am also grateful to our contributors for allowing me to collect these essays, and for their patience. And thanks most of all to Amy Gutmann and Dennis Thompson, for inspiring so impressive an array of scholars to think deeply and productively about central problems of modern democratic life. I hope that this volume is itself a contribution to the democratic deliberation that Gutmann and Thompson have so ably championed and advanced.

Contents

PART II: EXPANDING THE LIMITS OF DELIBERATIVE DEMOCRACY

PART III: REPLY TO THE CRITICS

Contributors

Daniel A. Bell is associate professor, Department of Philosophy, University of Hong Kong. He is the author, most recently, of *East Meets West: Human Rights and Democracy in East Asia.*

Norman Daniels is Goldthwaite Professor, Department of Philosophy, and Professor of Medical Ethics, Department of Community Medicine, at Tufts University. He is the author most recently of *Justice and Justification: Reflective Equilibrium in Theory and Practice.*

Stanley Fish is Dean of the College of Liberal Arts and Sciences at the University of Illinois at Chicago. He is the author of the forthcoming *How Milton Works.*

William A. Galston is Professor, School of Public Affairs, University of Maryland, and Director of the University's Institute for Philosophy and Public Policy. He is the author of *Liberal Purposes.*

Robert P. George is Professor of Politics at Princeton University and a former Presidential Appointee to the United States Commission on Civil Rights. He is author of *In Defense of Natural Law.*

Amy Gutmann is the Laurance S. Rockefeller University Professor of Politics and the founding Director of the University Center for Human Values at Princeton University. She is author, most recently, of a new edition of *Democratic Education* and co-author, with Dennis Thompson, of *Democracy and Disagreement*.

Russell Hardin is Professor of Politics at New York University. He is the author of *One for All: The Logic of Group Conflict* and *Liberalism, Constitutionalism, and Democracy*.

Jack Knight is Professor of Political Science and Resident Fellow of the Committee on Social Thought and Analysis at Washington University in St. Louis. His works include *Institutions and Social Conflict*.

Stephen Macedo is the Laurance S. Rockefeller Professor of Politics and the University Center for Human Values at Princeton University. He is the author most recently of *Diversity and Distrust: Civic Education in a Multicultural Democracy*.

Jane Mansbridge is the Charles F. Adams Professor of Political Leadership and Democratic Values at the John F. Kennedy School of Government, Harvard University. She is the author of *Beyond Adversary Democracy*.

Frederick Schauer is Academic Dean and Frank Stanton Professor of the First Amendment at the John F. Kennedy School of Government, Harvard University. He is the author of *Playing By the Rules: A Philosophical Examination of Rule-Based Decisionmaking in Law and in Life* and *The Philosophy of Law*.

Ian Shapiro is Professor of Political Science at Yale. He is author, most recently, of *Democratic Justice*.

William H. Simon is Kenneth and Harle Montgomery Professor of Public Interest Law at Stanford University. He is the author of *The Practice of Justice: A Theory of Lawyers' Ethics*.

Cass R. Sunstein is the Karl N. Llewelyn Distinguished Service Professor of Jurisprudence, Law School and Department of Political Science, University of Chicago. He is the author, most recently, of *One Case At a Time: Judicial Minimalism on the Supreme Court*.

Dennis F. Thompson is the Alfred North Whitehead Professor of Political Philosophy at Harvard University, with appointments in the Department of Government and the Kennedy School of Government. He is also the founding Director of the University's Program in Ethics and the Professions. His most recent book is *Democracy and Disagreement*, co-authored with Amy Gutmann.

Michael Walzer is Professor of Social Science at the Institute for Advanced Study in Princeton, New Jersey. He is the author most recently of *On Toleration*.

Alan Wertheimer is the John G. McCullough Professor of Political Science at the University of Vermont. He is the author of *Coercion* and *Exploitation*.

Iris Marion Young is Professor of Public and International Affairs at the University of Pittsburgh, where she is also affiliated with the departments of Philosophy, Political Science, and Women's Studies. She is author and editor of several books, including the award-winning *Justice and the Politics of Difference*. Her most recent book is *Intersecting Voices: Dilemmas of Gender, Political Philosophy and Policy*.

Deliberative Politics

Introduction

STEPHEN MACEDO

*T*hat we are in the midst of a renewal of interest in democratic principles and practices seems hard to deny. In the world's older democracies no less than the newer ones, the banner of deliberative democracy has attracted increasing numbers of supporters.

In part at least, this revival often seems to be motivated by profound currents of dissatisfaction with the dominant school of liberal political thought. Critics from Right and Left charge that an overreliance on individual rights means that too many of the most significant moral issues are withdrawn from the political agenda. When moral controversies such as those over abortion, gay rights, affirmative action, and assisted suicide are routinely decided by the courts, critics charge that it is no wonder that the office of citizenship comes to seem of marginal importance. Citizens deprived of the opportunity and the responsibility to grapple with the most significant moral questions lose a vital part of the training in responsibility and self-control that citizenship should bring. When the process of citizen negotiation and consensus-building is bypassed, moral decisions may lack political balance and legitimacy.[1]

There are other ways in which the turn toward deliberative democracy is often a turn against liberalism. Deliberative democrats often complain that the liberal emphasis on the authority of certain kinds of reasons—or "public reason"—restricts the agenda of public discussion, defines in advance what can

3

count as legitimate political reasons, and neglects the distinctive viewpoints of groups at the margins of the dominant culture.[2] Religious people and their advocates increasingly add their voices to this critical chorus, charging that liberalism rests on the authority of a secular, scientific rationality that discounts the concerns of religious people and unfairly silences the religious voice in our politics.[3] Deliberative democratic ideals respond to many of these disparate sources of complaint by arguing for a more wide-open and inclusive model of democratic discourse.

As with other large political categories, such as "liberalism" and "identity politics," the phrase "deliberative democracy" does not signify a creed with a simple set of core claims. Those who seek to advance the cause of democratic deliberation do not altogether agree about what the democratic ideal is or how it should be fostered. So the question remains: Why deliberative democracy? What are the distinctive political aspirations, the defining ideals, of a deliberative democratic approach to politics?

To the extent that deliberative democracy is about widening the agenda of public discussion beyond what liberalism allows, just how wide and open-ended should deliberation be? Is it ever proper to impose prior limits on democratic deliberation, in the form, say, of a Bill of Rights and judicial review? Should we limit permissible democratic outcomes based on prior and independent commitments to basic individual rights and other principles of justice? Are there any limits at all on the sorts of reasons that are legitimate reasons for determining how the coercive powers of the modern state will be deployed?

Is popular deliberation about politics simply an end in itself, or does it lead to good political outcomes? If popular reflection on moral questions is valued as an end in itself by deliberative democrats, is this direct engagement with moral reflection purchased at the cost of other political goods, such as the rule of expertise, and perhaps political stability?

Is deliberative democracy, as some assert, utopian? Is it simply too far removed from politics as we know it, and from the characteristics of citizens as we can realistically expect them to be? Should deliberative democracy be rejected as a political aspiration on account of its disconnection from the real politics of interests, bargaining, and power?

Is deliberative democracy, finally, best conceived of, as it usually is, as an alternative to the liberalism of John Rawls, Ronald Dworkin, and others, or has this oppositional stance with respect to liberalism misled much prior discussion of deliberative democratic politics?

All of these questions and more are addressed in the essays that follow. The purpose of this collection of essays is not, however, to attempt a comprehensive survey of the various versions of deliberative democracy. A rich sampling of the central debates over democratic theory is on display here. This collection has an organizing focus, however: to assess the strengths and weaknesses of the distinctive approach to deliberative democracy offered by Amy Gutmann and Dennis Thompson in *Democracy and Disagreement*.[4]

The essays that follow are not book reviews: They are substantial and original contributions to political theory that probe the value and limits of deliberative democracy as such. The essays pick up on or play off of some aspect of Gutmann and Thompson's approach, but many of the essays articulate and defend alternative political visions. Prior familiarity with the argument of *Democracy and Disagreement* is not a prerequisite, as this introduction will present the main contours of Gutmann and Thompson's arguments. Students of deliberative democracy may start here. If they do, we hope that they will go on to *Democracy and Disagreement* armed with an understanding of the basic design of Gutmann and Thompson's edifice, along with a sense of the landscape in which it is situated.

Those who have contributed to this volume are divided over many things, but all agree that the revival of interest in deliberative democracy is worthy of sustained critical attention. All of our contributors also agree that *Democracy and Disagreement* represents a distinctive and important contribution to political theory, a contribution that allows our contributors to critically probe the leading disagreements over the defensibility of deliberative democracy.

At the core of deliberative democracy as Gutmann and Thompson portray it is a conviction that much of our politics is made up of a broad swath of moral conflicts that should not be usurped by the courts but that are also not properly resolved by mere interest group bargaining. The moral conflicts of what Gutmann and Thompson call "middle democracy" include debates over health policy and welfare reform, affirmative action and preferential treatment, environmental protection, surrogate motherhood, and doctor-assisted suicide. These moral conflicts call upon citizens themselves to act as reason givers and reason demanders: Our institutions and practices should be arranged so as to encourage citizens to grapple with these moral conflicts, to seek reasons that can be accepted by their fellow citizens who will be bound by political action.

Gutmann and Thompson share some of the concerns of other deliberative democrats: They argue, for example, that many liberals are too preoccupied with the most fundamental issues of basic rights and principles of justice, at the expense of the moral disagreements that are and should remain at the center of ongoing political debate. In fact, however, *Democracy and Disagreement* represents not simply a democratic alternative to liberalism, but a deliberative alternative to those versions of democratic theory that flatten the landscape of politics into a low contest among interests and preferences. Gutmann and Thompson set out to counterbalance not only liberal constitutionalism's preoccupation with the courts but also those democratic theorists who, in the name of a hard-headed, "realistic" science of democratic politics, give short shrift to the politics of serious moral deliberation.

Gutmann and Thompson usefully distinguish between constitutionalism and proceduralism as two inadequate approaches to the problem of moral disagreement in politics.

Constitutionalists are too apt to withdraw moral disagreements from ordinary politics and assign them to elite institutions above the political fray, such as the courts. The judicial blunderbuss of rights that trump the results of democratic deliberations is not to be wholly discarded, but we need to recognize that it is often not the best way of coming to grips with moral conflicts in politics, especially when the conflict is among genuinely moral and not unreasonable positions. Gutmann and Thompson allow that the courts may rightly step in when a political majority acts on the basis of altogether unreasonable considerations, such as sheer racism, but they insist that such cases are rarer than liberals typically think. When parties to a political conflict are acting on the basis of not unreasonable moral positions, then the courts should typically exercise restraint and allow democratic deliberation to go forward.

The error of constitutionalists is an excessive readiness to shift serious moral argument out of politics and into judicial fora. The error of proceduralists, on the other hand, is to discount the very possibility of serious democratic deliberation on moral controversies. Proceduralists seek to domesticate moral disagreement by getting citizens to agree to some basic rules of the political game. Once the rules are agreed to, politics can be allowed to operate as a realm of bargaining over policy preferences and interests. Democratic procedures and institutions help structure political bargaining so that the same groups do not win all the time and so that broader coalitions of interests tend to win out over narrower ones; otherwise, the process should remain neutral about value choices.

Proceduralism is internally problematic, Gutmann and Thompson note, for different procedures in fact embody substantive values. Using lotteries or waiting lists to decide who will benefit from the scarce supply of organ transplants may give everyone an equal shot, but those procedures prevent us from favoring a host of other values, such as the greater long-term benefits of giving transplants to the young or to those who may do more for society. Ordinary people know perfectly well that procedures embody substantive values and that it is not possible to altogether separate debates over procedures from debates over outcomes.

The core conviction of Gutmann and Thompson's version of deliberative democracy is the belief that our shared political life would go better if we encouraged a wider discussion of moral values by citizens and their representatives. Moral disagreement in politics is to be expected, even under the best conditions. For even when people are motivated by a desire to find fair terms of social cooperation (and of course they often have other motives), disagreement will still result from the fact that different people hold incompatible values. In addition, people have incomplete understandings of many vexing issues, as well as of the consequences of different courses of action (18). Serious moral disagreement is with us to stay. Nevertheless, Gutmann and Thompson argue, even when agreement is not reached, deliberation contributes to the health of a democratic society.

At the core of Gutmann and Thompson's version of deliberative democracy is reciprocity: "the capacity to seek fair terms of cooperation for its own sake." Gutmann and Thompson know that certain expectations properly follow from the fact that "the results of democratic deliberation are mutually binding." The most important implication is that "citizens should aspire to a kind of political reasoning that is mutually justifiable" (52–53). Each of us has a right to expect that others will make their claims "on terms that I can accept in principle"; in return "I make my claims on terms that you can accept in principle" (55).

Deliberative democrats often object to the constraints that liberals seem to impose on the kinds of reasons that are appropriate for citizens and public officials who are shaping fundamental principles of justice. Gutmann and Thompson, likewise, eschew much of the apparatus that Rawls uses to define what he calls "public reason." Nevertheless, Gutmann and Thompson allow that "in deliberative democracy the primary job of reciprocity is to regulate public reason, the terms in which citizens justify to one another their claims regarding all other goods" (55). When deliberating about the merits of a "middle democratic" controversy such as universal health care, citizens should appeal to their own best understanding of mutually recognized moral principles such as the importance of basic opportunity for all citizens.

In sum, Gutmann and Thompson may relax and reformulate, but they do not reject, the notion that public reason has a certain form: "A deliberative perspective does not address people who reject the aim of finding fair terms for social cooperation; it cannot reach those who refuse to press their public claims in terms accessible to their fellow citizens" (55). Citizens, say Gutmann and Thompson, "must reason beyond their narrow self-interest" and consider "what can be justified to people who reasonably disagree with them" (2, and see 255).[5] It is one of the signal achievements of Gutmann and Thompson's book that they help point the way beyond the stale suggestion that deliberative democracy is best conceived of as a radical alternative to liberalism.

Reciprocity has an empirical dimension as well as a moral one. When we rely on empirical evidence, say Gutmann and Thompson, we should honor "relatively reliable methods of inquiry" and eschew implausible assertions. Here again, the point is to try and ensure that public discussions are carried on in terms that are mutually acceptable. It is illegitimate to appeal to "*any* authority whose conclusions are impervious, in principle as well as practice, to the standards of logical consistency or to reliable methods of inquiry that themselves should be mutually acceptable." Gutmann and Thompson importantly insist that the point is not to exclude appeals to religious authority per se but to exclude appeals to *any* authority impervious to critical assessment from a variety of reasonable points of view. Here again the aim of deliberative reciprocity is continuous with liberal public reason: Public power belongs to us all and is exercised over us all, and we should exercise it together based on reasons and arguments we can share in spite of our differences. Deliberative reciprocity promotes the authority of reasons we can share in public as fellow citizens.

Some religious people may reply to all this that their religious reasons are readily accessible to anyone who leads a good life as defined by their religion. Gutmann and Thompson insist that this will not do, for "any claim fails to respect reciprocity if it imposes a requirement on other citizens to adopt one's sectarian way of life as a condition of gaining access to the moral understanding that is essential to judging the validity of one's moral claims." According to deliberative reciprocity, citizens honor a basic duty of civility to one another when they accept the fact of reasonable pluralism and try to discern principles that can be assessed and accepted by individuals who are committed to a wide range of different ways of life (56–57). Citizens ignore this duty of civility when they cast aside the concern with mutually acceptable reasons and seek to have their own comprehensive morality enshrined into law, whether or not it is plausible to think that others can accept this.

In their elaboration of the value of reciprocity, Gutmann and Thompson seem to me to capture nicely the core aspirations of public reasonableness. They extend public reason into the realm of middle democracy. The reciprocity they seek is a reasoned, deliberative reciprocity. Deliberative reciprocity helps bring public reason firmly within the ambit of ordinary citizens. In particular, Gutmann and Thompson provide a nuanced discussion of how principled conflicts not properly resolvable by the courts should be discussed and negotiated democratically so as to honor our shared commitment to reasoned deliberation. Rather than rejecting public reason, as some deliberative democrats seem to want to do, Gutmann and Thompson help make it clear that the aspiration to mutually accessible reasons is a worthy part of democratic politics: the keystone of a democratic community of principle.

Is deliberative democracy utopian? It is worth emphasizing that the moral motivation that Gutmann and Thompson count on lies between altruism, on the one side, and narrow self-interest, on the other: It is a willingness to do your fair share (and to try and discern what your fair share is) in cooperative schemes, including the sovereign political cooperative scheme, so long as others will do the same.

As mentioned above, the widespread good-faith commitment to deliberative reciprocity does not mean that moral agreements will necessarily be found on many issues. When agreement is not forthcoming, deliberative democracy argues for the importance of moral accommodation to maintain conditions of mutual respect. Mutual respect goes beyond toleration, for it insists on the value of keeping open the channels of continued interaction and conversation with those with whom one disagrees, in the hope of eventually arriving at improved understandings and closer agreement (79–80).

Moral accommodation requires no sacrifice of integrity. In the face of disagreement, citizens should "affirm the moral status of their own political positions" (81). Personal integrity is not enough from a civic standpoint, however, for citizens should also practice what Gutmann and Thompson call civic magnanimity: They should acknowledge the moral standing of reasonable views opposed to their own and demonstrate their desire to find a mutually acceptable position that can be accepted by all. To this end, citizens should practice an "economy of moral disagreement," seeking rationales for their own positions that minimize the rejection of the positions they oppose (83–85). In these ways, good citizens respond to serious moral disagreement by fostering conditions of mutual respect within which deliberation can continue.

Reciprocity is the moral core of deliberative democracy for Gutmann and Thompson, but it is complemented by principles of publicity and accountability. "The reasons that officials and citizens give to justify political actions, and the information necessary to assess those reasons, should be public" (95) Of course, sometimes secrecy is necessary for the attainment of some important public goal, and public officials as well as our fellow citizens have a right to a sphere of privacy. In such cases, the reasons for keeping some things secret and private should themselves be publicly announced. In addition, Gutmann and Thompson provide principles of accountability that take into account the claims of electoral constituents, as well as what they call "moral constituents" (chap. 4).

Why should citizens and public officials take the trouble to engage in deliberative democratic argument? What will deliberative democracy do for us? Gutmann and Thompson identify four principal benefits.

First of all, deliberative democracy should help promote the *legitimacy* of collective decisions. Under the best foreseeable conditions, serious moral disagreements are bound to remain, and given the fact of scarce resources, some people will not get what they want or even what they believe they deserve on the basis of justice. The assurance that serious moral claims have at least been fairly considered should do more than a process of interest group bargaining to reconcile those who lose out to the legitimacy of the collective decision.

A fair process is not, however, simply a way of promoting feelings of legitimacy and democratic goodwill, nor is legitimacy simply an end in itself. A deliberative democratic process can help promote better outcomes over the course of time. As Gutmann and Thompson note, the conviction that organ transplants are being distributed fairly may well generate more organs for transplantation in the future.

A second purpose of deliberation is to *encourage public-spirited perspectives* on public issues. Moral deliberation introduces all citizens to considerations of the common good. Public talk does not, of course, necessarily lead to genuine public spiritedness; the task remains to design deliberative processes that favor broader over narrower interests, that are inclusive with respect to different groups in society, and that put a premium on moral deliberation rather than power politics and bargaining. Well-designed institutions can help favor the right sorts of attitudes, but there is no substitute, Gutmann and Thompson emphasize, for citizens with the character and the will to behave in accordance with their moral duties.

The third purpose of deliberation is to *promote mutually respectful decision-making.* Given that different moral values are often incompatible, it will be impossible to reconcile many moral conflicts beyond a reasonable doubt. The practice of deliberation, civility, and an economy of moral disagreement should help citizens and public officials recognize the merit in their opponents' claims.

Finally, the practice of deliberation should help democracies *correct the mistakes of the past.* Given that our understanding of complex issues of public policy are bound to be incomplete, it is crucial that the channels of critical scrutiny and reexamination be kept open. We are bound to learn more as time goes on and we see the consequences of implemented policies. Maintaining conditions of mutual respect and civility should make it easier to acknowledge mistakes and should increase our willingness to correct them.

Such is the ideal, in thumbnail sketch, of deliberative democracy as presented in *Democracy and Disagreement.* Of course, much of Gutmann and Thompson's book is taken up with applications and illustrations designed to show how deliberative democracy should work, and sometimes has worked, in actual practice. Many of these practical controversies—over abortion, and welfare and health care reform, and surrogate motherhood—are discussed in the essays below.

The critical essays that follow fall, roughly speaking, into two parts. The first group thinks that Gutmann and Thompson put too much emphasis on the deliberative components of democratic politics. The essayists in Part II allow that deliberation is an appropriate response to the enduring fact of moral conflict. Some in this group argue, however, that Gutmann and Thompson's political conception needs to be revised, while others argue that there should be even more room for deliberation than Gutmann and Thompson provide.

Several of our essayists in Part I question whether Gutmann and Thompson have put too much emphasis on deliberation and so perhaps present an overly idealized picture of democratic politics. Frederick Schauer wonders what the consequences are of combining an idealized deliberative procedure, such as that sketched by Gutmann and Thompson, with the very nonidealized conditions that prevail in politics as we know it. Placing too much emphasis on "talk-based decision procedures" may, paradoxically, undermine the deliberation that Gutmann and Thompson seek, given the tenor of so much actual political talk (such as that on talk radio and television talk shows). Ian Shapiro argues, on the other hand, that Gutmann and Thompson do not pay sufficient attention to the ways that moral disagreements are shaped by differences of interest and power: Debates over issues such as health care reform are all too easily derailed and dominated by special interests who fund misleading public relations campaigns.

Several of our essayists argue that the agenda of deliberative democratic politics is too broad and that it leaves too little space for the private beliefs of parents and communities, especially religious communities, in tension with deliberative aspirations. William A. Galston suggests that the deliberative ideal of Gutmann and Thompson verges on a "republicanism that diminishes the claims of liberty" and a "rationalism that denies the public claims of faith." William H. Simon charges that deliberative democrats such as Gutmann and Thompson promote a style of politics that denies the legitimacy of alternative political styles that may be especially important to marginalized groups and identity politics. Political activity, according to Simon, offers opportunities for groups "to define and constitute themselves through the assertion of their claims." Putting too much emphasis on the search for mutually acceptable reasons and the practice of civility may actually undermine some groups' political energy.

Michael Walzer argues that deliberative democracy leaves too little room for the nondeliberative political activities—educating, organizing, mobilizing, demonstrating, lobbying, campaigning, fund-raising, and ruling; these, and not deliberation, are at the center of democratic politics. Placing too much emphasis on deliberation may actually bespeak an antipolitical bias, Walzer asserts. Daniel A. Bell also questions whether "open and fair moral deliberation" should always have the centrality to democratic politics that Gutmann and Thompson claim for it. Bell moves in quite a different direction from Walzer, however, for Bell attempts to muster support for the notion that deliberation is an elite activity, for which specialized elite institutions should be contrived. Of course, the appeal and justifiability of elite institutions is liable to vary across societies, Bell notes: Elite deliberative institutions may have special appeal within the Confucian traditions of East Asia, and this may help indicate that there are cultural limits to particular deliberative schemes.

Stanley Fish goes much further in arguing for the limits of deliberative democracy. There is no such thing, for Fish, as a deliberative point of view that all parties can accept as reasonable or fair. Gutmann and Thompson's version of deliberative democracy is just one more variation, for Fish, of the wider liberal tendency to try and seize a moral high ground defined by such values as reasonableness or reciprocity, objectivity, impartiality, or fairness. All of these terms represent devices of exclusion: They are among the rhetorical tricks used to bolster one's preferred outcomes and to disparage the preferences of others.

Russell Hardin, in concluding the first section, argues that Gutmann and Thompson do not adequately distinguish between questions of institutional design and questions of policy assessment. We should not assess the working of institutions according to the same standards or with the same directness that we assess policies. Democratic institutions should be assessed based on their instrumental usefulness, not their intrinsic qualities.

Our second group of essays concede that deliberation is an appropriate response to the enduring fact of moral conflict, but they suggest that Gutmann and Thompson's version of deliberation needs to be reformulated or that deliberation should be taken further.

Cass Sunstein elaborates on his own proposal for the centrality of what he calls "incompletely theorized agreements." He offers some interesting suggestions about how we might extend Gutmann and Thompson's notion of an "economy of disagreement." Iris Marion Young, on the other hand, argues that inclusion needs to be taken more seriously than Gutmann and Thompson allow. The legitimacy of democratic decisions would be more adequately secured if a principle of inclusion were explicitly announced.

Jack Knight worries that Gutmann and Thompson may not be adequately distinguishing between the procedural and substantive elements of democratic theory. Unless we keep these elements distinct, Knight argues, it will be impossible to say for sure which elements have priority: whether basic liberties constrain democratic procedures, for example, or whether a substantive guarantee of equality is a precondition of procedural legitimacy.

Alan Wertheimer and Robert George pose interesting questions about the extent to which it is proper to respect persons or positions that one views as wrong. Wertheimer and George emphasize that if a moral position is to be worthy of respect as a matter of principle, it must be not only moral but also plausible. Wertheimer in particular worries that Gutmann and Thompson are in danger of according too much respect to the pro-life position in the abortion debate. George argues just the opposite: Gutmann and Thompson accord too much respect to the pro-choice position. Both of these essays have provocative things to say about the sorts of mutual respect that are appropriate in the face of deep disagreements over such issues as abortion, surrogate motherhood, and slavery.

Building on the renewal of interest among political theorists in "civil society" institutions, our final two essays argue for a broadening of democratic conversation into nonpublic and informal settings. Norman Daniels argues for an extension of deliberative principles into the important sphere of managed care organizations and the decisions that such organizations make regarding coverage for new technologies.

Jane Mansbridge brings our essays full circle, ending where Schauer began, with the question of the role of "everyday talk" in a deliberative democratic theory. Mansbridge argues that a fuller account of "the deliberative system" would include the everyday talk about serious moral issues outside of formal political institutions. Everyday conversations about what it means to be a "male chauvinist," for example, help shape social meanings and social norms, which are repositories of important public moral judgments. Conversation that issues in lawmaking or policy change is not the only, and may not even be the most important, locus of democratic deliberation.

In their spirited reply, Gutmann and Thompson clarify and deepen their deliberative democratic vision. They flesh out the ways in which their version of deliberative democracy is not intended as a substitute for constitutionalist and proceduralist values. Deliberative democracy should govern across the important swath of "middle democratic" controversies, but not every moral controversy should be subject to democratic deliberation. Bargaining is sometimes appropriate. Moreover, to argue for more democratic deliberation is not necessarily to argue against judicial deliberation. Unlike most deliberative democrats, Gutmann and Thompson do not posit a zero-sum game in which greater deliberation by courts necessarily undercuts deliberation by the people. It is time, according to Gutmann and Thompson, for the proponents of public moral argument to take more seriously the deliberative capacities of citizens and their elected officials, but doing so does not require that we disparage the uses of constitutional politics and judicial review. It is equally time, they assert, for students of democratic politics to give the people and their representatives credit for being able to do more than blindly pursue interests and preferences without regard for the reasonableness or morality of their aims.

Like *Democracy and Disagreement* itself, this volume poses fundamental challenges to both "liberals" and "democrats": to those adherents of justice who regard democracy with hostile suspicion and to those who defend popular self-government by disparaging the concern with justice and rights. To the moralistic critics of popular self-rule, Gutmann and Thompson insist that the best way to strengthen the moral voice in our politics is to place more confidence in the moral capacities of the people and their representatives. To those who would raise the banner of "deliberative democracy" against a politics of justice and public reason, Gutmann and Thompson insist that the best way to elevate and invigorate democratic politics is by challenging democracy to live up to a genuine public reasonableness of its own.

Much of modern political theory grows out of the tension between democratic and liberal political ideals. Gutmann and Thompson's *Democracy and Disagreement* does more than any other recent contribution to political theory to bridge the gap between democratic and liberal aspirations. But can this be done, and, if so, do Gutmann and Thompson succeed? The essays that follow shed important light on the question of whether the principles of liberalism and democracy are complementary, at base, rather than opposed.

Notes

1. Criticisms such as these have long been leveled at the practice of judicial review in America. See James Bradley Thayer, "The Origins and Scope of the American Doctrine of Constitutional Law," in Thayer, *Legal Essays* (Boston: Boston Book Co., 1908), pp. 7–12; the opinions of Justice Felix Frankfurter, including his dissenting opinion in *West Virginia State Board of Education v. Barnette*, 319 U.S. 624 (1943); Alexander Bickel, *The Least Dangerous Branch: The Supreme Court at the Bar of Politics* (New Haven: Yale University Press, 1986); John Hart Ely, *Democracy and Distrust* (Cambridge: Harvard University Press, 1980).

2. Seyla Benhabib argues that liberals conceive of public reason "not as a process of reasoning among citizens but as a regulative principle imposing limits upon how individuals, institutions, and agencies ought to reason about public matters": "Deliberative Rationality and Models of Democratic Legitimacy," *Constellations: An International Journal of Critical and Democratic Theory* 1, no. 1 (April 1994): 26–52. See also Michael Sandel's review of *Political Liberalism, Harvard Law Review* 107 (May 1994): 1765–94, esp. 1789–94.

3. See for example, Stephen L. Carter, *Culture of Disbelief: How American Law and Politics Trivialize Religious Devotion* (New York: Basic, 1993).

4. Gutmann and Thompson, *Democracy and Disagreement* (Cambridge: Bellnap Press of Harvard University Press, 1996). Page references to this book are given in parentheses in the text.

5. Compare John Rawls's discussion of the "burdens of judgment" and his broader account of reasonableness, which seem to me quite similar in spirit to the parallel ideas of Gutmann and Thompson: *Political Liberalism* (New York: Columbia University Press, 1993), 56–57.

PART I

*Challenging the Value of
Deliberative Democracy*

1

Talking as a Decision Procedure

FREDERICK SCHAUER

*I*t is a source of continuing astonishment for me that such a small percentage of even my soundest opinions command widespread assent. Indeed, my only source of solace in this is the knowledge that most others experience life in similar ways and thus must confront daily the obtuseness of their fellow citizens. For many of us, the resistance of other members of the community to even our strongest arguments is a continuing and puzzling frustration.

Behind my irony is a serious empirical claim. As we experience communal life, we experience having beliefs with varying amounts of strength. My beliefs in the falsity of astrology, for example, and in the truth of the propositions that the Holocaust occurred and that child molestation is morally wrong are stronger than my beliefs that psychoanalysis is frequently effective, that a large meteor crash caused the extinction of the dinosaurs, and that mandatory retirement ages are morally suspect. Yet as we experience having beliefs of fact and value with differing degrees of firmness, we also experience a world in which there is more or less disagreement within the political community. In the contemporary United States, for example, the degree of disagreement about welfare policy, race relations, and health care is greater than the degree of disagreement about the desirability of public nudity, the undesirability of top marginal tax rates in excess of 80 percent, and the wisdom of ending fluoridation of the water supply. The falsifiable empirical claim, therefore, is that the strength of belief for an individual citizen, or the aggregate strength of belief for the citizenry, is predictive of the extent of disagreement among that population.

Although it would be nice if this hypothesis—that strength of belief is negatively correlated with the extent of disagreement—were correct, much around us, sadly, suggests just the opposite. Rather, the political world we inhabit forces us to consider the possibility that serious disagreement even as to matters that the disagreers believe beyond disagreement is an endemic feature of modern political life. Confronting the fact of disagreement has not traditionally been high on the agenda of political theory, which all too often has assumed away the problem of disagreement by implicitly treating the disagreers as irrelevant. At times theorists appear to have assumed either that the disagreers would be swayed by good theory into relinquishing their recalcitrance or that the extent of disagreement, compared to the degree of agreement, was minor and friendly, not unlike a competition between two bowling teams or a 1950s election-night party in which Democrats and Republicans gathered together to watch the returns, secure in the knowledge that their amiable disagreements were far less important than their rock-solid agreement about the strength of the system. Under either assumption, the problem of political and moral disagreement was not central to the agenda of political theory.

In recent years, however, the agenda of political theory has shifted, and disagreement itself has become an important topic and an important datum. John Rawls's *Political Liberalism*[1] was a noteworthy stepping stone on the path to taking the fact of disagreement as being as important a topic for political theory as equality, liberty, authority, and representation, and in *Democracy and Disagreement*[2] Amy Gutmann and Dennis Thompson have provided us with a superb example of serious and normative philosophical confrontation with the fact of disagreement in contemporary political life.

Gutmann and Thompson rely heavily on several detailed examples, and these examples illustrate the type of disagreements they believe, properly, that contemporary political life and contemporary political theory cannot avoid. In delving deeply into the problems of abortion, affirmative action, environmental risk, surrogate motherhood, organ transplants and the allocation of scarce health care resources, and work requirements for welfare recipients,[3] Gutmann and Thompson demonstrate not only that deep disagreement is all around us but also that on many important issues of current policy the nature of the disagreement is *moral* to the core. Although we may disagree about some of the empirical and policy efficiency dimensions of each of these debates, even total agreement about the nonmoral facts and implications would leave much deep moral disagreement remaining and thus leave the resolution of the issue dependent on some method of dealing with the fact of moral disagreement.

One of the curious things about this book is that perhaps its most outstanding feature is not the one that Gutmann and Thompson intended. Although Gutmann and Thompson set out to write about *public* deliberation as a method of navigating the shoals of public disagreement, they are at their most outstanding in demonstrating their *own* deliberation about these problems. Setting out background conditions for the deliberation—reciprocity, publicity, and accountability—as well as constraints on acceptable solutions—basic liberty, basic opportunity, and fair opportunity—Gutmann and Thompson provide a wonderful model of how people should go about thinking about these thorniest of political and moral issues. Without fail they make things hard for their own views, they assume the least rather than the most favorable answer to unknown facts, they confront the best arguments on both sides, they acknowledge the importance of compromise, they recognize contested empirical claims for what they are, they avoid inflammatory or question-begging rhetoric, they respect those with whom they disagree, and they come up with solutions that seem like those that a large number of similarly open-minded and cooperative citizens could accept as a reasonable outcome. Without exception, Gutmann and Thompson avoid the why-I'm-so-right-and-you're-so-wrong approach that dominates not only contemporary moral and political public debate, but contemporary academic moral and political theory as well. Instead, they negotiate with great skill the difficult task of simultaneously recognizing the strengths in seemingly opposed arguments and recognizing the importance of making their arguments acceptable and respectful to those who might disagree with their conclusions.

Despite the tone of many of their discussions of the cases, however, *Democracy and Disagreement* is not primarily a book about substantive policy, nor is it primarily a book devoted to offering morally acceptable outcomes to morally difficult public policy issues. Rather, it is a book about decision *procedure*—about how a democracy should make its decisions on pressing policy questions that are pervaded by moral and political disagreement. Indeed, although a plausible inference for others reading this book might be that a pretty good decision procedure would be for society to let Gutmann and Thompson make the decisions, that, unsurprisingly, is not the procedure they advocate. Rather, they advocate *public deliberation* as the decision procedure of choice, and their own analyses are largely exemplars or ideal types of how such a public deliberation would proceed.

Because so much has been written about deliberation in recent years,[4] it is worthwhile to note the features that distinguish Gutmann and Thompson's approach. For one thing, unlike Habermas and his followers, Gutmann and

Thompson make no epistemological claims for or about deliberation. The wisdom of public policy and the truth of propositions about politics and morality are, for them, logically antecedent to deliberation. Consequently, truth is not defined by the deliberation (although policy might be produced by it), making it possible to understand how it is that participants *in* a deliberation can attempt to argue that other participants are mistaken, and also making it possible for anyone to argue that a deliberation has produced an erroneous conclusion.[5]

Gutmann and Thompson not only avoid making deliberation desirable by definition; they also acknowledge the deficiencies of many real-world public deliberations. They do not assume away the problem of deliberative deficiencies or ignore the character of the deliberations we see on a daily basis in the mass media (and in faculty meetings) but instead make a normative argument for a particular form of deliberation, one that is constrained not only by the substantive requirements of basic liberty, basic opportunity, and fair opportunity but also by the procedural mandates of publicity, reciprocity, and accountability. A public deliberation that fails any of these requirements, as so many real-world deliberations do, does not for them count as the kind of deliberation that *Democracy and Disagreement* aims to promote. "Deliberation" is thus for Gutmann and Thompson a normatively thick term, and to refer to collective talk as deliberation is, in part, to praise it.

If deliberation is not constitutive of moral or political truth, however, and if many real-world instances of public collective talk do not qualify as "legitimate" public deliberations, then the nature of Gutmann and Thompson's claims becomes more elusive. In order to see this, it is important to understand that there are alternatives to deliberation and that some of them are not only commonly employed in working democracies but are also not self-evidently undesirable. What makes a claim about and for deliberation important, rather than vacuous, is that we can imagine numerous decisional opportunities in a society in which a public deliberation is not the only procedure available but is one among several.[6] One such procedure is a nondeliberative preference measurement, possibly by public opinion poll but more commonly by secret ballot.[7] Although deliberation might precede such a ballot, the key feature here is that the preferences of citizens, however those preferences might be formed, are taken as dispositive, and the majority preferences prevail, if only because the only alternative, as Gutmann and Thompson argue, is for minority preferences to prevail. Still, a procedure simply calling for reflection of majority preferences is not the same as public deliberation, and the very secrecy of the secret ballot stresses the ultimate individuality, and thus nondeliberativeness, of the typical voting procedure.

Another alternative to deliberation is expert (or elite) decision-making. Just as some people are better mathematicians or pianists or carpenters than others, so the argument goes, so might some people be better policymakers or even moral reasoners than others, and if this is so, then a possibly more desirable decision procedure in a democracy might be for such people to simply make the decisions within their areas of expertise. We accept such a model when scientific or other technical expertise is at issue (one of the things we do not see on the side of cigarette packages is "the public in a deliberative process has determined that cigarette smoking causes cancer, emphysema, heart disease, and birth defects"), and thus it is conceivable that we might promote the same form of decision-making even when the relevant expertise is less technical, or at least use such a form of decision-making when it is acknowledged that there is an available but potentially inaccessible body of expertise.

Third, decisions might be made by deliberative processes within a select group, as with a representative legislature, or with an appellate court.[8] Here there does exist a deliberative process, and many of the features advocated by Gutmann and Thompson and other deliberation theorists are present, but the deliberation does not take place within the population at large. Deliberation is recognized as an appropiate decision procedure within these forums, but the public is not perceived to be the best group to do the actual deliberating.

Finally, there is public deliberation, a decision procedure that is usually distinguished from procedures that are public but not necessarily deliberative, as with the referendum and the plebiscite, and procedures that are deliberative but not necessarily public, as with the conferences of the Supreme Court. As conceived by Gutmann and Thompson and by many other deliberative theorists, the central features of public deliberation are an active discourse by an engaged citizenry and a preference for designing the discourse so that it works toward a resolution satisfactory to the deliberators.[9] In two important respects, however, Gutmann and Thompson distinguish their model of deliberation from the models that pervade the literature. In the first place, they impose strong procedural constraints on the nature of deliberation, and their constraints of reciprocity, publicity, and accountability, stressing the importance of deliberators' actually giving reasons that all of the other deliberators could accept, makes it clear that for them deliberation is not simply a synonym for talking but rather represents talking of a certain kind. Second, and relatedly, Gutmann and Thompson plainly do not have a romantic vision of the kinds of public deliberations that now take place. They recognize the demagogic, ad hominem, and inflammatory nature of much of existing public rhetoric and thus recognize as well that for talking to be a viable decision procedure, it must be public talk substantially different from the kind that now dominates so much of American public life.

This willingness to see the warts in existing public talk, however, exposes the central question raised by Gutmann and Thompson's approach. Now that we see that there are at least three decision procedures (secret ballot reflecting antecedent preferences; decision by experts authorized to make the decisions; deliberation by a multimember group of decision-makers such as a legislature) other than public deliberation that are widely used in most modern democracies, it is incumbent on the theorist of deliberation to make the case for using public deliberation rather than one of the other three as a method of reaching a decision. Gutmann and Thompson recognize this, but in making their case for public deliberation, they rely largely on philosophical rather than empirical arguments for the superiority of public deliberation. Although they do at times give examples of successful deliberative processes, the deliberation they promote is hardly the dominant form of American public discourse, as even the briefest sojourn into talk radio, sound-bite television, and tabloid print journalism will attest. In the world as we know it, a decision to prefer a talk-based decision procedure to some other alternative plainly runs a substantial risk not only of departing dramatically from Gutmann and Thompson's ideal but also of producing less rather than more of the features that Gutmann and Thompson would like to see in an idealized deliberation.

Gutmann and Thompson would likely object to this line of argument, claiming that it is an unfair misreading of their argument to saddle them with the burdens of Geraldo Rivera, Larry King, Oprah Winfrey, Jerry Springer, Don Imus, Rush Limbaugh, the *New York Post, Vanity Fair*, and *The Mc-Laughlin Group* when they have been so careful to insist that their idea and ideal of public deliberation is so different from these unfortunate exemplars of contemporary public talk. In the world they advocate, they would rightly say, such models would wither, and the more engaged, reason-giving, and respectful discourse they describe at length would prosper.

Were this book an exercise an ideal theory, their response would be persuasive. There is, appropriately, a utopian, or at least an aspirational, element in much of the best of political theory, and this book is no exception. Gutmann and Thompson want to point us to a better way, they would say, and not merely to describe or endorse existing practices. But at the same time that they are giving us an aspirational vision of public deliberation as an exercise in ideal theory, they claim that this vision is the appropriate decision procedure for dealing with the fact of disagreement in a nonideal world. The central anomaly in their argument, I believe, is the tension between, on the one hand, the nonideal world that they rightly claim gives rise to the problems they address and, on the other, the idealized dimension of the solution they propose for resolving or at least managing those problems.

Pointing out the tension between a nonideal view of the problems that deliberation is supposed to solve and an ideal view of the deliberative processes that are supposed to solve them is my central task here, so I want to pause over it. Consider first a nonideal view of the terrain of political disagreement and an equally nonideal view of the procedures available for negotiating that terrain. Here we have the existing state of substantive disagreement about affirmative action, smoking, health care, welfare policy, flag desecration, airline safety, and any of a host of other topics that dominate American policymaking. But from this perspective we also have the existing pathologies of the various systems that we might deploy in the resolution or management of these disagreements. Were we to suggest simple voting, we would properly worry about the method of formation of the preferences that such voting would reflect and thus worry about the effect of misleading political and other issue advertising, the effect of excess selfishness, and the effect of private and unjustified prejudice that the secret ballot has no way of excluding. If, instead, expert decision-making were the model, we would then worry about the lack of democratic accountability, the effect of autonomous subcultures of experts, the capture of expert communities by special interests, and an expert community more concerned with its own welfare and power than with the population in whose name it is entrusted to make decisions. Much the same could be said about deliberation by representatives or other small groups, where we would again be concerned, in this nonideal scenario, with the lack of accountability, with the pursuit of private rather than public interests, with the effect of special interest groups, and with deliberators out of touch with the actual concerns of those whose interests are in fact at stake. And when we consider having the decision made by public deliberation, we confront the problems of demagoguery, of sound-bite democracy, of the persistent inability of facts and evidence to transcend background normative belief, and of the extent to which the inequalities of society in general are reflected and replicated in its deliberative environments.

This list of decision-making options that our nonideal world presents us with is not attractive. But decisions must be made, including decisions at the level of institutional design, so we must choose among these options for various sorts of decisions. Many of these decisions of institutional design, of course, appear to us as already having been made, and perhaps there is little we can do to change them. But at other times we actually have a choice. Consider the fact that California employs the referendum considerably more than any other state. This suggests that in the nonideal world California presents a model that other states and even smaller subdivisions may or may not choose to emulate. So given that affirmative action is one of the examples that Gutmann and Thompson use, we could ask in a nonideal world whether nonideal referendum procedures (Proposition 209) are better or worse than executive decision-making, legislative decision-making, or judicial decision-making as a way of resolving, if only temporarily, the quandary of affirmative action. This is a real choice and is one seemingly best made by engaging in serious empirical enquiry about the effects of various procedures on the ultimate inquiry. Indeed, if we understand many areas of moral and political disagreement as having right and wrong answers independent of the fact of disagreement, as Gutmann and Thompson properly understand it, then the empirical task becomes slightly more tractable, since we could evaluate each of the putative decision procedures according to how closely or how often it reached the correct result.[10]

There are many ways in which such an empirical study could proceed, and it is not my intention here to engage in a lengthy methodological excursus. Moreover, I do not claim that the results of such a study should be dispositive. The epistemological preferability of a decision procedure would not answer important questions of democratic accountability and participation, and it may very well be that democracy entails a commitment to certain epistemologically suboptimal decision procedures in the service of optimizing democratic values. Especially when we are not dealing with issues involving individual rights, democracy may at times require that the people be granted the authority to make what can be expected to be, values of participation and decision-making authority aside, worse decisions. At its core, democracy may entail, with respect to some issues, the people's right to be wrong.

Even though the empirical questions are thus not the only ones that are relevant, it remains the case that choosing decision procedures in a nonideal world should involve *some* empirical evaluation of the likely consequences and outcomes of the alternatives. And at least as a preliminary first cut, it is far from self-evident that the existing state of decidedly nonideal public talk has as much to recommend it as a decision procedure as one would surmise from reading much of the existing deliberation literature.[11]

Gutmann and Thompson, as I have tried to make clear, do not take the existing state of public talk as a given or as a model for their deliberative ideal. Their model of public deliberation is thus, in important ways, an idealized one—a normative aspiration. So now let us consider the question in exactly the opposite way that we considered nonideal deliberation in a nonideal world of political and moral disagreement. Rather, let us look at ideal deliberation in an ideal world. In doing so, we have to think about what disagreement would look like in an ideal world. One possibility is that it would disappear entirely, since in an ideal world people would all agree on the correct moral and political outcomes. But this picture may be too ideal, which is why we reserve the mildly pejorative word "utopian" for something different from our conceivably attainable normative aspirations. Still, all disagreement in an ideal world is at least reasonable, in Rawls's sense of that word, and the perspectives that inform those disagreements would be untainted by prejudice, selfishness, and related pathologies. In an ideal world, people would not have the kinds of beliefs that deliberation would talk them out of. Public deliberation in an ideal world, therefore, might be nice but would hardly be necessary, since any other form of decision procedure would also produce, essentially by stipulation, ideal results.

Because Gutmann and Thomson so explicitly relinquish any claims to be doing ideal theory, I will not dwell on the conjunction of ideal deliberation in an ideal world. But I mention the possibility, as well as the possibility that deliberation would again have no necessary advantage in such a world, precisely to highlight the anomaly of attaching an idealized model of deliberation to a nonideal political environment. What reason is there to think, we might ask, that we could have much better deliberation than we now have without also thinking that we might simply have a much better substantive political environment than we now have?

Gutmann and Thompson, I suspect, would not take the foregoing question as a rhetorical one. They might argue that in a nonideal world there is a greater chance of improving the quality of public deliberation than there is of improving the deliberation-independent quality of the substantive political terrain, and, if so, then aiming toward the former would be a good way to get us closer to the latter. And perhaps this is so. But now the empirical task is even trickier, for it involves an empirical assessment of the likelihood of change in some segment of our nonideal political life. And it may very well be that Gutmann and Thompson are correct in believing that pushing on the quality of public deliberation will yield more fruit than pushing on other parts of our nonideal world. But perhaps their faith is misguided, with certain features of deliberation making it less rather than more likely that the flaws in existing deliberative practices will yield to persuasive normative arguments. Moreover, it is possible that some of the flaws in other decision procedures are even more correctable, in which case we might want to correct what is wrong with them rather than correcting what is wrong with deliberation, even if a corrected deliberative procedure was superior to its corrected alternatives. It may well be that an improved nondeliberative decision-making procedure is better than an unimproved deliberation, and in a nonideal world, that we wish to improve this possibility must be taken seriously as well.

My reference to "talk" in the title of this essay was hardly accidental. Much of the contemporary discussion of discourse and deliberation trades on the normative and valuational dimensions of these terms, enabling their advocates to disassociate themselves from the seamier side of real-world political and moral talk. It is to Gutmann and Thompson's credit that they are so explicit about this move, and here, as elsewhere in the book, they provide a wonderful model of what talk at its best can be. But the fact that Gutmann and Thompson have the intellectual honesty and analytic acuity to acknowledge the move from talk to deliberation, and the reasons for it, does not make the issue itself less problematic. At its core the normative political theory of discourse or deliberation is at least partly about *talking*, and by calling it what it is, we may better position ourselves to evaluate talk as a contingent device of institutional design. "Let's talk about it" is different from "Let's vote." "Let's fight," "Let's split the difference," and "Let's let Gutmann and Thompson (for example) decide for us." If "Let's talk about it" is superior as a matter of nonideal theory, then we need more empirical investigation than contemporary deliberation theorists have provided. And if "Let's talk about it" is superior as a matter of ideal theory, then we have to know more about the other conditions that would obtain in the ideal world, conditions that might make "Let's talk about it" unnecessary. Gutmann and Thompson are to be commended for making so explicit their idealized version of deliberation, and in doing so they have greatly the advanced the state of deliberation theory. But in overlaying this idealized version of deliberation onto the nonideal world of existing political disagreement, they leave for skeptical examination and empirical inquiry the possibility that moving to their ideal deliberative world may be riskier and more difficult than other ways of improving our moral life and our political decisions.

Notes

1. John Rawls, *Political Liberalism* (New York: Columbia University Press, 1993).

2. Gutmann and Thompson, *Democracy and Disagreement* (Cambridge Belknap Press of Harvard University Press, 1996).

3. These are their major examples, but one of the many virtues of the book is that points are frequently illustrated with less extensively detailed examples as well, such as the Senate debate on the patentability of the Confederate flag insignia (135–36), international cooperation on environmental issues (161), and public and political responses to the practice of "dwarf tossing" (252–54).

4. For the uninitiated, a good start would be the works cited by Gutmann and Thompson at 364, n. 4.

5. For a fuller version of my argument against a truth-constitutive notion of deliberation, see Frederick Schauer, "Discourse and Its Discontents," *Notre Dame Law Review* 72 (1997): A much earlier version is in Frederick Schauer, *Free Speech: A Philosophical Enquiry* (Cambridge: Cambridge University Press, 1982), chap. 2.

6. I wish Gutmann and Thompson had devoted more space to describing in detail the occasions for choosing public deliberation over an alternative decision procedure. Although they describe substantive controversies in rich detail, rarely do they do the same about procedural controversies or opportunities for choice. Given its focus on public deliberation as a decision procedure, the book would have been better if the authors had identified concrete instances in which there is or was a choice between a certain form of public deliberation and an alternative decision procedure.

7. For a rare willingness to confront the tensions between a deliberative perspective and the traditional admiration of the secret ballot, see Geoffrey Brennan and Philip Pettit, "Unveiling the Vote," *British Journal of Political Science* 20 (1992): 311–33.

8. On the Supreme Court as a potential model for and example of deliberative decision-making, see Frank I. Michelman, "Foreword: Traces of Self-Government," *Harvard Law Review* 100 (1986): 4–98.

9. Gutmann and Thompson admirably recognize that even ideal deliberations will have losers, and one of their stronger arguments, echoing and improving on arguments made by Alexander Meiklejohn in *Political Freedom: The Constitutional Powers of the People* (New York: Harper & Row, 1965), is that public deliberation is advantageously suited to give the losers reason to feel respected and thus reason to accept and obey political decisions with which they disagree. In recognizing that public deliberations will often not lead to unanimous consensus, Gutmann and Thompson confront an issue—we might call it *impasse theory*—that many other deliberation theorists unfortunately bracket.

10. For recent formal and economic theory casting doubt on some of the more extravagant epistemological claims of some deliberation theorists, see Alvin I. Goldman and James C. Cox, "Speech, Truth, and the Free Market for Ideas," *Legal Theory* 2 (1996): 1–32; David Charny, "The Economic Analysis of Deliberative Procedures," Harvard Law School Seminar in Law and Economics Paper, April 15, 1997.

11. For related critiques, see James A. Gardner, "Shut Up and Vote: A Critique of Deliberative Democracy and the Life of Talk," *Tennessee Law Review* 63 (1996): 421–51; Lynn M. Sanders, "Against Deliberation," *Political Theory* 25, no. 3 (June 1997): 3.

2

Enough of Deliberation

Politics Is about Interests and Power

IAN SHAPIRO

Many of the substantive arguments in *Democracy and Disagreement* resonate favorably with me, but it should be said that this is not a particularly demanding test. To know how effective Amy Gutmann and Dennis Thompson's deliberative model would be, either at reducing moral disagreement or at promoting accommodation of irresolvable differences in American politics, one would have to see it in action in debates among pro-lifers and pro-choicers, parties to the *Mozert v. Hawkins* litigation, or protagonists in debates over redistricting, affirmative action, welfare reform, child support, and the other contentious issues that Gutmann and Thompson describe. Their claim is that if the various protagonists "seek fair terms of cooperation for their own sake," committing themselves to appeal, in their arguments, "to reasons that are recognizably moral in form and mutually acceptable in content," then disagreements will be minimized and accommodation will be promoted.[1] Gutmann and Thompson report how they believe these and other public policy debates ought to come out when the model is applied, or, in some cases, that it cannot resolve them. This is different, however, from demonstrating that it would actually happen in practice. Gutmann and Thompson do offer qualified praise of some actual deliberative processes, such as the 1990 meetings that were held in Oregon to help set health care priorities for Medicaid recipients (see below). But I did not detect mention in their discussion of any actual deliberative process that they did not insist falls significantly short of their deliberative ideal. Nor can I think of one. Accordingly, the assertion that the model would have the beneficial effects claimed for it remains speculative.

I start with this observation because I doubt that the failure to resolve many of the issues discussed by Gutmann and Thompson has much to do with a "deliberative deficit" resulting from insufficient attention to "the need for ongoing discussion of moral disagreement in everyday political life." (12). Sometimes, perhaps, people might better resolve differences and accommodate themselves to views they reject by more deliberation of the prescribed sort. But what reason is there to think that failure to attempt this is the principal reason why the public policy issues they examine are not resolved along the lines Gutmann and Thompson advocate? It is one thing to think, as I do, along with them, that much of what divides people politically is susceptible to rational analysis more often than people realize; it is quite another to believe that what prevents better resolution of prevailing disagreements is insufficient deliberation of the Gutmann Thompson sort. In my view, Gutmann and Thompson's emphasis on deliberation attends too little to the degree to which moral disagreements in politics are shaped by differences of interest and power. I think they give a plausible account of the nature of some moral disagreements and of possible argumentative strategies for constructive responses to them when protagonists are appropriately inclined. It is as response to moral disagreement *in politics* that their account seems to me to be lacking.

Gutmann and Thompson never claim that deliberation will, or even that it should, vanquish all moral disagreement in politics. But certainly they expect it to reduce disagreements and to help people who disagree better to converge on mutually acceptable policies. Deliberation both presumes and promotes the value of their leading principle of reciprocity, which requires people to find "mutually acceptable ways of resolving moral disagreements."(2). Thus Gutmann and Thompson tell us that democratic citizens with moral disagreements "should deliberate with one another, seeking moral agreement when they can, and maintaining mutual respect when they cannot." Although they defend the deliberative perspective as a method of resolving some moral disagreements in politics, they suspect that "its greater contribution can be to help citizens treat one another with mutual respect as they deal with the disagreements that invariably remain" (346, 2, 9).

Why deliberation? The principal reason that suggests itself to Gutmann and Thompson is that there seems to be so little of it in the political debate they observe. "In the practice of our democratic politics, communicating by sound bite, competing by character assassination, and resolving political conflicts through self-seeking bargaining too often substitute for deliberation on the merits of controversial issues." Nor is the deficiency limited to public debate. It is reflected in academic commentary on democracy as well, which is "surprisingly silent about the need for ongoing discussion of moral disagreement in everyday political life. As a result, we suffer from a deliberative deficit not only in our democratic politics but also in our democratic theory." Gutmann and Thompson think that we are unlikely to lower the deficit in our politics if we do not also reduce it in our theory (12).

Yet it is by no means obvious that deliberation exhibits the felicitous political properties Gutmann and Thompson attribute to it. As they concede at one point, sometimes deliberation can promote disagreement and conflict (44). The cases they have in mind here are moral issues that arouse intense passions, paradigmatically the issues liberals have sought to defuse politically since the seventeenth-century wars of religion. Skeptics of deliberation in these areas proceed from the assumption that there are "moral fanatics as well as moral sages, and in politics the former are likely to be more vocal than the latter." Gutmann and Thompson's response to this claim is that although moral argument "can arouse moral fanatics," it can also "combat their claims on their own terms." Deliberation undermines moral extremists, who "must assume that they already know what constitutes the best resolution of a moral conflict without deliberating with their fellow citizens who will be bound by the resolution." In the everyday political forums, Gutmann and Thompson insist, "the assumption that we know the political truth can rarely if ever be justified before we deliberate with others who have something to say about the issues that affect their lives as well as ours." Accordingly, they conclude with a presumption in deliberation's favor: "by refusing to give deliberation a chance, moral extremists forsake the most defensible ground for an uncompromising position" (44–45).

Alluring as this reasoning might be to you and me, I find it hard to imagine a fundamentalist being much impressed by it, particularly when she learns that any empirical claims she makes must be consistent with "relatively reliable methods of inquiry" (56). Nor will she be much comforted by Gutmann and Thompson's gloss to the effect that this does not "exclude religious appeals per se" (why not, one wonders?), so long as these do not include taking the Bible literally. The reason for this latter constraint is that "virtually all contemporary fundamentalists subject biblical claims to interpretation, accepting some as literally true and revising the meaning of others. To reject moral claims that rely on implausible premises is therefore not to repudiate religion" (56). If the syllogistic force of this claim was not lost on the fundamentalist in the abstract, surely it would be once it was explained to her that it denies her the right to insist on the literal truth of *any* particular biblical imperative.[2] From her perspective it would look as though she were being told that it is fine to be a fundamentalist so long as she abandons her fundamentalism. At bottom, the difficulty here is that the fundamentalist believes exactly what Gutmann and Thompson decry as illegitimate: that it is necessary to adopt her "sectarian way of life as a condition for gaining access to the moral understanding that is essential to judging the validity" of her moral claims. (57). She will agree with Gutmann and Thompson that she cannot justify her views on grounds they can accept, but for her this will be conclusive evidence of the inadequacy of those grounds. She will rightly expect to come out on the short end of any deliberative exchange conducted on that terrain. The Gutmann/Thompson model works only for those fundamentalists who also count themselves fallibilist democrats. That, I fear, is an empty class, destined to remain uninhabited.

Gutmann and Thompson are plausibly skeptical of those, like Owen Fiss and Ronald Dworkin, who believe that courts are better suited to achieving principled resolution among contending moral perspectives in the public realm than are other political institutions (45–47). Neither a compelling theoretical argument nor any persuasive evidence has ever been adduced in support of this view. Contrary to what they seem to suppose, however, this is scarcely relevant to the standard constitutionalist argument for avoiding, or limiting, public deliberation about intense, particularly religious, differences. This turns not on any illusion that courts can resolve them in a principled fashion but rather on the recognition that no one can. The idea is that their explosive potential is so great that it is better, for the welfare of both religious adherents and the democratic polity, if they are kept out of organized politics as much as possible, subjected to what Stephen Holmes describes as "gag rules."[3] Hence such devices as the Establishment Clause of the First Amendment. That is the serious constitutionalist case against promoting attempts to resolve religious disagreements in the public sphere. Perhaps there is a reply to it from the deliberative democratic perspective, but Gutmann and Thompson do not supply it.

Their brief remarks on the disquieting possibility that deliberation might move politics away from the agreement and accommodation they value seem to me to skirt the tip of another rather large and multifaceted iceberg. Leaving uncompromising religious values to one side, Adam Przeworski has recently reminded us of a different class of circumstances in which deliberation might promote disagreement and enhance conflict.[4] People with opposed interests are not always aware of just how opposed those interests actually are. Deliberation can bring differences to the surface, widening the political divisions rather than narrowing them. This is what Marxists hoped would result from "consciousness-raising." It would lead workers to discover that they share interests that are fundamentally at odds with those of employers, assisting in the transformation of the proletariat from a class-in-itself to a revolutionary class-for-itself. These hopes proved naive. The general point remains, however, that there is no particular reason to think deliberation will bring people together, even if they hope it will and want it to. A couple with a distant but not collapsing marriage might begin therapy with a mutual commitment to settling some long-standing differences and learning to accommodate one another better on matters that cannot be resolved. Once honest exchange gets under way, however, they might unearth new irreconcilable differences, with the effect that the relationship worsens and perhaps even falls apart in acrimony. Deliberation can reasonably be expected to shed light on human interaction, but this may reveal hidden differences as well as hidden possibilities for convergence. It all depends on what the underlying interests at stake actually are.

Another respect in which Gutmann and Thompson's appeal to deliberation pays insufficient attention to the contending interests at stake is revealed in their discussion of health care reform in Oregon in the early 1990s. Rationing of health care procedures for the non-elderly poor by the legislature followed a series of "town meetings" in which citizens and various health professionals were asked to rank medical procedures.[5] The object was to find a way of settling disagreements about priorities in health care insurance, given the hard choices that public budget constraints impose. Gutmann and Thompson note that this procedure was flawed because the plan covered only the nonelderly poor. They describe this as a "basic injustice" that "may have adversely influenced the surveys and community meetings, which in any case fell short of the deliberative ideal." Yet they commend the process on the grounds that it "forced officials and citizens to confront a serious problem that they had previously evaded and to confront it in a cooperative ('first-person plural') spirit." They go on to claim that the process helped ameliorate the underlying injustice, because when the legislators "finally saw what treatments on the list would have to be eliminated under the projected budget, they managed to find more resources and increased the total budget for health care for the poor" (143–44).

Notice that the legislature's decision to appropriate additional funds was unrelated to the substance of the deliberative meetings, which never dealt with what the overall budget should be or how health care resources should be traded off against other demands on the state treasury. It was not a product of citizens with moral disagreements reducing them through reciprocal deliberative exchange. It was, rather, a fortunate externality, for the uninsured poor, of the deliberative process, such as it was, in that the publicity it generated helped spotlight their plight in the media and the legislature. If this is the proffered defense of the Oregon process, one would have to compare it to other ways in which the condition of the uninsured poor might have been publicized with similar or better effect, such as publicity campaigns, public protests, or class action lawsuits. I will not pursue this issue further, since, as I have said, it does not bear on Gutmann and Thompson's defense of deliberation: that it reduces disagreement and increases mutual accommodation of differences that cannot be resolved.

In fact, as a device for settling disagreements about how hard choices should be made in rationing health care resources, the Oregon deliberative process was a notable failure. Gutmann and Thompson acknowledge, as have others, that it is hard to find a relationship between the final rankings and the results of the deliberative process, which eventually became little more than a vehicle for public outrage at attempts to introduce a measure of prudence into Oregon's health care priorities.[6] Nonetheless, Gutmann and Thompson conclude that the deliberations "evidently helped citizens, legislators, and health care professionals arrive at an improved understanding of their own values— those they shared and those that they did not" (144). But whose values are we really talking about? The "citizens, legislators, and health care professionals" by and large excluded those who would be covered under the Oregon Plan: the nonelderly poor. I am not talking here about the injustice that Gutmann and Thompson acknowledge—that in effect this choice was really about "making some poor citizens sacrifice health care that they need so that other poor citizens can receive health they need even more urgently, while better-off citizens can get whatever treatment they need" (143). Rather, my question is; Why should we attach any legitimacy at all to a deliberative process that involved very few of those whose health care priorities were actually being discussed?[7] Gutmann and Thompson themselves make a similar point in criticizing workfare and welfare reform later in the book. There they suggest the need for participatory processes that "encourage the participation of economically and educationally disadvantaged citizens" (303–6). That seems right to me, and generalizable, so far as it goes. But it needs to be taken further.

Notice that only part of the infirmity in these cases is that those who must live with the results go more or less unrepresented in the decision-making; the other part is that most of those making the decisions know that they will never depend on the good whose rationing or provision is under discussion. In countries like Britain and Canada, where the great majority of the population use collectively rationed medical services, their participation in democratic decision-making through the political process lends legitimacy to the resulting policies. By contrast, in Oregon, more than 80 percent of the population is unaffected by the rationing program.[8] The general point here is that the legitimacy of decision-making processes varies with the degree to which they are both inclusive and binding on those who make them. Deliberative processes are not exceptions. Gutmann and Thompson acknowledge this in principle. They define political decisions as collectively binding, adding that "they should therefore be justifiable, as far as possible, to everyone bound by them" (13). However, their discussion is not sensitive to the reality that different people are differently bound by collective decisions. When there is great variation in the impact of a decision, then interests diverge in ways that are relevant to assessing the decision's legitimacy.

This is most obviously true when there are substantial differences in the capacities of different groups to escape the effects of policies on which they are deciding. Those who can easily avoid them do not have the same kind of interest at stake in a decision as those whose exit costs are prohibitively high. The story of apartheid in American public schools is eloquent testimony of what happens when this fact goes unrecognized. Urban public schools are starved of resources by middle-class voters who opt out either fiscally (to private urban schools) or physically (to suburban schools). It should be added that the latter may live in towns that are paragons of deliberative democracy. In 1995, for instance, a statewide Connecticut plan to reduce segregation in schools was duly deliberated upon at great length in New England town meeting in which the inner-city residents of Hartford and New Haven had no effective voice at all. As a result, their interests were simply ignored and the plan was easily defeated. Gutmann and Thompson place great stress on the importance of adequate elementary and secondary education, like adequate health care, in providing the necessary basic opportunities for living in a democracy. But they seem not to appreciate that as deliberation operates on the ground in what Douglas Rae has described as the "segmented democracies" that Americans increasingly inhabit, it can be an obstacle to providing these goods.[9] When there are great differences in capacity for exit, what is often needed is not widespread deliberation but firm action from above to protect the vulnerable.[10]

Another area in which Gutmann and Thompson's account suffers from lack of due attention to conflicting interests has to do with what shapes the terms of deliberation in modern democracies. There are circumstances in which more deliberation would be a healthy thing in the formation of public policy, but often the principal obstacle is not the lack of will on the part of people with differing moral convictions to deliberate in ways that can minimize their differences. Rather, it results from decisions by powerful players who make it their business to shape the terms of public debate through the financial contributions they make available to politicians and political campaigns. Engels once described ballots as "paper stones." In the post–*Buckley v. Valeo*[11] world, when any credible political campaign requires multi-million-dollar war chests to buy the requisite television time to do political battle, public deliberation all too often consists of verbal stones hurled across the airwaves, with victory going to whoever has the most bountiful supply. Granted, this is a long way from what Gutmann and Thompson have in mind when they advocate deliberation, but I find it stunning that a book about the importance of enhancing deliberation in contemporary American politics can ignore the reality it creates.

For instance, in their discussion of the failure of the Clinton administration's attempt at national health care reform, Gutmann and Thompson seek to lay blame on the secret meetings of Hillary Clinton's Task Force on National Health Care Reform, along with other unmentioned factors. Endorsing the claims of critics who, at the time, said that support for the plan would be more difficult to achieve "if the policymakers did not show that they were responding to criticisms and taking into account diverse interests in the process of formulating the plan," they conclude that even when "secrecy improves the quality of a deliberation, it may reduce the chances that a well-reasoned proposal will ever become law" (117). Perhaps Hillary's secret meetings contributed something to the failure, along with the Clinton administration's ineptitude in failing to get essential Capitol Hill barons like Senators Moynihan and Nunn on board; the administration's inability to come to grips with the sheer economic scope of the proposal (12 percent of a $3 trillion economy);[12] and the structural deficit inherited from the Reagan and Bush administrations.[13] But how can anyone who lived through the huge amounts of public misinformation that contributed to the steady decline in the bill's popularity, and its eventual abandonment by the administration, not be struck by the importance of the $50 million public relations and lobbying campaign that the medical, insurance, and other corporate establishments waged to kill the legislation?[14]

I am not taking issue, here, with Gutmann and Thompson's convincing argument that secrecy is generally a bad thing in government. Rather, my point is that if we ask the question "What prevented meaningful public discussion of health care reform in 1993 and 1994?," secrecy's significance seems trifling when compared to the way the options were presented in the war of words on television and the activities of political lobbyists. They ensured that important options (notably a Canadian-style single-payer system) were never seriously discussed and that the entire debate came to focus on issues that are irrelevant to the bill's basic goal of achieving universal health care coverage. Arguments about the feasibility of managed competition and the freedom people may or may not have in selecting their own physicians dominated the discussion, as the plight of the 40 million uninsured fell by the wayside. It is difficult for me to see how any aspect of Gutmann and Thompson's "deliberative deficit" was responsible for this, since the problem had nothing to do with reaching agreement among the contending views or finding an accommodation among those who could not agree. Rather, the problem was that some of what ought to have been the contending views never confronted one another in the public mind. This seems to me to have been due, more than any other single factor, to the blank check the United States Supreme Court has given those who have large amounts if money, or the capacity to raise it, to shape the terms of public debate. It creates a reality in which, rather than compete in the realm of ideas, politicians actually must compete for campaign contributions. The ideas they advance are those of their financial backers, and those they avoid advancing all too often are ideas that, though they may be in the interests of many in the public, would cause vast sums of money to be given to electoral opponents if they were seriously advanced. How else is one to explain the fact that a single-payer system could not be seriously mooted, even at the start of the public debate, despite a substantial body of academic commentary suggesting that it is easily the most cost-effective way of achieving affordable universal coverage?[15] How else can one explain the fact that neither political party ever proposes massive hikes in the estate tax, although this move would be in the interest of all but a tiny fraction of the electorate?[16]

For anyone who is worried about the lack of deliberation in the health care debate, worrying about how money structured it seems to me to be the obvious first order of business. Yet Gutmann and Thompson never mention it. Perhaps they would say their book is simply not concerned with this subject, but I would find that difficult to square with the claims they make for their argument. They insist that their focus is on "the everyday forums of democratic politics," differentiating their deliberative perspective from other academic discussion, which is said to be "insensitive to the contexts of ordinary politics: the pressures of a power, the problems of inequality, the demands of diversity, the exigencies of persuasion" (2–3). As my discussion has indicated, their own account pays surprisingly little attention to these very features of politics. They are heartened by the fact that although "the quality of deliberation and the conditions under which it is conducted are far from ideal in the controversies we consider, the fact that in each case some citizens and some officials make arguments consistent with reciprocity, suggests that a deliberative perspective is not utopian" (2). I do not think we should be so easily fortified. Until it can be shown that these arguments can be made on a sufficient scale and garner enough institutional force to influence the ways that politics is structured by powerful interests, Gutmann and Thompson's case for deliberation's undernoticed *political* value is not established.

Notes

1. Amy Gutmann and Dennis Thompson, *Democracy and Disagreement* (Cambridge: Belknap Press of Harvard University Press, 1996), 57, 53.

2. The example Gutmann and Thompson discuss (56) is the literal proscription of miscegenation, but if their argument is accepted in this case it must surely apply to every literal assertion in the Bible.

3. Stephen Holmes, "Gag Rules," in *Constitutionalism and Democracy*, ed. Jon Elster and Rune Slagstad (Cambridge: Cambridge University Press, 1988).

4. Adam Przeworski, "Minimalist Conception of Democracy: A Defense," in *Democracy's Value*, ed. Ian Shapiro and Casiano Hacker-Cordon, (Cambridge: Cambridge University Press, 1999), 23–55.

5. In 1990, forty-seven community meetings were held across Oregon, attended by about a thousand people total. The attendees were asked to rank categories of treatment by importance and articulate the values that guided their decisions. The state legislature then used the list as a yardstick to appropriate Medicaid funds. The Oregon Plan was intended to expand Medicaid eligibility from 68 percent of those at the federal poverty level to 100 percent and to finance the increased cost by prudent rationing of procedures. Although Oregon did end up expanding coverage to some 126,000 new members by February 1997, much of this expansion was actually achieved by appropriation of new funds by the legislature rather than from savings generated by the deliberations about rationing priorities. See Norman Daniels, "Is the Oregon Rationing Plan Fair?" *Journal of the American Medical Association* 265, no. 17 (May 1, 1991): 2232–35; Jim Montague, "Why Rationing Was Right for Oregon," *Hospitals and Health Networks* (February 5, 1997): 64–66

6. See David C. Hadorn, "Setting Health Care Priorities in Oregon: Cost-Effectiveness Meets the Rule of Rescue," *Journal of the American Medical Association* 26, no. 17 (May 1, 1991): 2218–25.

7. Daniels reports that the meetings were attended predominantly by "college-educated, relatively well-off, and white" audiences, half of which consisted of health professionals. Of the attendees, 9.4 percent were uninsured (whereas 16 percent of the state's population was uninsured at the time), and Medicaid recipients (among other things, the only direct representatives of poor children) were underrepresented by half. "Is the Oregon Rationing Plan Fair?," 2234.

8. Daniels, "Is the Oregon Rationing Plan Fair?," 2233–34.

9. Douglas Rae, "Small tyrannies of Place," in *Democracy's Edges*, ed. Ian Shapiro and Casiano Hacker-Cordon (Cambridge: Cambridge University Press, 1999), 165–92.

10. See Jennifer Hochschild, *The New American Dilemma* (New Haven: Yale University Press, 1984).

11. In *Buckley v. Valeo*, 424 U.S. 1 (1976), the Supreme Court held, inter alia, that Congress may regulate financial contributions to political parties or candidates, but it cannot otherwise regulate private expenditures on political speech, which are protected by the First Amendment. Although the Court has since allowed some minor constraints on corporate expenditures in *Austin v. Michigan State Chamber of Commerce*, 110 S.Ct. 1391 (1990), for all practical purposes the *Buckley* rule makes it impossible to limit privately funded political advertising.

12. See Theodore Marmor, *Understanding Health Care Reform* (New Haven: Yale University Press, 1994), 2–3, 184.

13. For accounts of the failure, see Jacob Hacker, *The Road to Nowhere: The Genesis of President Clinton's Plan for Health Security* (Princeton: Princeton University Press, 1997), and Theda Skocpol, *Bommerang: Health Care Reform and the Turn against Government* (New York: Norton, 1997).

14. The $50 million figure is reported by Tim Rinne, "The Rise and Fall of Single-Payer Health Care in Nebraska," *Action for Universal Health Care* 3, no. 10 (May 1995): 4–5. See also Tom Hamburger and Ted Marmor, "Dead on

Arrival: Why Washington's Power Elites Won't Consider Single Payer Health Reform," *Washington Monthly* (September 1993): 27–32.

15. See the papers collected in Marmor, *Understanding Health Care Reform.*

16. I am indebted to James Tobin's comments at the conference entitled "Rethinking Democracy for a New Century" held at Yale University, February 28–March 2, 1997, for this last point.

3

Diversity, Toleration, and Deliberative Democracy

Religious Minorities and Public Schooling

WILLIAM A. GALSTON

*I*t is said that during medieval times, Bulan, king of the Khazers, summoned four wise men to his kingdom—a secular philosopher, a Christian scholar, a Muslim scholar, and a rabbi. After interrogating them seriatim on the content and basis of their beliefs, Bulan called his people together in an assembly, declared that he accepted Judaism, and decreed that all Khazers would thenceforth be instructed in and practice Judaism as their communal faith.[1]

I suspect that this chain of events strikes most readers today as strange. Would it be less strange if—rather than one man deciding for all—the people had assembled themselves and, after the most scrupulous democratic deliberation, settled on Judaism as the official religion of the Khazer nation? I think not. For believers in *liberal* democracy, there is a threshold question: Does the state possess the legitimate power to make collectively binding decisions on this matter? If not, the question of how such decisions should be made is never reached.

For liberal democrats, religion is a clear example of a matter that in principle should not be subject to collective determination. There are many others. Imagine a young single man coming home one day to find an official-looking letter (certified, return receipt requested):

Dear Mr. X:

Last week, after the most careful fact-finding and deliberation, your state legislature unanimously decided that you should marry Ms. Y. She lives at . . . ; her telephone number is . . . ; she can also be reached by fax at. . . . Please send us written proof of marriage within one month. While we are sure that you will respond appropriately to this decision, let is remind you that under Title 6, section A, subsection I, paragraph (i), failure to comply with this determination is punishable by a prison term of up to three years.

Absurd? Of course—not because the decision was undemocratic or nondeliberative (it wasn't) but because the state had no business making such a decision in the first place.

The proposition that some matters are none of the state's business carries an important discursive consequence: With regard to those matters, individuals and civil associations are not regarded to give an account of—or justify—themselves before any public bar. So, for example, representatives of minority religions could not rightly be compelled by a congressional committee to explain the essentials of their faith.

Indeed, as Ira Katznelson has recently argued, such individuals are not morally required to give an account of themselves to anyone, public or private: A meaningful pluralism entails "the right not to offer a reason for being different." Katznelson builds on Susan Mendus's metaphor of "neighborliness." We owe our neighbors civil behavior that is mindful of our actions' impact on them, but ordinarily "neighbors do not owe each other reasons" for the way they choose to lead their lives.[2]

For liberal democrats, in short, there are two critical questions: the *nature* of democratic decision-making, and the *scope* of legitimate democratic authority. It seems to me that Amy Gutmann and Dennis Thompson deal far more adequately with the first question than with the second. One comes away from *Democracy and Disagreement* with a very clear (albeit contestable) sense of how democratic deliberation should be conducted, but with (at best) a general conception of the limits of state power. To be sure, there is a guiding concept—the preservation of "personal integrity."[3] But in nearly all cases, the movement from general concept to specific conception is mediated by democratic deliberation—not the most secure and comforting basis for the maintenance of liberty: "In keeping with the spirit of a deliberative constitution, we argue that citizens and public officials are responsible for setting limits to . . . liberty . . . through a deliberative process" (200–201). By contrast, liberal constitutionalism both specifies basic liberties and tries to keep them outside the normal processes of democratic revision.

To be fair, Gutmann and Thompson do identify a few core violations of personal integrity. Unless individuals have the right to resist "certain kinds of constraints on their personal beliefs (for example, on their religious or moral convictions), their mental integrity is in jeopardy" (204). The question I want to raise in this essay is whether their conception of democratic deliberation proves in the end to be compatible with this account of individual liberty. I will focus on what I take to be the linchpin of deliberation for Gutmann and Thompson—the principle of reciprocity—and on their application of this principle to the controversy between religious fundamentalists and public education that erupted in Hawkins County, Tennessee, a decade ago. Gutmann and Thompson contend that fidelity to reciprocity as they define it entails the rejection of the fundamentalists' attempts to have their children shielded from reading materials they found offensive to their faith. I argue that reciprocity, so understood, requires an intolerable sacrifice of personal integrity but that a more generous and defensible conception of reciprocity does not.

Claims based on personal integrity (understood in familial, communal, and religious terms) have proved especially powerful limits on state action in the arena of public education, as shown by two famous cases in U.S. constitutional law.

Reflecting the nativist passions stirred by World War I, the state of Nebraska passed a law forbidding instruction in any modern language other than English. A teacher in a Lutheran parochial school was convicted under this statute for the crime of teaching a Bible class in German. In *Meyer v. Nebraska*, decided in 1923, the Supreme Court struck down this law as a violation of the liberty guarantee of the Fourteenth Amendment. Writing for the Court, Justice McReynolds declared:

> That the State may do much, go very far, indeed, in order to improve the quality of its citizens, physically, mentally, and morally, is clear; but the individual has certain fundamental rights which must be respected. . . . The desire of the legislature to foster a homogeneous people with American ideas prepared readily to understand current discussions of civic matters is easy to appreciate. . . . But the means adopted, we think, exceed the limitations upon the power of the State and conflict with rights assured to plaintiff.[4]

The majority decision identified the underlying theory of the Nebraska law with the plenipotentiary state of Sparta, as well as with Plato's *Republic*, which it quoted at length and sharply distinguished from the underlying premises of liberal constitutionalism.

Consider, second, *Pierce v. Society of Sisters*, decided in 1925.[5] Through a ballot initiative, the people of Oregon had adopted a law requiring parents and legal guardians to send all students between the ages of eight and sixteen to public schools. The Society of Sisters, an Oregon corporation that among other activities maintained a system of Catholic schools, sued to overturn this law as inconsistent with the Fourteenth Amendment. The Supreme Court emphatically agreed:

> The fundamental theory of liberty upon which all governments in this Union repose excludes any general power of the State to standardize its children by forcing them to accept instruction from public teachers only. The child is not the mere creature of the State; those who nurture him and direct his destiny have the right, coupled with the high duty, to recognize and prepare him for additional obligations.[6]

These two cases rest, it seems to me, on a plausible understanding and specification of the limits on state power inherent in the idea of liberal democracy. Taken together, they stand for two propositions. First, in a liberal democracy, there is in principle a division of authority between parents and the state. The state has the right to establish certain minimum standards, such as the duty of parents to educate their children, and to specify some minimum content of that education, wherever it may be conducted. But parents have a wide and protected range of choices as to how the duty to educate is to be discharged.

Second, there are some things the liberal state may not do, *even in the name of forming good citizens.* The appeal to the requisites of civic education is powerful but not, in the end, dispositive when opposed by claims based on personal integrity.

With these cases and considerations as a backdrop, I turn to the specifics of the argument. The essentials of Gutmann and Thompson's account of reciprocity are by now well-known. Building on the work of Rawls and Scanlon, they say that the

> foundation of reciprocity is the capacity to seek fair terms of social cooperation for their own sake. . . . From a deliberative perspective, a citizen offers reasons that can be accepted by others who are similarly motivated to find reasons that can be accepted by others. . . . [Thus,] a deliberative perspective does not address people who reject the aim of finding fair terms for social cooperation; it cannot reach those who refuse to press their public claims in terms accessible to their fellow citizens. (52–53, 55)

This understanding of reciprocity raises some deep questions (for example, about the nature of moral motivation), but I won't pursue them here. Instead, staying within the bounds of Gutmann and Thompson's account, I want to offer three caveats. First, the phrase "social cooperation" tends to suggest a common course of action that all citizens (must) pursue. But there are other equally legitimate forms of cooperation, including agreements to disagree, to go our various ways without hindrance or cavil, to "live and let live." Neighborliness as Katznelson and Mendus define it is a form of cooperation.

In addition, there are different kinds of "public claims." Individuals may argue that the political community as a whole ought to pursue a particular course of action. (This is, I think, the core case that Gutmann and Thompson have in mind.) But they may also argue that the question at hand should not be treated as a public matter in the first place, or that even if it is a legitimate public matter, some individuals and groups may (or must) be exempted from the constraints of otherwise general decisions. Some public claims are "offensive"—you (all) should do what I say—while others are "defensive"—I need not do what you say, even if you speak in the voice of the entire political community. The kinds of reasons offered in support of defensive claims may rightly differ from those for offensive claims.

Finally, the requirement that the terms of public argument should be "accessible" to one's fellow citizens turns out to be highly restrictive: "Any claim fails to respect reciprocity if it imposes a requirement on other citizens to adopt one's sectarian way of life as a condition of gaining access to the moral understanding that is essential to judging the validity of one's moral claims" (57). Over the past two decades, a substantial debate has developed over the nature of what Rawls calls "public reason," a debate that Gutmann and Thompson seem to resolve by definitional fiat. For purposes of clarity, let me be equally categorical: The norm of reciprocity should not be interpreted to screen out the kinds of foundational beliefs that give meaning and purpose to many lives. This caveat is especially important in the United States, where levels of religious belief and observance are far higher than in any other industrialized democracy. It is difficult to imagine that any liberal democracy can sustain conscientious support if it tells millions of its citizens that they cannot rightly say what they believe as part of democratic public dialogue.

I want to suggest that an inclusive understanding of public reason is especially appropriate in the context of what I have called defensive public claims. It is one thing to take the offensive—for example, by claiming that the United States should be a "Christian nation" and should restore official Christian prayer to public schools. That was the situation that existed in the grade schools of my youth, when I (a Jew) was compelled to recite the Lord's Prayer. I do not see how such a regime could possibly be defended through legitimate public reasons. It is quite a different thing to seek, on conscientious grounds, defensive exemption from general public policies that may seem legitimate and acceptable to a majority of citizens.

Suppose a fundamentalist parent said to a secular philosopher,

> Because of the content of your deepest beliefs, you happen not to experience a conflict between those beliefs and the content of the public school curriculum. But if *you* believed what *I* believe, you would experience that conflict, and you would seek for your child what I am seeking for mine. Moreover, the accommodation I seek is one that I would readily grant, were our positions reversed. I am not asking you to enter

into the perspective of my particular religious beliefs. But I am asking you to enlarge your sympathies by imagining what it would be like to be in my shoes.

This fundamentalist is offering as a public reason not the specific *content* of religious belief but rather the *fact* of that belief and of the resulting clash with secular public policies. The secular interlocutor is being asked to imaginatively experience that clash as part of a process that could create a wider shared understanding—even if the particulars of faith are not easily communicable. I do not see why such a request is outside the legitimate bounds of public reason.[7]

Gutmann and Thompson insist that "there is a public interest in educating good citizens, and no citizen can fairly claim that what constitutes good citizenship is whatever happens to conform to his or her particular religion" (67). This proposition is true as far as it goes. But as applied to the clash between the fundamentalist parents and the public schools, it raises three issues.

The first is empirical: Is it the case that the accommodation sought by the fundamentalist parents would significantly impair the development of democratic citizens? The Hawkins County School Board never offered evidence on this point, and it is hard to see how they could have done so. Besides, the fundamentalist parents are constitutionally permitted to withdraw their children from the public schools and send them instead to Christian academies. It is hard to believe that the consequences of such a choice for democratic citizenship are more favorable than a policy of accommodation with the public schools would have been. (Perhaps Gutmann and Thompson believe that *Pierce v. Society of Sisters* was wrongly decided and that the logic of deliberative democracy requires that all children be sent to public schools. Or perhaps they believe, as Stephen Macedo does, that the sphere of legitimate state regulation of private schools is so wide as to obviate this problem.)[8]

The second issue raised by Gutmann and Thompson's assertion is conceptual: How is the good citizenship whose development we seek through education to be defined? The answer is contested, and in any event it is likely to be complex. The capacity for deliberation is surely one element, but there are others, such as law-abidingness, personal responsibility, and the willingness to do one's share (through taxes, jury duty, military service, etc.) to sustain a system of social cooperation. In comparing the civic consequences of different educational strategies, one must examine all relevant dimensions, not just one. It is possible that on average the graduates of Christian academies are less well prepared for democratic deliberation than are graduates of the best public schools (I know of no evidence bearing on this idea one way or the other). Nonetheless, they may be better citizens in other respects.

The final issue cuts even deeper. Suppose it is the case that a particular public policy is conducive to the cultivation of democratic citizenship. Does it follow that this policy is always right or permissible? The liberal answer is no, not always. The claims of liberty (or, in Gutmann and Thompson's terms, personal integrity) serve to limit the state's power to mold individuals into citizens. That is what it means to affirm a sphere of parental power not subject to state control. And as we saw, that is the clear meaning of *Meyer v. Nebraska* and *Pierce v. Society of Sisters*. There is, as Gutmann and Thompson rightly insist, an important public interest in educating good citizens. But there are other morally significant interests with which the formation of citizens sometimes comes into conflict and to which the claims of citizenship must sometimes give way.

I believe that a genuinely liberal society will organize itself around the principle of maximum feasible accommodation of diverse ways of life, limited only by the minimum requirements of civic unity. This principle expresses (and requires) the practice of tolerance—the conscientious reluctance to act in ways that impede others from living in accordance with their various conceptions of what gives life meaning and worth.

Gutmann and Thompson criticize this principle on the grounds that it

> would not go far enough for the purposes of deliberative democracy. It provides no positive basis on which citizens can expect to resolve their moral disagreements in the future. Citizens go their separate ways, keeping their moral reasons to themselves, avoiding moral engagement. This may sometimes keep the peace. . . . But *mere toleration* also locks into place the moral divisions in society and makes collective moral progress far more difficult. (62, emphasis added)

In my view, Gutmann and Thompson are far too optimistic about the actual possibilities of resolving moral disagreements, and much too grudging about the practical worth of toleration. In most times and places, the avoidance of repression and bloody conflict is in itself a morally significant achievement—all the more so if it is based on internalized norms of restraint rather than a modus vivendi reflecting a balance of power. The agreement to disagree is a way of dealing with moral disagreement that is not necessarily inferior to agreement on the substance of the issue. In the real world, there is nothing "mere" about toleration. As Michael Walzer says, "Toleration itself is often underestimated, as if it is the least we can do for our fellows, the most minimal of their entitlements. In fact, . . . even the most grudging forms and precarious arrangements [of toleration] are very good things, sufficiently rare in human history that they require not only practical but also theoretical appreciation."[9]

I do not deny that "collective moral progress" is possible. But it is much rarer than one would like and (if history is any guide) at least as likely to be achieved through the exercise of political power, or military force, or slow unplanned processes of social abrasion and influence as through democratic deliberation. Liberals have never scorned (indeed, they have rightly prized) principles of social organization that "lock into place" *religious* divisions in society. A society that makes room for a wide (though not unlimited) range of cultural and moral divisions is no less an achievement.

But to what extent is it possible to implement policies based on this principle? Wouldn't the kind of accommodation sought by the fundamentalist parents lead to a slippery slope of endless claims against public school systems? The actual sequence of events in Hawkins County suggests otherwise.

The parents raised objections not to the public school curriculum as a whole but to one specific line of English readers. They initially proposed removing their children from reading classes every day and personally teaching them out of different textbooks somewhere on the school grounds. The principal of the middle school rejected that proposal but said, "I can understand why you feel the way you do." He offered a counterproposal approved by the school superintendent and the chairman of the school board: The children could go to the library during reading period, where they would read from an alternative textbook on their own, without parental involvement or supervision. The fundamentalist parents quickly accepted this offer and agreed on alternative readers. Within a few weeks, ten middle school children were using the readers.

If this accommodation had been accepted by all schools in Hawkins County, that would have been the end of the matter. But it was not. A number of elementary school principals refused to go along, and some children were suspended. The next month, after a contentious meeting, the school board changed course and suppressed the policy that had been implemented by the middle school with the approval of the board chairman. It was only at that juncture that the parents felt compelled to escalate a limited policy dispute into a broader legal controversy.[10]

In short, the parents were willing to play by the rules, enter into a civil dialogue with school officials, and accept proposals that fell short of their original desires. The logic of their position was perfectly compatible with the principles of constitutional order and with a workable system of public education. There was no slippery slope.

This should not be surprising: The limited public education accommodation for the Old Order Amish approved by the Supreme Court in *Wisconsin v. Yoder*[11] a quarter of a century ago has not led to an escalation of faith-based demands. Indeed, few other groups have even sought similar treatment for themselves. Properly interpreted, the constitution of a liberal democracy is capacious enough to accommodate groups whose beliefs and practices do not much resemble those of most college professors.

Still, accommodation cannot be unlimited; a constitution is not a suicide pact. A liberal democracy must have the capacity to articulate and defend its core principles, with coercive force if needed. I agree with Gutmann and Thompson that democracy cannot be understood simply as a set of procedures. The issue between us concerns the extent and substance of the principles that a democracy must enforce.

In my view (which I have discussed at length elsewhere), these principles include what is required for civil order, justice, and the basics of human development.[12] Beyond this limited uniformity, a liberal democracy insists on the priority of liberty—that is, on the importance of allowing human beings to live their lives in ways congruent with their varying conceptions of what gives life meaning and purpose. It is only on this basis—in theory and in practice—that a political community can embrace divergent views concerning the ultimate source of moral authority.

For two millennia, political orders have grappled with the challenges posed by revealed religions that are not "civil" religions. Liberal democracy, rightly understood, represents the most nearly adequate response to this challenge. At the heart of the liberal democratic settlement is a principled refusal to allow religion to engulf the political order or to let politics invade and dominate religion.

By contrast, Gutmann and Thompson's brand of deliberative democracy seems almost indifferent to this delicate but vital balance. In the name of democracy, it verges on a kind of republicanism that diminishes the claims of liberty. In the name of deliberation, it verges on a kind of rationalism that denies the public claims of faith.

The motivation that leads Gutmann and Thompson to their account of deliberation is admirable. A more deliberative politics along the lines they suggest would be a great improvement over the mindless sloganeering and special interest deals that dominate our politics today. My argument is not against deliberation as such, only against a restrictive understanding of deliberation that rules out so much of what is central to the lives of so many of our fellow citizens. The "civic magnanimity" that Gutmann and Thompson propose in what for me is the most compelling section of their book (82–84) can and should be capacious enough to include the dissenting parents of Hawkins County.

Notes

1. See Jehuda Halevy, *Kuzari: The Book of Proof and Argument*, edited with an introduction and commentary by Isaak Heinemann (Oxford: East and West Library, 1947), 50–51.

2. Ira Katznelson, *Liberalism's Crooked Circle: Letters to Adam Michnik*

(Princeton: Princeton University Press, 1996), 171–73. Katznelson takes the first quotation from an article by Partha Chatterjee.

3. Gutmann and Thompson, *Democracy and Disagreement* (Cambridge: Bellnap Press of Harvard University Press, 1996), 204. Page references to this book are given in parentheses in the text.

4. *Meyer v. Nebraska,* 262 U.S. 401, 402 (1923).

5. *Pierce v. Society of Sisters,* 268 U.S. 510 (1925).

6. *Pierce v. Society of Sisters,* 268 U.S. 535 (1925).

7. Especially for Gutmann, who praises the cultivation of the imagination as an important (and politically relevant) goal of education ("Civic Education and Social Diversity," *Ethics* 105 [April 1995]: 572). She properly raises the question of how imaginative powers are to be strengthened. But the answer is hardly obvious. Recently, at my son's bar mitzvah, our rabbi commented that students' engagement with the lives of Jewish patriarchs and matriarchs—especially the portions of their lives that seem strangest to modern readers—can be a powerful force for the cultivation of imaginative sympathies. That was certainly true for my son, who wrestled productively (if not wholly successfully) with the question of why Sarah asked Abraham to have a child by Hagar, and why Abraham consented.

8. Macedo, "Liberal Civic Education and Religious Fundamentalism: The Case of God v. John Rawls?," *Ethics* 105 (April 1995): 486. I find it difficult to believe that the "exposure to diversity" Macedo believes is essential to the inculcation of liberal tolerance in children is likely to succeed if it is crammed down the throats of their parents. I believe that in the long run the *practice* of toleration— the policy of providing the widest possible scope for diversity consistent with the minimum requirements of liberal social unity—offers the best hope of generating gratitude toward the regime that makes this possible and hence support for the principle of toleration itself.

9. Michael Walzer, *On Toleration* (New Haven: Yale University Press, 1997), xi.

10. This history is drawn from Stephen Bates, *Battleground: One Mother's Crusade, The Religious Right, and the Struggle for Control of Our Classrooms* (New York: Poseidon, 1993), 71–85.

11. *Wisconsin v. Yoder,* 406 U.S. 205 (1972).

12. See my *Justice and the Human Good* (Chicago: University of Chicago Press, 1980); *Liberal Purposes: Goods, Virtues, and Diversity in the Liberal State* (New York: Cambridge University Press, 1991); and "Two Concepts of Liberalism," *Ethics* 105 (April 1995): 516–34.

4

Three Limitations of Deliberative Democracy

Identity Politics, Bad Faith, and Indeterminacy

WILLIAM H. SIMON

*I*n *Democracy and Disagreement*, Amy Gutmann and Dennis Thompson elaborate a liberal political style designed to complement the substantive liberalism they and others have developed in recent years. The style they portray is deliberative, and its essence is the appeal to principle.[1]

Although deliberation is necessarily open-ended, it flounders without some structure. So Gutmann and Thompson suggest three broad substantive principles as starting points—liberty, basic opportunity, and fair opportunity. These principles are supposed to be definite enough to help us frame issues but not so definite as to constitute a program. Finally, they give us extended illustrations of how deliberative democracy might play out with respect to three current debates—surrogate motherhood, welfare reform, and affirmative action.

There is a paradoxical quality to their demonstration. Gutmann and Thompson's conclusions on the three illustrative issues pretty much track the prevailing views on the Center-Left portion of the American political spectrum. (They oppose criminalization of surrogacy contracts but also reject coercive enforcement of unexecuted contracts where the mother changes her mind; favor work requirements for welfare recipients but only where decent jobs are available; and support affirmative action for historically disadvantaged minority groups.) If, as I do, you find their arguments powerful and their conclusions convincing, you have to wonder why we need the actual, large-scale deliberation for which the authors call initially, since Gutmann and Thompson make their strong cases on these issues entirely with simulated armchair-style deliberation. Of course, if you don't buy their conclusions, then you may be inclined to wonder whether the deliberative style they argue for doesn't have a programmatic bias that limits its appeal.

I don't intend this as a criticism, however. The paradox seems largely unavoidable in any effort to give concreteness to a picture of a style or process. Anyone who has tried to envision what kind of politics might follow from Jürgen Habermas's ideals of "communicative action" has to be grateful to Gutmann and Thompson for their effort to illustrate their norms in detail.

So I want to engage Gutmann and Thompson's examples, not as substantive policy arguments but as illustrations of a political style. It's an attractive style, but it has some drawbacks that Gutmann and Thompson do not adequately credit.

Identity Politics and the Mobilization Problem

Gutmann and Thompson make deliberative democracy seem so attractive that you tend to forget that many people reject it.

One notable mode of rejection is politically engaged religious fundamentalism, which in several sectarian varieties is booming throughout the world. Another is the various forms of "identity politics" prominent in the United States, especially in the universities. Fundamentalism is explicitly hostile to deliberation, and "identity politics" is occasionally so. Even when the latter is not openly hostile, it is often implicitly so.

On this point, I offer two pieces of evidence from my own experience: First, many minority students and academics regard the demand to deliberate over issues of racial justice, notably affirmative action, as offensive or oppressive. For them, merely to treat such questions as open for debate is a personal assault. Their positions on these issues are so bound up with their sense of self-worth that they cannot "deliberate" about them any more than they can deliberate about their sense of self-worth.

Second, student activists of various types often seem to prefer dealing with conservative over liberal administrators, even though the substantive commitments of the former are closer to their own. They often speak contemptuously of "liberals." In doing so, they usually seem to be referring not to substantive disagreements but to just the matters of political style that Gutmann and Thompson's notion of deliberation captures. These students dislike the deliberative style. They prefer the more "straightforward" style of the conservative bureaucrat. This is the style that forgoes invocation of principles in favor of assertions of power and appeals to self-interest—a style that Gutmann and Thompson distinguish and disparage as "bargaining," in contrast to "deliberation" (56–57).

Gutmann and Thompson do not deal adequately with this type of rejection of deliberation. They speculate that it arises from a fear on the part of subordinated groups that they are not as skilled at deliberation and will hence lose out. They dismiss this fear as ungrounded, noting that disadvantaged groups have historically been able to find able representatives to speak on their behalf, and they mention Martin Luther King Jr. as an example. "The lack of political success of marginalized groups stems not from a deliberative deficit but from a lack of power," they say, and they argue that the commitment to reciprocity on the deliberative playing field can only benefit disadvantaged groups (133).

This response misses the point in important respects. Gutmann and Thompson are right to suggest that fear of being bested at deliberative discourse should not be a major concern for disadvantaged groups generally, but they ignore two more important concerns.

First, politics offers occasions for groups to define and constitute themselves through the assertion of their claims. A group's political power is partly a function of its cohesion and confidence. Public political action is an occasion for building both, and nothing in Gutmann and Thompson's argument suggests that deliberative styles will be optimal from this point of view. Malcolm X is perhaps the most famous activist to insist on the tension between the self-constitutive dimension of identity politics and deliberative political styles. "Don't change the white man's mind," he said. "We've got to change our own minds about each other. We have to see each other with new eyes."[2] From this perspective, the rhetorical equality of the deliberative style can leave unabated a psychological inequality that distorts a subordinated group's sense of its interests and capacities.

Second, some people seem to experience the connotations of mutuality or commonality of the deliberative ideal as oppressive or presumptuous. Deliberation seems to presuppose a closeness or solidarity that seems false or suffocating. One might say that to such people, deliberation is objectionable because it disrespects the "plurality of groups." I adapt this phrase from a prominent liberal complaint about communitarianism, which is that it ignores the "plurality of persons."[3] In contrasting itself to communitarianism, liberalism prides itself on its relative impersonality, but the complaints of identity politics suggest that the deliberative style of liberalism is not impersonal enough, as compared to, say, the style of "bargaining."

However, the most salient alternative of identity politics to the deliberative style is not "bargaining" but a style that could be called "carthartic." Vis-à-vis opposing groups, the cathartic style seeks to engender respect and cooperation by appealing to fear and/or empathy (the Hegel effect).[4] Vis-à-vis the group itself, the cathartic style strengthens and unifies the group through the articulation and dramatization of shared experiences and goals and through confrontation with opposing groups (the Sartre effect).[5]

Of course, the great master of the cathartic style in modern America was Martin Luther King Jr. Gutmann and Thompson are surely wrong to claim him for deliberative politics. No part of his most famous achievements was based on deliberation. His genius was to assert age-old claims in a manner that mobilized African Americans and their allies and to maneuver liberal officials into positions where they felt compelled to make good on principles they already espoused.

The example of identity politics suggests a broader complaint against Gutmann and Thompson. Why take "disagreement" as the agenda-defining problem for democrats, rather than, say, *demobilization*? To be sure, Gutmann and Thompson are proponents of "participation," but they seem to have a fairly constricted notion of it, and they tend to portray it as a means to forging agreement rather than an end in itself.

While the goals of engaging people in politics and bringing them to agreement are partly complementary, they're partly in tension. Political mobilization often increases both the experience and the articulation of disagreement. Of course, the tension between consensus and mobilization is another long-standing problem of liberalism, which alternately finds itself appealing to consensus to ground its prescriptions and appealing to more transcendent norms against consensus. I wouldn't criticize Gutmann and Thompson for failing to resolve this tension, but I am inclined to fault them for overvaluing consensus.

Gutmann and Thompson make good use of the tradition of Aristotle and Mill to defend the idea of public conversation against utilitarianism and libertarianism, but they seem unfortunately allergic to the tradition of Hegel, Marx, and Sartre. Yet both the broader notion of political practice and the emphasis on collective self-constitution in the latter tradition seem essential to understanding an important range of contemporary practices and aspirations.

Bad Faith

Gutmann and Thompson don't have much to say about strategic issues in deliberation—indeed, they tend to counterpose the strategic mentality to the deliberative. Surely, however, just as it's important to choose one's battles, it's important to choose the occasions on which one will deliberate. Gutmann and Thompson seem insufficiently discriminating in their commitment to deliberation.

For Gutmann and Thompson, deliberation is appropriate for disagreements over moral principles. This seems to me overbroad in two respects. First, where your opponent takes a position in bad faith, it can be a mistake to deliberate. By "taking a position in bad faith" I mean being either consciously dishonest or simply not open to reflection. It can be a mistake to deliberate with a person in bad faith because at best it could be a waste of time, and at worst you could help the person present himself to others as more reasonable than he is. Moreover, the deliberative process may put some pressure on people who hold extreme positions in good faith to modify their positions simply not to appear to disrespect the deliberative process.

Second, note that disputes cannot be readily categorized as moral or nonmoral prior to efforts to resolve them. Disputes may be moral for some people and not for others, or partly moral and partly something else. Some people will typically be in good faith and some not. So the decision to intervene with a deliberative style is partly a decision about how a dispute is to be constituted, not just about how it will be resolved.

Gutmann and Thompson's discussion of welfare reform illustrates some of these difficulties. The basic problem is that it presupposes that disputes over welfare reform are based on good-faith moral differences, but it seems clear to me that they are not.

Note three features of the debate:

1. Hardly any liberals believe that the government should provide public assistance to someone who has the capacity to earn a minimally decent living under minimally decent conditions. Hardly any conservatives deny that the government should provide public assistance to people who cannot support themselves through no fault of their own. If there is any ground of good-faith disagreement among liberals and conservatives, it would be over factual matters concerning the availability of private sources of support in the event of various welfare cutbacks and interventions.

Yet one finds very little interest in these factual matters among either legislators or Gutmann and Thompson. Instead one finds effusive debate over propositions that are largely undisputed or unespoused. For example, a substantial segment of the debate takes the form of conservatives imputing to liberals the virtually nonexistent belief in unconditional welfare and proceeding to refute it, with liberals futilely denying that they hold the belief.

Gutmann and Thompson fall into this conservative trap by devoting a substantial part of their argument to refuting the claim for unconditional welfare, even though they confirm its virtual nonexistence by offering as their sole citation for it a work by a Belgian philosopher unknown to the participants in the American welfare debates (277–82).

2. Nearly everyone in the debate, now including Gutmann and Thompson, asserts or assumes that there is a strong connection between long-term

welfare receipt and a psychological trait that can be appropriately described as "dependence" and loss of self-respect (285–86, 302–3). The usually implicit comparison is to earnings in the low-wage labor market, which are assumed to be connected with relative independence and dignity. Although this position now has the status of uncontestable dogma in the debates, no one has made any effort to substantiate it, and many people have good reason to believe it is wrong. Most ethnographic studies of low-wage work emphasize the same psychologically debilitating features the welfare reform debate associates with welfare.[6]

3. Finally, at the risk of triteness, let me remind you that dozens of packages of "corporate welfare" programs and dozens of features of Social Security involve expenditures of greater magnitude and weaker normative support (even on conservative principles) than Aid to Families with Dependent Children. Yet these big-ticket items command not a fraction of the space on the public agenda that welfare reform does.

The point here is not that the deliberation has been faulty. It is that welfare reform is by and large not a matter of moral disagreement. Viewed charitably, it is a matter of factual disagreement over the availability of earnings from low-wage employment. Viewed uncharitably, it is a campaign of vicious demagoguery. On the first assumption, treating it deliberatively diverts attention from the key issues. On the second assumption, treating it deliberatively gives an undeserved legitimacy to the demagogues.

Liberal Indeterminacy

Here I want to reassert the familiar complaint of leftist lawyers that liberal principles are too indeterminate to do the work that political theorists assign them. I am not forgetting that the indeterminacy of Gutmann and Thompson's substantive principles plays a considered role in their scheme. It makes room for deliberation. Nevertheless, the principles are supposed to provide structure and chart the path to answers, and in this capacity, Gutmann and Thompson's basic liberty, basic opportunity, and fair opportunity will leave us stranded or lead us astray more often than they allow.

I think this happens in the surrogate motherhood example. Gutmann and Thompson treat this under the liberty principle, but I think this is a mistake. I don't disagree with their conclusion that the surrogacy contracts should not be criminalized but should be unenforceable against a mother who changes her mind before or shortly after birth. However, I don't think liberty provides much support for the conclusion.

Granted, as against the moralistic position that would criminalize surrogacy arrangements, liberty does seem a relevant and strong consideration. But compared to the position Gutmann and Thompson characterize as paternalistic that would make executory contracts unenforceable, liberty seems irrelevant.

The liberty to which Gutmann and Thompson appeal is the liberty to make contracts, which they suggest implies that the government should "enforce contracts necessary for citizens to carry out their plans" (235). They see contract enforcement as a presumptive incident of autonomy, but this view is not tenable in any a priori or categorical sense. The type of contracts exemplified by the surrogate mother example are "executory" in the sense that they contemplate, not simultaneous exchange, but a future performance by at least one of the parties. When the state enforces such contracts against a promisor, it potentially enhances the promisor's liberty by making it possible for her to enter a variety of exchanges that her contract partners would not have been willing to make without the assurance of enforcement. But at the same time, such an enforcement regime potentially restricts the promisor's liberty by subjecting her to state coercion at the time for performance. Enforcement protects liberty to enter into contracts only at the cost of restricting liberty to change your mind. It facilitates your ability to plan your life at the time of commitment but frustrates it at the time of enforcement.[7]

As a matter of abstract logic, there is no reason to think that the liberty-enhancing effects of an enforcement regime will outweigh the liberty-limiting effects. To make a plausible assessment of the matter, we have to begin by asking how many people will, like the surrogate mother Mary Beth Whitehead, regret their commitment when enforcement time comes. To the extent that they do regret, we have to ask whether the initial choice facilitated by the enforcement regime or the later one frustrated by it is more important in liberty terms.

Of course, for some libertarians, the mere fact that the promisor "agreed"—gave some formal manifestation of consent—makes it consistent with liberty values to enforce even where she regrets agreement. But such arguments strike most people, surely including Gutmann and Thompson, as dogmatic and circular. For Gutmann and Thompson, liberty is not a formal property but an actual experience of self-expression and control. There is no reason to presume that executory contract enforcement is consistent with this thicker version of liberty.

And indeed there is no such presumption in our culture. Contract enforceabililty has been limited and even banished throughout large areas of the American landscape. These areas include not only much of family law, where the surrogate mother case arises, but also much of the law of political rights, where one would expect liberty values to be especially important. Citizenship rights, including the rights of residence and voting, are typically inalienable, which means that a vast range of potential executory contracts are unenforceable. Note also that while the contract enforceability is the starting point in the realm of business matters, the dominant justification for the principle appeals not to liberty but to efficiency.

Gutmann and Thompson recognize the indeterminacy of the liberty principle when it comes to extreme situations like contracts to sell yourself into slavery. Here they acknowledge that there's something wrong with characterizing a choice that precludes all future capacity for choice as an expression of liberty. They respond to this problem by carving out an exception to their presumption for contracts that impair "personal integrity," and they suggest that the exception applies to surrogacy contracts (264–72).

But every executory contract is like a slavery contract in that it involves a choice that impairs the chooser's capacity for future choice. True, the impairment in most contracts is less than in the slavery contract. But if the question is whether enforcement furthers liberty, the issue is not the magnitude of the impairment but whether this sacrifice in liberty is outweighed by some gain in liberty from the benefit the promisor receives. In situations where the promisor regrets her commitment, we have no reason for presuming this to be so.

On the issue of whether surrogacy contracts should be enforced against a mother who changes her mind, I think Gutmann and Thompson reach the right answer. They decide that the "personal integrity" exception rebuts the liberty-based presumption in favor of enforcement. Nevertheless, I think Gutmann and Thompson are wrong in thinking that liberty supports any presumption in favor of enforcement. Their framing of the issue in liberty terms and their invocation of the presumption gives more weight to the enforcement argument than it deserves. The issue calls for a comparison of the choices made possible by an enforcement regime with those foreclosed by one (for the promisee as well as the promisor). There is no a priori reason to think liberty weighs more heavily on either side of the comparison.

Conclusion

Having made my criticisms, I want to reaffirm my admiration for *Democracy and Disagreement*. Gutmann and Thompson have vividly illustrated a way of talking about issues that many people believe can't be productively discussed. They have also made an eloquent plea for more participation and more civility. The political style they favor will be attractive to much of the professional class.

I don't intend the "professional class" qualification as a put-down. I like deliberative politics; it's my kind of politics. But I see situations, including several of those Gutmann and Thompson discuss, in which some people are likely to find that the deliberative style doesn't suit their most fundamental political aims, makes them vulnerable strategically, or just doesn't get them very far even in the quest for "agreement."

Notes

1. Two other components—publicity and accountability—are important but secondary. Gutmann and Thompson, *Democracy and Disagreement* (Cambridge: Belknap Press of Harvard University Press, 1996). Page references to this book are given in parentheses in the text.

2. *Malcolm X Speaks: Speeches and Statements* 40 (New York: Grove Press, press, 1965).

3. E.g., Michael Sandel, *Liberalism and Limits of Justice* (Cambridge, Mass.: Harvard University Press, 1982), 50–51.

4. G. W. F. Hegel, *Phenomenology of Spirit*, trans. A. V. Miller (New York: Oxford University Press, 1977), 113–19) (on "lordship and bondage").

5. Jean-Paul Sartre, *Critique of Dialectical Reason: Theory of Practical Ensembles*, trans. Alan Sheridan-Smith (London: NLB, 1976) 345–404 (on the transition from "seriality" to the "fused group").

6. See, for example, Elliot Liebow, *Tally's Corner* (Boston: Little Brown, 1967), chap. 2, and for a survey, Regina Austin, "Employer Abuse, Worker Resistance, and the Tort of Intentional Infliction of Emotional Distress," *Stanford Law Review* 41, no. 1 (1988).

7. On these matters in general, see Robert Hale, "Coercion and Distribution in a Supposedly Noncoercive State," *Political Science Quarterly* 38, no. 470 (1923); Walter Wheeler Cook, "The Privileges of Labor Unions in the Struggle for Life," *Yale Law Journal* no. 163 27 (1919).

5

Deliberation, and What Else?

MICHAEL WALZER

*T*he recent outpouring of books and articles on deliberative democracy is very impressive, and many of the arguments are persuasive. But there has been so little disagreement about deliberation—and no effort at all to consider its contexts and complements—that the idea is in danger of becoming common-place and sterile.[1] So I intend to indulge a contrarian impulse and try to make a list of all the nondeliberative activities that democratic politics legitimately, and perhaps even necessarily, involves. I doubt that the list is exhaustive, though I have not knowingly left anything out. As will quickly become ob-vious, I have not made deliberation synonymous with thinking; mine is not a list of thoughtless activities. Deliberation here describes a particular way of thinking: quiet, reflective, open to a wide range of evidence, respectful of different views. It is a rational process of weighing the available data, consid-ering alternative possibilities, arguing about relevance and worthiness, and then choosing the best policy or person. Now, what else do we do? What is going on in the political world besides deliberation?

The point of these questions is not to deny the importance of deliberation or to criticize theoretical accounts of what it requires, like that provided by Amy Gutmann and Dennis Thompson in *Democracy and Disagreement*.[2] Nor do I mean to suggest that those two, or any other theorists of deliberation, would deny the importance of the activities that I shall list in my answer—

though they might describe them somewhat differently than I do. For I do mean to offer, in almost all the cases, a strongly sympathetic description. But my main purpose here is to figure out how deliberation fits into a democratic political process that is, as my list makes clear, pervasively nondeliberative. So let's assume, but for the moment set aside, the value of "reasoning together" as Gutmann and Thompson describe it, where reason is qualified by reciprocity, publicity, and accountability. Politics has other values in addition to, and often in tension with, reason: passion, commitment, solidarity, courage, and competitiveness (all of which also require qualification). These values are exemplified in a wide range of activities in the course of which men and women sometimes find occasion to "reason together" but which are better described in other terms.

1. *Political education.* People have to learn how to be political. Some of what they learn they are taught in school: a rough outline of the history of democratic politics, the crucial events and actors; basic information about the federal system, the three branches of government, the structure and timing of elections; perhaps also an account of the leading ideologies, at least in caricature; and so on. But parties, movements, unions, and interest groups are also schools of a sort, teaching their members the ideas that the groups are organized to advance. What the old communist parties called "agitprop" is a form of political education. Theorists committed to deliberation will say that this is a bad form of education, really indoctrination; and it is literally true that parties and movements seek to indoctrinate their members, that is, to bring them to accept a doctrine—and, whenever possible, to represent it, to repeat its central tenets (even when it is unpopular to do that), so that each indoctrinated member becomes an agent of doctrinal transmission. Whether this sort of thing is good or bad, it is enormously important in political life, because the political identity of most people, or, better, of most of the people who are engaged by politics, is shaped in this way. This is how they become agents with opinions. Of course, political identities are also shaped by familial life: Agents with opinions marry agents with similar opinions and raise children to whom they try, most often successfully, to pass on those opinions. Socialization in the family, the earliest form of political education, is just agitprop with love. But the opinions that are transmitted reflect doctrines developed outside the family and inculcated in public settings through a great variety of public media.

2. *Organization.* One of the aims of political education, or, at least, of agitprop and indoctrination, is to induce people to identify with and work for particular organizations. But organizing itself is a highly specific activity, which involves getting people to actually sign up, carry a card, accept a discipline, pay their dues, and learn to act in accordance with a script that they don't write themselves. "The union makes us strong!" is a democratic maxim, even

if it is also true in nondemocratic settings; it reflects democracy's majoritarianism, which puts a premium on association and combination. But unions, like armies, are not strong if their members stop to deliberate about every action that the leadership commands. The leaders deliberate on behalf of everyone else, and this process is more or less public, so that the members can speculate about what the deliberations of the leaders will come to. But organizers try to persuade people to act in unison, rather than as speculating or deliberating individuals.

3. *Mobilization.* Large-scale political action requires more than organization. Individual men and women have to be stimulated, provoked, energized, excited, called to arms. The military metaphor is appropriate: An army can be an inert organization, held in reserve, the soldiers sitting in camps, cleaning their weapons, occasionally exercising. If they are to fight a war, they have to be mobilized. Something similar is true in political life. Ordinary members must be turned into militants, at least for the duration of a particular activity. An especially intense sort of agitprop is necessary here, to capture their interest, focus their energies, draw them tightly together—so that they actually read the party's manifesto, say, and argue on its behalf, and march, carry banners, and shout slogans in the party's parades. I know that the image of masses of people shouting slogans will suggest to deliberative democrats an antidemocratic politics. But the character of the politics depends on the slogans, and these have often been prodemocratic. Indeed, what might be called the struggle for deliberative democracy—that is, for political equality, a free press, the right of association, civil rights for minorities, and so on—has required a lot of slogan shouting. It is not easy to imagine a democratic politics to which popular mobilization has become superfluous. (Whether that should be our ideal is a question I will come to only at the end of my list.)

4. *Demonstration.* The point of a democratic mobilization is not to storm government offices and literally seize state power but rather to demonstrate personal intensity, numerical strength, and doctrinal conviction—all of which are critical to popular power. Hence the march or parade, the party rally, the placards and banners, the shouting of the participants, the oratory of the leaders, and the fierce applause it is meant to elicit. There is no room here for quiet deliberation, for that would not show to the world the force of these people's concern, their passionate commitment and solidarity, their determination to achieve a particular political object. Once again, the aim is demonstrative: to deliver a message—sometimes more generally to one's fellow citizens, sometimes more narrowly to an entrenched elite. The message goes like this: Here we stand; this is what we believe must be done; and we don't believe it casually, it isn't an "opinion" of the sort that might be captured by an opinion poll, it's not what we think today and might or might not think tomorrow; we will keep coming back until we have won; and if you want to

get on with the ordinary business of politics, you had better accommodate us on this point (or on this series of seventeen points). Of course, all this can be said in a fanatical way, reflecting ideological or religious absolutism rather than political determination. But demonstrating intensity and conviction now doesn't necessarily preclude negotiating later on, and this combination can be used, and has been, in defense of democratic rights—to vote, or strike, or associate freely—as well as in defense of substantive but contested reforms like prohibition, or gun control, or the minimum wage.

5. *Statement.* "Making a statement" is the aim of the demonstration, but it can also take a more literal form. I have already mentioned the party manifesto, which the militants endorse and repeat. Sometimes it is politically useful to reduce the manifesto to a credo or declaration, affirming this or that ideological conviction (something like the profession of faith of a religious community), or staking out a position on some more immediate issue, and then ask people to sign on. The publication of the credo, with names attached, signals to the world the commitment of these people, their readiness to take a stand in a public way. The authors of the credo may have deliberated about what to say, more likely about how to say it; the people asked to sign presumably deliberate about whether to sign or not. But the credo itself has the form of an assertion, which is not likely to be modified as a result of counterassertions. At moments of intense political conflict, newspapers and magazines will be filled with statements of this sort—declarations for and against this or that policy, say; but all of them taken together do not constitute a democratic deliberation, since the different sets of authors and signatories don't always make arguments, and when they do, they rarely read each other's arguments.

6. *Debate.* Statement and counterstatement make for something like a debate, though we usually expect debaters to speak directly to one another, arguing back and forth in a quicker, more spontaneous, more heated way than is possible in the formal exchange of credos and declarations. Debaters do have to listen to one another, but listening in this case does not produce anything like a deliberative process: Their object is not to reach an agreement among themselves but to win the debate, that is, to persuade the audience that this position, rather than any of the alternatives, is the best one. (Some members of the audience may then deliberate among themselves or within themselves— going over the different positions in their own minds.) A debate is a contest between verbal athletes, and the aim is victory. The means are the exercise of rhetorical skill, the mustering of favorable evidence (and the suppression of unfavorable evidence), the discrediting of the other debaters, the appeal to authority or celebrity, and so on. All these are plain to see in party debates in parliaments and assemblies and in debates between or among candidates at election time. But they are also standard on the lecture circuit and in newspapers and magazines, whenever representatives of different positions are chal-

lenged to engage each other's arguments. The others are rivals, not fellow participants; they are already committed, not persuadable; the objects of the exercise, again, are the people in the audience—though many of them have come just to cheer for their own side, which can also be a useful political activity.

7. *Bargaining.* Sometimes the positions defended in this or that demonstration or manifesto or debate have been deliberated on, but very often they are the products of long and complicated negotiations among interested as well as opinionated individuals. That means that they don't represent anyone's idea of the best position; they are compromises with which no one is entirely satisfied they reflect the balance of forces, not the weight of arguments. Commonly, bargaining doesn't begin until the relative strength of the different parties has been tested; sometimes its purpose is to avoid further costly or bloody tests. So the parties agree to split the differences between them, the precise split depending on the previous tests of strength. "Balanced tickets" are worked out in the same way. And government policy in a democracy is more often the result of a negotiating process of this sort than of any deliberative process. The best policy is the one that accommodates the largest number of interests or, better, that accommodates precisely those interests that are able to assert themselves politically (hence the importance of organization and mobilization). I can imagine people arguing about how to serve the common good, above and beyond all the particular interests, given the constraint that the particular interests must also be served. But that is a pretty severe constraint, and the result is surely closer to give-and-take than to deliberation. Gutmann and Thompson argue for a distinction between "self-interested" bargaining and mutual accommodation—the latter representing a properly deliberative process.[3] But I suspect that mutuality in political life is always qualified by interest and tested by conflict. What marks off deliberation is better seen if we consider the example of the jury. We don't want the jurors in a criminal case bargaining with one another or even accommodating one another: "I'll vote your way on the first count if you vote my way on the second and third counts." We want them to weigh the evidence as best they can and come up with a verdict, that is, a true statement about guilt or innocence. But politicians can legitimately act in exactly the way jurors are barred from acting; indeed, a bargain is often the better part of political wisdom.

8. *Lobbying.* The cultivation of public officials by private parties is pervasive in politics, in both democratic and nondemocratic settings. It may well be the case that in democracies the private parties are more likely to argue with the officials (rather than bargain with them), or at least to provide them with arguments, since democratically responsible officials will have to defend their positions in one or another open forum. Still, lobbying at its most effective involves the forging of close personal relations; it depends on social

networks and individual friendships. A good lobbyist makes up in charm, access, and insider knowledge whatever he lacks in arguments. And the arguments he makes will probably have less to do with the issue at hand than with the political future of the official he is lobbying.

9. *Campaigning.* Sometimes this military metaphor is used to refer to any coordinated program of organizing, mobilizing, demonstrating, and so on, for a particular cause. But I mean here to describe only electoral campaigns, the democratic search for voter support. This obviously involves most of the activities that I have listed so far, but it also has its own specific character—in part because it is focused, even when political parties are strong, on specific characters, on leaders with names and faces and life histories as well as programs. It is these leaders who bear the brunt of the campaigning, actively soliciting the votes of their fellow citizens, making promises, trying to look trustworthy, and trying to suggest the untrustworthiness of their opponents. We can imagine them working within a set of limits, legal or moral rules, say, defining "fair campaign practices"—though in fact virtually no effective limits exist today except those enforced by public opinion. What would the rules of a fair campaign be like? They would certainly bear little resemblance to the rules about what can and can't be said in a courtroom, and the reason for that, again, is that we don't believe that voters, any more than politicians, are like jurors.

10. *Voting.* What should citizens do when they vote? Clearly, they should attend to the arguments being made by the different candidates and to the platforms of the parties. They should think about the consequences of this or that candidate's victory, not only for themselves but for the various groups to which they belong, and for the country as a whole. Nonetheless, the body of citizens is not a search committee, deliberating on the most qualified candidate for the Senate, say, or the presidency. The members of a search committee are like jurors in that they are assumed (sometimes wrongly) to have a common understanding of the relevant qualifications and to deliberate impartially among the candidates. But neither of those assumptions is justified in the case of citizens. Some of them may believe that it is toughness and commitment on this or that issue that qualifies someone for the presidency, while others believe that the capacity to produce compromises on all the issues is the best qualification. Some of them may identify with candidate X because she has defended their interests or their values in the past or with candidate Y because he is a member of their ethnic or religious community, or of their union or interest group, or because he has a political history similar to their own. Certainly, again, we want voters to consider the available evidence carefully and to reflect long and hard on the arguments of the contending candidates and parties. But they don't have to disqualify themselves if, because of their current interests or previous commitments, they can't or won't pay equal attention to

each of the contenders. Nor are they barred from choosing the issues on which they focus their considerations and reflections for nondeliberative reasons. Indeed, voters have a right to choose issues and candidates alike with reference to their interests, or their passions, or their ideological commitments, and most of them do just that. Perhaps it is a general truth that the issues on which citizens deliberate (or do not) arise through a political process that is largely nondeliberative. It is through the mobilization of passions and interests that we are forced to address what is (only now) the "question" of poverty, or corruption, or exploitation.

11. *Fund-raising.* Not much can be done in politics without money. Even before the age of television, money had to be raised to pay for salaries and offices; leaflets, newsletters, advertisements, and mass mailings; travel, meeting halls, and party conferences. Nothing is more common in political life than the varied activities that come under the rubric of fund-raising. Historically, in the United States, these activities have probably provided the best examples of participatory democracy—precisely because they don't involve studying the issues, arguing in public, making speeches, or sitting on deliberative committees. Of course, asking rich individuals for their money isn't the work of the demos, but fund-raising on a smaller scale—raffles, rummage sales, bake sales, dinners and dances, "passing the hat"—is in fact a mass activity, one that involves thousands of men and women. And there can't be any doubt that money raised in this way is a bond: People who have given it, and people who have helped to get it, are more loyal to the cause, or loyal longer, than those who merely have reason to think that the cause is just.

12. *Corruption.* This powerful censorious term describes a set of activities, outright bribery and extortion the most obvious and probably the most common, that ought to be excluded from democratic politics. These activities, taken together, constitute my only negative example, and what I am interested in is the argument for their exclusion. Bribery is a nondeliberative activity like many others (though its protagonists might well reason together about whom to bribe and how much to offer); more important, it is an activity that interferes with deliberation. That's why it is barred from some social and governmental settings, but not why it is barred from the primary political setting, the arena of electoral politics. Bribing judges and jurors is wrong precisely because it produces a result that doesn't reflect an impartial deliberative process. Bribing government officials who dispense licenses and grants is wrong because it produces a result that doesn't reflect an honest search for qualified people and worthy projects. But bribing voters is wrong only because it interferes with the democratic representation of the voters themselves, not with any activity required of them: we don't get an accurate picture of their interests, concerns, or opinions. The result lacks democratic legitimacy, but it isn't

illegitimate because impartial reason and reflection have played no part in its production. A candidate who promises to reduce unemployment is appealing, let's say, to the unreflective interests of the unemployed (and all their friends and relatives), yet her appeal doesn't corrupt the political process. In fact, it is an important and entirely legitimate result of her appeal that we find out how many people share those particular interests and give them high priority. But she can't hire the unemployed to vote for her.

13. *Scut work.* A lot of what passes for political participation, a lot of the activity that is critical to the success of organizations and campaigns, is simply boring and repetitive work that has no intrinsically political character at all— like stuffing envelopes, setting up chairs, preparing placards, handing out leaflets, making phone calls (to ask for signatures or money, or to get people to go to meetings or to vote on election day), knocking on doors (for the same purposes), sitting at the literature table at party conferences, and so on. None of this requires much thought, though it often takes a lot of thought, and even some ingenuity, to motivate oneself to do it. Since scut work is necessary— "someone has to do it"—it's worth dwelling for a moment on how it gets done. Obviously, commitment plays a major part, but I think it is important that this commitment exists within a competitive system. The excitement of the competition, the sense of possible victory, the fear of defeat—all these things press people to take on tasks they would otherwise be reluctant to perform. Even when politics begins to get dangerous, there isn't much difficulty recruiting people to do scut work: Danger has its own excitements. Properly deliberative men and women, of course, might be reluctant to stuff envelopes even if no one was threatening to beat up all the envelope stuffers. They might be too busy reading position papers; they might be unmoved by competitive emotions. That scut work regularly gets done may well be the clearest example of the appeal of nondeliberative political activity.

14. *Ruling.* If scut work is the low end of politics, ruling is the high end. Aristotle defined citizenship in a democracy as "ruling and being ruled in turn." But it is the first of these that is commonly valued; the acceptance of "being ruled" is an accommodation to democratic doctrine. If everyone is to have the experience of ruling, we have to take turns. In practice, of course, some people rule for long periods of time; others are ruled all the time. What distinguishes democratic ruling from undemocratic domination is the legitimation of the former through consent. But whatever its legitimacy (and there is domination even in democracies), ruling is for most rulers a pleasurable activity. Aristotle probably believed that some part of the pleasure derived from the exercise of reason on a large scale, over the whole agenda, so to speak, of public issues. In this sense, ruling is a deliberative activity. But the pleasures of command are by no means wholly rational, else people would not seek to

rule with such passion. And we sometimes want rulers who are not likely to deliberate too much—whose "native hue of resolution" is not, like Hamlet's, "sicklied o'er with the pale cast of thought."[4]

That is my list, and it is a hard question whether, if I had not started by asking *What else?*, deliberation would have a place on it. Does deliberation belong in the same series that includes "organization," "mobilization," "demonstration," and so on? If we take what jurors do as the model of a deliberative process, it probably doesn't. Of course, courts are political institutions insofar as they exist within constitutional structures and sometimes find themselves in conflict with officials exercising legislative and executive authority. But political considerations are supposed to be ruled out when a civil or criminal trial is in progress. The reason for ruling them out is our standard assumption that there is a single just outcome of the trial, which the jury is or should be united in pursuing. No such assumption is possible in political life, which is not merely adversarial but inherently and permanently conflictual. Very few political decisions are "verdicts" in the literal sense of that term. I don't mean that we can't, sometimes, insist that it is morally right and perhaps imperative to do X; but even the people who agree on what X is and on the necessity of doing it are likely to disagree about how to do it, or how soon, or at whose expense.

It isn't necessary to adopt Carl Schmidt's view of politics to recognize that different interests and ideological commitments are often irreconcilable. Of course, parties in conflict negotiate, and settle, and then reconcile themselves to the settlement, but they are likely to feel that something has been lost in the negotiating process and to reserve the right to reopen the discussion whenever conditions seem more propitious. We protect criminals against second prosecutions for the same crime, but we don't protect politicians against repeated challenges on the same issue. Permanent settlements are rare in political life precisely because we have no way of reaching anything like a verdict on contested issues. Passions fade; men and women disengage from particular commitments; interest groups form new alignments; the world turns. But certain deep disagreements, like those between Left and Right, are remarkably persistent, and local forms of religious or ethnic conflict are often so embedded in a political culture as to seem natural to the participants. So politics is the endless return to of these disagreements and conflicts, the struggle to manage and contain them, and, at the same time, to win whatever temporary victories are available. The democratic way to win is to educate, organize, mobilize . . . more people than the other side has. "More" is what makes the victory legitimate, and while legitimacy is strengthened if good arguments can be made about the substantive issues at stake, the victory is rarely won by making good arguments.

But it isn't only the permanence of conflict that accounts for the omission of deliberation from my list but also, more particularly, the prevalence of inequality. Political history, when it doesn't take an ideological form, is mostly the story of the slow creation or consolidation of hierarchies of wealth and power. People fight their way to the top of these hierarchies and then contrive as best they can to maintain their position. The "ruling class" may be much less coherent than Marxist theory suggests; nonetheless, something like it exists, with more or less self-awareness, and aims to sustain itself. Popular organizations and mobilizations are the only ways to oppose this aim. Their effect is not—at least it never has been—to level the hierarchies, but only to shake them up, bring new people in, and perhaps set limits to the differentiations they define and entrench. So democratic politics makes possible an amended version of political history: Now it is the story of the establishment *and partial disestablishment* of inequality. I don't see any way to avoid the endless repetition of this story, any way to replace the struggles it involves with a deliberative process. Who would deliberate? On what issues? With reference to what facts and theories? And why would dissatisfied citizens accept the outcome of the deliberations? Couldn't they always claim that the best thinking of the best thinkers, deliberating under the best conditions, reflects nothing more than the interests of the powers-that-be? Of course, one can design a deliberative process that excludes those interests altogether—by requiring the participants to deliberate behind a veil of ignorance, say, and strictly controlling the facts and theories to which they have access. But that is a utopian design, not realizable in any extant political world.

Should we aim at realizing it? Is this our utopia, the dream of committed democrats—a world where political conflict, class struggle, and ethnic and religious differences are all replaced by pure deliberation? As Joseph Schwartz has recently argued, left-wing political theorists have often written as if this were their ultimate goal.[5] But theories of this sort, as Schwartz correctly claims, reflect an antipolitical bias, and they are unlikely to be realized except by the repression of conflict. No doubt, repression would be undertaken only in defense of policies that the theorists and their friends had thought about long and hard, in imperfect but not implausible deliberative settings, like academic seminars, or communities of exiled intellectuals, or the committees of vanguard parties far from political power. Still, committed democrats can hardly endorse the repression.

Deliberation does have a place, in fact an important place, in democratic politics, but I don't think it has an independent place—a place, so to speak, of its own. There is no setting in the political world quite like the jury room, in which we don't want people to do anything *except* deliberate. Similarly, though politics is often said to involve more committee work than anything else, there are no political committees quite like a search committee looking to appoint a professor or a prize committee trying to identify the best novel of the year. The work of searching out candidates and awarding prizes is often politicized, of course, but when it is, the results are likely to be called into question. By contrast, one expects political considerations to prevail in the committees of a party or movement and even in legislative and administrative committees—at least, such considerations are legitimately invoked; something would be wrong with the democratic process if they had no role at all. Imagine a group of bureaucrats deliberating with great seriousness for many hours, and then doing what they have concluded is the right thing to do—without taking into account the recorded preferences of a majority of the people or the interests of whatever coalition of groups currently constitutes the majority (which is exactly what juries are supposed to do). The chosen policy of the deliberating bureaucrats might well be the "best" one, but it would not be the right policy for a democratic government.

Deliberation's proper place is dependent on other activities that it doesn't constitute or control. We make room for it, and should do that, in the larger space that we provide for more properly political activities. We try to introduce a certain measure of calm reflection and reasoned argument into, say, the work of political education. Even agitprop can be better or worse, and it is clearly better if its arguments are honestly informed and addressed to the hardest questions, the most difficult challenges that the party or movement confronts. Similarly, we can imagine the party platform drawn up by a group of people who are not only good negotiators but reflective men and women aiming at proposals that are morally justified and economically realistic as well as politically appealing. We can imagine a negotiating process in which people try to understand and accommodate the interests of the other side (while still defending their own) rather than just driving the hardest possible bargain. We can imagine parliamentary debates where the rival speakers listen to one another and are prepared to modify their positions. And finally, we can imagine citizens who actually think about the common good when they evaluate candidates or party programs, the deals their representatives strike or the arguments they make.

It is an interesting question, one that has been addressed most inventively by James Fishkin,[6] what practical arrangements might help citizens think about the common good. But I don't believe that these arrangements, whatever they are, can or should replace the settings and activities that I have listed. Fishkin's argument for citizens' juries, where scientific sampling substitutes for electoral politics, suggests the central problem of deliberative democracy: Deliberation is not an activity for the demos. I don't mean that ordinary men and women don't have the capacity to reason, only that 100 million of them, or even 1 million or 100,000 can't plausibly "reason together." And it would be a great mistake to turn them away from the things they can do together. For then there would be no effective, organized opposition to the powers-that-be. The political outcome of such a move is readily predictable: The citizens who turned away would lose the fights they probably wanted, and may well have needed, to win.

Notes

1. The continental analogue and possible source of the American arguments, Habermas's communication theory, has been the subject of a vast critical literature, most of it focused on the technical philosophical aspects of the theory. American writers, who mostly avoid technical argument, have escaped the criticism. But see Lynn Sanders, "Against Deliberation," *Political Theory* (June 1997), and my own "Critique of Philosophical Conversation" (aimed only in part at Habermas), *Philosophical Forum* (Fall–Winter 1989–90).

2. Amy Gutmann and Dennis Thompson, *Democracy and Disagreement* (Cambridge: Belknap Press of Harvard University Press, 1996).

3. Ibid., 352–53.

4. William Shakespeare, *Hamlet*, act 3, scene 1.

5. Joseph M. Schwartz, *The Permanence of the Political: A Democratic Critique of the Radical Impulse to Transcend Politics* (Princeton: Princeton University Press, 1995).

6. James Fishkin, *Democracy and Deliberation: New Directions for Democratic Reform* (New Haven: Yale University Press, 1991). If the purpose of the juries is simply to add their own conclusions to the mix of ideas and proposals that are already being debated in the political arena, then they are useful in the same way that think tanks and presidential commissions are useful. If any sort of democratic authority is claimed for them, if the sample displaces the sampled, they are dangerous.

6

Democratic Deliberation

The Problem of Implementation

DANIEL A. BELL

*T*he most influential political philosophers today divide their work into two tasks. The first task is to present and rigorously defend morally desirable political principles, and the second is to think about how to implement them. Quite often, the first task proves to be overwhelming, and it is left to others to think about feasibility. The problem, of course, is that the political principles often prove to be useless or counterproductive in practice, which undermines the first task. One might have thought that the political principles themselves should be assessed partly by the extent to which they can be usefully implemented in practice, but philosophical purists seem to worry about the possible implication that there may not be one unique, universally applicable, and eternally valid set of political principles.

Amy Gutmann and Dennis Thompson's *Democracy and Disagreement* is a first-class contribution to political philosophy, but it suffers from the same basic flaw as other leading works in the field. The "core idea" of their book, they say on page 1, is simple: "When citizens or their representatives disagree morally, they should continue to reason together to reach mutually acceptable decisions." The rest of the book is a tightly argued presentation and defense of six moral principles of deliberation that should guide political argument in democratic systems. But instead of discussing the preconditions for the successful implementation of their moral principles and developing the institutional implications of their theory, the coauthors explain that they concentrated on the "prior task" of developing the principles to assess the institutions of deliberative democracy (358).

As we will see, this approach has the effect of weakening Gutmann and Thompson's case for the importance of moral deliberation in democratic societies like the United States. Even in cases of political disputes that are marred by conflicts of moral principle, further deliberation among ordinary citizens may be unnecessary if not counterproductive. Given that things can go wrong, it is important to specify some of the preconditions for effective deliberation. In this chapter, I discuss three preconditions that, if present, make constructive moral deliberations more likely: a relatively fair distribution of resources, a sense of community and trust between participants, and, more controversially, a political culture that values decision-making by intellectual elites. These conditions are sorely lacking in the United States, which is the main focus of Gutmann and Thompson's book. But they are present to a greater extent in some East Asian countries, which may be a more promising context for the institutionalization of political deliberation. The second half of this chapter develops a proposal for institutionalization in an East Asian context.

I. The Appropriate Context for Democratic Deliberation[1]

1. The Pitfalls of Deliberation

To be fair, Gutmann and Thompson go out of their way to use examples from everyday, real-life politics, and the use of actual examples does help to answer the question of feasibility. The coauthors show that the principles of democratic deliberation already inform the political process of "actually existing" democracies to a certain extent, which implies that it is not entirely unrealistic to expect that more can be achieved. But on the other hand, Gutmann and Thompson tend to select examples that lend themselves to philosophical debate over moral principles. No doubt the issue of whether surrogate mothers have an obligation to give away their babies if they change their minds is important for the people involved, but how typical is this of everyday politics?

The point here is to cast doubt on the coauthors' argument that open and fair moral deliberation should have a more prominent role to play in contemporary democratic societies. While Gutmann and Thompson argue that democratic deliberation offers a way of dealing with moral disagreement in political life, many important political issues are not in fact areas of moral disagreement. Every sensible person condemned the carnage in Bosnia, but the really crucial political issue was not moral but strategic—how best to end the war? This was accomplished by means of a closed meeting with several leading thugs in Dayton, Ohio, but it doesn't really matter. The important thing was to end the killing, not to worry over the process of democratic deliberation. More generally, sound foreign policy does not readily lend itself to open debate.[2] It is no coincidence that the coauthors' examples come almost entirely from domestic policy.

Of course, Gutmann and Thompson can reply that deliberation is not meant to be a cure for all modern political ailments: Only political controversies marred by conflicts of moral principle should be dealt with by means of further deliberation. And since conflicts of moral principle (arguably) tend to be most prominent in the domain of domestic policy, (perhaps) that is why the coauthors spend a disproportionate share of the book exploring such issues. Even in domestic policy, however, one might question the coauthors' advice that when citizens disagree morally, they should continue to engage in open debate on the matter. Many Canadians wish that the Meech Lake constitutional accord with Quebec had gone through, as it nearly did. This accord was negotiated behind closed doors in a meeting with a dozen politicians or so. Instead, the country was condemned to many years of fruitless and frustrating debates on the question of Quebec's role in the country. The lack of resolution eventually poisoned the atmosphere to the point that no one wanted to talk about it anymore. Canadians breathed a collective sigh of relief when the government decided to focus on more pressing economic matters instead of wasting more taxpayers' money on Royal Commissions designed to provide forums for deliberation on constitutional matters. Even the pro-independence government of Quebec announced a plan to remove the language/identity issue from the public agenda for the next two or three years.

Nor is it obvious that open deliberation has a significant role to play in the formulation of economic policies. Many economic issues are so complex that it is difficult for nonexperts to contribute meaningfully to the "debate." Gutmann and Thompson themselves confront the fact that the powerful Federal Reserve Board, which is composed largely of professional economists, conducts its meetings behind closed doors, on the grounds that going public would undermine the efficacy of its policies. They say that "exceptions" to the publicity principle are acceptable from a deliberative perspective if they are fully discussed, approved in advance, and regularly reviewed (104), but these "exceptions" may well be the rule when it comes to important questions of economic policy.[3]

One might also ask whether deliberation is necessary for the purpose of securing social justice. Gutmann and Thompson argue that the least advantaged citizens must be empowered with habits of political deliberation as a condition for welfare reform, but it is worth recalling that East Asian countries such as Taiwan, Japan, and South Korea have managed to achieve a relatively egalitarian distribution of wealth without relying on inclusive structures for political deliberation.[4] Instead, social justice in the East Asian region was promoted (at least partly) by means of clever policies devised by meritocratically chosen bureaucrats.[5]

2. Some Preconditions for Deliberation

In short, deliberation is not always necessary for resolving political controversies marred by moral conflict. Worse, deliberation can sometimes be counterproductive, in the sense that it actually intensifies disagreement about public policy and increases the risk that things could go drastically wrong.[6] There is, in short, a need to qualify the "core idea" of Gutmann and Thompson's book, the claim that citizens should resort to political argument guided by moral principles when they disagree with each other about public policy. Sometimes they shouldn't do that. Things can go wrong when public debate is prolonged, which is a reason for caution.

This is not to deny that democratic deliberation might offer a way of dealing with moral disagreement in some policy areas. Gutmann and Thompson effectively draw on the abortion controversy in the United States to make their case.[7] But this leads to the question of when—in what context—deliberation is most likely to be an effective remedy for dealing with political controversies marred by moral conflict. Gutmann and Thompson do not discuss this issue, so let me point, in a very preliminary way, to some of the more obvious preconditions that seem to underpin constructive deliberation. First, proponents of deliberation since Jean-Jacques Rousseau have argued that a relatively egalitarian society is more likely to produce the conditions for constructive deliberation. The more just the distribution of wealth—or the more it is seen to be just by the participants involved in political debate—the less worry there is that some people with more bargaining power will take advantage of others. In a society deeply polarized between rich and poor, it is difficult to imagine that people will be willing to set aside their differences to discuss controversial issues in good faith. In such a context, the solution might be expropriation rather than deliberation.

Second, the sense of belonging to a common political project might be essential for lowering the passions and inducing a willingness to compromise. There is not much point in discussing things if people don't trust each other, and citizens might not be motivated to abide by the principles of democratic deliberation if they regard each other as strangers from foreign lands.[8]

Of course, these two conditions are interrelated. On the one hand, it is difficult to establish a sense of community in a grossly unequal society. On the other hand, a sense of community often underpins the willingness to share resources with "fellow" citizens.[9] This might seem obvious, but it is worth noting because Gutmann and Thompson fail to make these points. Empowering disadvantaged citizens with the habits of political deliberation is not likely to bring about welfare reform unless these conditions are present. Without a certain degree of material equality and a sense of community between participants, relying on deliberation to resolve moral conflicts may turn out to be useless or counterproductive.

In any case, I would like to say more about a relatively controversial (in a Western context) precondition for constructive deliberation. My claim is that deliberation is more likely to be effective if the political culture values decision-making by intellectual elites. Why is that? Because talented elites with the motivation and the ability to understand and apply moral principles to complex political controversies with national (and international) implications are more likely to engage in constructive deliberations.

It is perhaps surprising that Gutmann and Thompson—who spend much of their time deliberating with America's "best and brightest"[10]—never seriously confront the possibility that some elected politicians, not to mention ordinary citizens, may lack the capacity and the motivation to follow their principles of democratic deliberation. Consider what Gutmann and Thompson say about politicians elected by ordinary citizens from the state of Arizona. The coauthors criticize Arizona legislators who voted to defund organ transplants in order to cover fees for prenatal and pediatric care on the grounds that "they said little about the standard of 'good' they were using, and therefore even less about the potential of prenatal and pediatric care to produce this good. This moral argument was far less developed than it could have been on the basis of deliberation, and its empirical assumptions were not subject to even a modest degree of scrutiny" (225).

Part of the explanation may be that democratic deliberation is intellectually demanding. The principle of accountability, for example, requires "citizens and public officials to give attention to the claims of everyone who might be affected by their political actions" (227), including their constituents, nonresidents, foreigners, and future generations. Besides an unusual capacity for overlooking the imperatives of reelection, the principle of accountability also seems to require a talent for processing large amounts of complex empirical information. And makers of public policy in Arizona would also need to consider the other five principles of democratic deliberation.

The point here is to suggest that not all citizens have the same capacity to reflect upon and apply principles of deliberation to complex cases; this suggests that it is incumbent upon defenders of political deliberation to identify mechanisms for the selection of political decision-makers with above-average intelligence (and virtue). One possibility that comes to mind is the House of Lords in the United Kingdom, which is composed largely of politically appointed persons who have demonstrated excellence in their fields.[11] Not coincidentally, the House of Lords is the political institution that comes closest to expressing the moral principles of deliberation defended by Gutmann and Thompson. Its debates are elegant, nonadversarial, and informative, and even critics acknowledge that the House of Lords performs its task of refining bills from the House of Commons with admirable competence and nonpartisanship.

American defenders of deliberation, however, immediately run into the problem of a profoundly anti-elitist culture, which helps to explain the reaction by "politically correct" critics of democratic deliberation. Peter Berkowitz, who acknowledges that "mastering the art of conversation requires a rare combination of gifts," asks rhetorically whether intellectuals who commend a politics of conversation, "like oligarchs of all ages, place themselves in the compromised position of advocating a general principle that directly advances their own class interest."[12] In a recent article entitled "Against Deliberation," Lynn Sanders argues that ordinary citizens would not recommend solving political problems by means of deliberation, since "some citizens are better than others at articulating their arguments in rational, reasonable terms." Instead, Sanders favors "testimony" by members of marginalized groups, who would tell their own story rather than seek common dialogue, as this would encourage "the democratic consideration of the worthiness of perspectives not obviously rooted in common ground and not necessarily voiced in a calmly rational way."[13] And these are the views of people who are themselves intellectuals at America's elite universities! Defenders of deliberation by intellectual elites are likely to have even less support when they try to gauge the reaction of Jesse Helms types.

Of course, those who can persuasively voice arguments "in a calmly rational way" still occupy leading positions in the real world, notwithstanding the dominant anti-elitist culture. The U.S. Supreme Court, which is composed largely of academic overachievers, seems to carry out constitutional debates in ways that approximate Gutmann and Thompson's ideals (not surprisingly, the coauthors often draw on examples from the Supreme Court). Intellectual elites also play an important role in more directly "political" domains: The Rhodes scholar Bill Clinton appointed many of his Oxford and Yale friends to important political posts, for example. But this must be done in quasi-hidden ways, in the sense that it would be a political mistake to officially acknowledge that the country is being ruled by America's "best and brightest."[14] So the fact remains that those recommending a political institution (beyond the Supreme Court) that is specifically designed to identify "philosopher kings" who can present and defend morally justifiable and rationally produced policy recommendations still face a nearly unsurmountable cultural obstacle in the American context. And if we remind ourselves of some of the other conditions for a workable "politics of conversation"—a relatively fair distribution of material resources and a strong sense of community—it turns out, somewhat ironically,[15] that the United States, an ethnically polarized country with the most unequal distribution of wealth in the developed world, seems to be a distinctly unpromising context for the institutionalization of deliberative democracy.

Let us then turn to the East Asian context, where things look better for deliberative democrats, at least on the surface. The Japanese development model, which has been adopted by several countries in the East Asian region, has helped to narrow the gap between rich and poor. Moreover, East Asian countries are relatively homogeneous (with the exception of Singapore), which makes it easier to sustain strong communal bonds between citizens. Most important, perhaps, there is strong social support for "political elitism," or the idea that political power should be given to ethical and intellectual elites. The value of political elitism, as we will see, can be traced to its Confucian origins, and its contemporary manifestations are still evident in East Asia.[16] "Actually existing" Confucianism, however, is deeply flawed from the perspective of deliberative democrats, and I will argue for an as yet unrealized political institution first suggested by the seventeenth-century Confucian scholar Huang Zongxi.

II. Institutionalizing Deliberative Democracy in East Asia

1. A Confucian Tradition of Conferring Respect and Authority on an Educated Elite

A basic assumption of Confucian ethics is that human excellence is best realized through public service. Consider the following passage from the *Analects* of Confucius: "Tzu-lu asked about the qualities of the true gentleman. The master said, he cultivates in himself the capacity to be diligent in his tasks. Tzu-lu said, can he not go further than that? The Master said, he cultivates in himself the capacity to ease the lot of other people. Tzu-lu said, can he not go further than that? The Master said, he cultivates in himself the capacity to ease the lot of the whole populace. If he can do that, could even Yao or Shun find cause to criticize him?"[17]

In contrast to Plato's philosopher king, burdened with the task of public duty among unenlightened "cave-dwellers," and to Aristotle's idea that intellectual contemplation is the highest pleasure, and to "the prophets of Israel and the West, who appear to be more free standing and less professionally committed to such secular functions,"[18] Confucius's superior men achieve complete self-realization in their public vocation.

Of course, not everyone can be a "gentleman": In Confucius's eyes, only ethical and intellectual elites have a vocation to lead society, as the bulk of persons are not thought capable of exercising such initiative.[19] Confucius does speak of "teaching" the people,[20] but Benjamin Schwartz points out that what they are taught "is presumably no more than the rudiments of family relationships. They are hardly in a position to achieve to extensive cultivation required for the achievement of full self-realization, and it is obvious that only those in public service can do anything substantial to order human society."[21]

In short, only those who acquire knowledge and virtue ought to participate in government, and the common people are not presumed to possess the capacities necessary for substantial political participation. This brand of political elitism does not differentiate Confucianism from, say, Plato's views in *The Republic,* but most distinctive is that Confucian societies *institutionalized* a stable mechanism capable of producing (at least on occasion) what was widely seen as a "government of the best men"—China's famous 2,000-year-old meritocratic civil service examination system. Entry into the civil service through competitive examination was open to all males with a few exceptions, and those who eventually succeeded in passing (often having to undertake half a lifetime to do so) were thought to be in sole possession of the moral and intellectual qualities necessary for public service. Moreover, the civil service examination system was widely viewed as a means of upward mobility (there are countless stories in Chinese folklore about talented young men from peasant backgrounds who study hard, pass the examinations, and rise to become important public officials), which undoubtedly contributed to the legitimacy of the system.[22] Generally speaking, then, scholar-officials who proved their ability by succeeding in a fair and open examination system were granted uncommon (by Western standards) amounts of legitimacy, respect, and authority.

2. Contemporary Manifestations of Confucian Elitism in East Asia

According to Tu Wei-ming, "the Confucian scholar-official mentality still functions in the psychocultural construct of East Asian societies."[23] This is not to deny that the Chinese Communist Party did its best to eradicate the Confucian political value of conferring respect and power on an intellectual elite. For thirty years, politics was driven by the slogan "Better red than expert," although ideology began to take a back seat to considerations of talent and expertise with the advent of economic reform. The Chinese communist leadership is once again promoting Confucian studies,[24] and competitive examinations for the civil service have recently been reinstituted in China. The most striking evidence for the continuing relevance of Confucian elitism, however, comes from the May–June 1989 prodemocracy demonstrations, when over 1 million ordinary Beijing citizens participated in a movement led by students and intellectuals from China's most prestigious universities.[25]

Contemporary manifestations of Confucian political elitism are even more evident in East Asian countries fortunate enough not to have experienced a full-scale "cultural revolution." In Japan, for example, the top candidates of the nationwide pre-university examination system enter the Law Faculty at

Tokyo University, and upon graduation they obtain posts with the most prestigious government ministries. The political system then empowers them to make most of their nation's policy, and they effectively answer to no one, including the nation's elected politicians. In Singapore, the top graduates from the National University compete not for lucrative jobs in the private sector but rather for posts in the civil service. Those who score highest on their "A levels" are given government scholarships to study abroad at top American and British universities, and when they return to Singapore they are almost immediately given responsible positions in the public sector. As a condition of having accepted the scholarship they are under a legal obligation to work for the government for a minimum of eight years.

3. The Need for Accountability, Publicity, and Participation

Whatever the merits of Confucian elitism, its drawbacks are becoming increasingly evident, for reasons well appreciated by deliberative democrats. Recent incidents in Japan, for example, have exposed the dangers of granting excessive power to unaccountable bureaucrats who make policies in mysterious ways hidden behind the façade of democratically elected politicians. In one particularly egregious case, bureaucrats at the Health Ministry resisted allowing imports of sterilized blood until 1985, well after they had been told of the risks of HIV contamination. This resulted in the death of several hundred Japanese hemophiliacs from AIDS.[26]

Things are even worse in Singapore, where "Confucian elitism" takes more authoritarian forms. Singapore is nominally democratic, but opposition candidates face retaliation in the form of bankruptcy, humiliation, and exile, with the result that few qualified individuals dare to contest the ruling People's Action Party at election time. In between elections, the government employs harsh measures against professionals and religious organizations critical of the government's policies. The predictable consequence is a pervasive atmosphere of fear in the country, as well as implicit encouragement for antisocial, narrowly self-interested behavior.[27]

In short, East Asian societies face the challenge of combining a commitment to rule by a talented and public-spirited elite with the democratic virtues of accountability, publicity, and participation (meaning, at minimum, free and fair competitive elections, including the right to run for the opposition without fear of retaliation).

4. Voting for the Wise?

A Western democrat might favor leaving it up to "the people." The idea here is that ordinary citizens can be trusted to make sensible choices as to capable rulers. If people want "Confucian" political rulers of talent and integrity, they will vote for them at election time.

The problem with this view, however, is that elected politicians may lack both the competence (as noted above) and the motivation to make sound political judgments. In developing countries, it may be easier to get elected by promising to provide the conditions for rapid economic development, regardless of the ecological costs for future generations by choosing politicians who promise to keep economically unsustainable welfare benefits. Politicians will thus feel constrained by the need to accommodate the interests of particular, present-day constituencies even if it conflicts with their view of the common good.

Perhaps the situation is different in East Asia. Ordinary people seem to have imbibed the Confucian ethic of respect and deference toward educated rulers, which may lead one to expect that voters will choose talented and public-spirited politicians. The fact that candidates for national office in Japan, South Korea, Singapore, and Taiwan often flaunt their educational qualifications, apparently with the hope that people will be more inclined to vote for a ruler with a Ph.D. from a prestigious university, lends some support to this hypothesis.

The situation in Japan, however, is not encouraging. Voters appear to be swayed primarily by short-term material benefits, and most political talent finds its way to the bureaucracy rather than the legislature. Even supposing that voters are motivated by a desire to identify "Confucian" political rulers, they may not be able to identify such men and women during the course of a free-for-all political fest held every four or five years. In the case of China, it is interesting to note that even Fang Lizhi and other democracy leaders "have expressed only horror at a democratic formula that would give equal voting rights to peasants."[28] The assumption seems to be that China's problems—overpopulation, pollution, increasing economic inequality, a risk of civil war—are so severe that many reformers are nervous about granting too much power to relatively uneducated people.

So what is the solution? Either elected politicians (and, indirectly, the people as a whole) rule, or an educated elite rules, but how can both rule in the same society?

5. *Huang Zongxi's Proposal for a Parliament of Scholars*

Let us turn for inspiration to a seventeenth-century Confucian scholar named Huang Zongxi.[29] Huang's book, *Waiting for the Dawn: A Plan for the Prince*, opens with a radical attack on despotic government: "In ancient times, all-under-Heaven were considered the master, and the prince was the tenant. The Prince spent his whole life working for all-under-Heaven. Now the prince is the master, and all-under-Heaven are tenants. That no one can find peace and happiness anywhere is all on account of the prince."[30]

The dynastic system, in Huang's view, was not to be reformed merely by finding a virtuous ruler of exemplary character. Unlike most Confucians, Huang argued for specific laws and institutions designed to curb imperial power, such as the establishment of a strong prime minister and relatively powerful ministers. Huang's proposal to strengthen the political role of the schools for the training of Confucian scholar-officials is particularly relevant. Schools of all levels, in Huang's view, should serve as forums for open public deliberation. He noted that during the Eastern Han, 25–220 A.D., scholars at the Imperial College, the top school for the training of scholar-officials, engaged in outspoken discussion of important issues without fear of those in power, and the highest officials were anxious to avoid their censure. Moreover, Huang proposed that the rector of the Imperial College, to be chosen from among the great scholars of the day, should be equal in importance to the prime minister and that once a month the emperor should visit the Imperial College, along with the prime minister and some other ministers. The emperor was to sit among the ranks of students while the rector questioned him on the administration of the country.[31] The primary function of the system, in short, would be to hold rulers accountable to what Theodore de Bary terms a "Parliament of Scholars."[32]

Moreover, Huang proposed to revise the Confucian examination system for selecting scholar-officials. He condemned the examinations of his day for rewarding superficiality and plagiarism, thus failing to identify scholars of "real talent." Examinations, he argued, should test for both the capacity to memorize and the capacity for independent thought: "After listing one by one what is said by the various Han and Sung scholars, the candidate should conclude with his own opinion, there being no necessity for blind acceptance of one's authority's word."[33]

6. *A "House of Scholars" for the Twenty-First Century*

While Huang's proposal for a Parliament of Scholars was too radical for his own day,[34] it is an idea—if combined with a democratically elected lower house—worth taking seriously in a modern context. The "modern" adaptation of Huang's proposal, in other words, would be a bicameral legislature with a democratically elected lower house and a "Confucian" upper house—let us call it a "House of Scholars"—composed of representatives selected on the basis of competitive examinations.

A House of Scholars would have several advantages from a deliberative standpoint. In contrast to democratically elected politicians, deputies engaged in political deliberations would not be constrained by the need to accommodate the interests of particular constituencies, which makes it more likely that decision-makers would "give attention to the claims of everyone who might be affected by their political actions" (227). Concerns that members be held accountable for abuses of power could be met by means of term limits and stiff penalties for corruption. Debates could be televised and transmitted directly to the public, which would help meet the requirements of publicity. Most important, perhaps, the examination process would help to ensure the selection of talented decision-makers. This is not to deny that the examination process is a highly imperfect mechanism for selecting decision-makers of talent and integrity. But arguably this procedure is more effective than other methods of political selection currently on offer, including democratic elections.[35] The social and economic achievements in Taiwan, Singapore, Japan, and Korea in the post–World War II era can be explained at least in part by the sound policy choices of rulers selected on the basis of competitive examinations.[36] In short, a House of Scholars would preserve the advantages of "actually existing" Confucian elitism, while meeting some of the concerns of deliberative democrats.

Finally, it is worth noting that the House of Scholars would be more meritocratic, and no less democratic, than the systems currently in place to select decision-makers in the House of Lords in the United Kingdom and the Senate in Canada—not to mention the practice of giving substantial political power to unelected First Ladies! Needless to say, many issues would still need to be resolved, including the question of scale,[37] the relationship between the two houses[38] and between national and provincial legislatures, how to administer the examinations for the House of Scholars, and how to further insulate members from political pressure. These are details to be ironed out during the course of deliberations at an actual constitutional convention, however.[39]

Conclusion

Whatever the virtues of the House of Scholars, there is no reason to expect that countries will jettison the political status quo in favor of an institution whose merits have yet to be demonstrated in reality. In the event of a serious crisis of legitimacy, however, it is not entirely unrealistic to expect that the House of Scholars will be considered as one option, among other ideas, for radical political reform. In mainland China, for example, it is unlikely that the current political system will be stable for the long term, and many reformers expect a constitutional convention on political reform sometime in the twenty-first century. Other East Asian countries, such as Japan and South Korea, have recently been experiencing difficult times, and they too may be receptive to new ideas for qualifying democratic populism with institutions representing intellectual elites.

Given that the United States lacks the preconditions for deliberative democracy and that it is not likely to radically overhaul its constitutional system in the foreseeable future, the chances that proposals for institutionalizing deliberative democracy (such as the House of Scholars) will be taken seriously seem quite remote. But it is not unrealistic to expect some ad hoc experimentation with ideas for promoting deliberative democracy, [40] and this may well help to resolve particular areas of moral conflict, as Gutmann and Thompson argue. Defenders of deliberation, however, need to be more explicit about the need to involve (relatively) capable and virtuous elites as a precondition for constructive deliberations concerning complex moral controversies with national (and international) implications. Relying (only) on deliberation by elected politicians and ordinary citizens to resolve such controversies is a recipe for failure, and this can only discredit the ideals that deliberative democrats care about.

Notes

I am most grateful to Stephen Macedo for his helpful comments on an earlier draft of this chapter.

1. This section draws partly on my review of *Democracy and Disagreement* in: *TLS*, 17 Jan. 1997, 25.

2. See George Kennan, *American Diplomacy: 1900–1950* (Chicago: University of Chicago Press, 1951).

3. Moreover, it is worth noting that the coauthors could have been more critical of the Federal Reserve Board's secrecy. They commend Fed chairman Alan Greenspan for (belatedly) honoring the requirement of public accountability for secrecy (104), but economist Alan Blinder—who recently resigned from the Fed, apparently because he failed to persuade his colleagues to change their secretive ways (see John Cassidy, "Fleeing the Fed," *New Yorker*, February 19, 1996, 45–46)—argues that much of the Fed's secrecy is in fact unnecessary and thus unjustifiable.

4. No doubt the current economic crisis in the region will make things worse for the poor in the short to medium term, but barring unforeseen disasters, the worst-off in East Asia will likely remain better off than the worst-off in the United States.

5. Of course, there may be other explanations for the relatively egalitarian distribution of wealth in East Asian countries. One common claim is that racial homogeneity underpins egalitarian economic policies, as people are more likely to accept economic redistribution to members of their own ethnic group. It is worth noting, however, that multiethnic Singapore does not have a significantly worse distribution of wealth than the relatively homogeneous countries of South Korea and Taiwan, whereas Thailand (95 percent Thai) and Hong Kong (98 percent Cantonese) have the most unequal distribution of wealth among developing East and Southeast Asian countries.

6. Perhaps it's easier to appreciate this point by extrapolating from everyday, "nonpolitical" life: Most of us have probably had discussions that left us feeling dissatisfied with if not downright hostile toward our "fellow" interlocutors, even when both parties had started off on friendly terms. In fact, it's precisely when disputes touch on deeply felt moral matters that tempers tend to flare and positions harden. Whatever the flaws of John Rawls's proposal that we should strive for an "overlapping consensus" that brackets controversial areas of the good life in discussions about politics, it is often a good policy to apply in our personal lives!

7. Even in this case, however, the coauthors come to a determinate policy recommendation (i.e., voluntary contributions through the tax system to subsidize abortions; see 89–90). This strikes me as a very sensible policy, but there wasn't a need to go through any actual dialogue to arrive at this conclusion.

8. This might have implications for educational policy. Gutmann and Thompson note that "in an effort to make democracy more deliberative, the single most important institution outside government is the educational system" (359). Schools should encourage students to understand different people's perspectives and teach them to engage in the "give-and-take of moral argument." That may well be the case, but the educational system also needs to build up a common sense of national identity so that future citizens will be willing to talk with each other in a civilized manner.

9. See, e.g., David Miller, "The Ethical Significance of Nationality," *Ethics* (July 1988): 647–62.

10. David Halberstam famously used this term as an ironic reference to academic overachievers such as Robert McNamara in the Kennedy/Johnson administrations who led the United States to disaster in Vietnam (see David Halberstam, *The Best and the Brightest* [New York: Random House, 1972]). One "lesson" from this experience is that intellectual skills are not always accompanied by moral virtue, and it is important to keep this cautionary tale in mind. But McNamara saw himself as a technocrat, applying "value-free" solutions to particular political controversies, which may help to explain why his solutions turned out to be so perverse. It is assumed (hoped?) that those engaging in Gutmann/Thompson-type deliberation would not be working under such illusions, since they would face the explicit task of deciding between different sides of *moral* controversies. Also, they would be constrained by the principles of publicity and accountability (McNamara et al. made their decisions in secret, without much of a need to answer for their decisions), and transparent public debate of this sort may help to filter out distinctly bad ideas.

11. The House of Lords also includes a minority of hereditary peers, but the current Labor government has pledged to reform the House of Lords by abolishing seats reserved for such persons.

12. Peter Berkowitz, "The Politic Moralist," *New Republic*, September 1, 1997, 37.

13. Lynn M. Sanders, "Against Deliberation," *Political Theory* 25, no. 3, (June 1997): 348, 372. I do not mean to suggest that Sanders is wrong to value testimony and to argue for "multicultural" representation in various political in-

stitutions. These are important goals, but they also need to be weighed against the value of constructive deliberation by those people who have the ability and the motivation to perform it.

14. There is less of a need for hypocrisy in the business world, where people are judged primarily by their contribution to the bottom line. The leading business consultancy firm, McKenzie and Co., offers jobs to all Rhodes scholars who apply, no experience necessary. The assumption seems to be that academic stars will do well at the job of applying their intelligence to the question of how companies can increase their profits. Investment banks like Goldman Sachs hire Ph.D.'s from top universities in fields completely unrelated to banking, on the assumption that real talent is transferable from one domain to another.

15. It is ironic because Gutmann and Thompson seem to have the American context in mind as the setting for their theory. They do claim that the principles of democratic deliberation "are relevant for societies other than our own" (5), but since they also say that the "best justification" for their conception of deliberative democracy is to show its contribution to actual debates (2) and they rely almost exclusively on examples from the American context, it is difficult to understand why the coauthors think democratic deliberation is relevant for societies outside the United States. This is not to deny that the principles of deliberation may in fact be relevant in non-American societies. Quite the opposite: My own argument is that the principles of deliberation (some principles, not necessarily the whole package) may be particularly relevant in the East Asian region, since the preconditions for constructive deliberation seem to be present to a greater extent (compared to the United States).

16. I do not mean to suggest that the value of respect for political decision-making by intellectual elites is not shared by countries outside East Asia. The "cultural" terrain for institutionalizing deliberation by intellectual elites may also be favorable in France, given the social and political importance of intellectuals in French public life.

17. *The Analects of Confucius*, trans. Arthur Waley (London: Allen & Unwin, 1938), bk. 14.45. According to Bruce Brooks, however, the person we refer to as "Confucius" was probably directly responsible only for the ideas expressed in chapter 4 of the *Analects*, and an interest in the well-being of the populace does not appear until book 12, which may date to more than 150 years after his death (Brooks, *The Original Analects* [New York: Columbia University Press, 1997]; I thank Chris Fraser for bringing this reference to my attention). For our purposes, however, what matters is that the dominant interpretation of Confucianism transmitted over the past 2,000 years has valued public service as the highest of life's achievements.

18. Theodore de Bary, "The Trouble with Confucianism," Institute of East Asian Philosophies (Singapore) Public Lecture Series, 1989, no. 13, 16.

19. See *The Analects of Confucius*, bk. 16.9, bk. 8.9, bk. 12.19.

20. Ibid., 13.9.

21. Benjamin Schwartz, "Some Polarities in Confucian Thought," in *Con-*

fucianism in Action, ed. D. Nevinson (Stanford: Stanford University Press, 1960), 53.

22. As one might expect, the reality often deviated from the "meritocratic" myth. But arguably, the civil service examination system allowed for more upward mobility than the systems in place elsewhere at the time.

23. Tu Wei-ming, *Confucian Traditions in East Asian Modernity* (Cambridge: Harvard University Press, 1996), 15.

24. Ibid., 259–60.

25. When we think of the (un)likelihood of the American equivalent—a few dozen students from Harvard and MIT leading a radical movement for social change with the enthusiastic support and participation of a million working-class Bostonians—it becomes clear just how distinctive the Confucian value of respect for rule by an intellectual elite really seems to be.

26. See Sheryl WuDunn, "Japan's Bureaucrats Fumble Away the Traditional Center of Power," *International Herald Tribune*, May 7, 1996, p. 4.

27. See my article "A Communitarian Critique of Authoritarianism: The Case of Singapore," *Political Theory* 25, no. 1 (February 1997): 6–32.

28. Vivienne Shue, "China: Transition Postponed?," *Problems of Communism* (January–April 1992): 163. Some reformers nervous about the prospects of a farmer-dominated legislature also favor maintaining a system of malapportionment that favors urban over rural voters. Andrew Nathan notes that he is "not aware of any proposal to move to one-man-one-vote" (Nathan, "China's Constitutionalist Option," *Journal of Democracy* 7, no. 4 [October 1996]: 48).

29. Needless to say, there are other possibilities for institutionalizing the role of decision-making by intellectual elites, such as J. S. Mill's suggestion that educated persons be given extra votes. I criticize alternative proposals in chap. 5 of my forthcoming book, *East Meets West: Human Rights and Democracy in East Asia* (Princeton University Press, Spring 2000).

30. Huang Zongxi, *Waiting for the Dawn: A Plan for the Prince*, trans. William Theodore de Bary (New York: Columbia University Press, 1993), 92.

31. Ibid., 107.

32. Ibid., 83.

33. Ibid., 113.

34. Huang was resisting the conquest of China by the Manchus, who went on to found the Qing dynasty, and it seems that he was addressing a future ruler inclined toward benevolence rather than the emperor of his day. Initially, his book was distributed to a few colleagues and friends, and it was circulated samizdat for two and a half centuries, finally seeing the light of day in the latter part of the Qing period, when the dynasty was in disarray. See de Bary's introduction in ibid., 7.

35. Winston Churchill's quip about democracy—that it is the worst possible system except for all the others—can also be used to defend the examination system as a procedure for selecting political talent.

36. Of course, the current Asian economic crisis may point to the "lesson" that there are some risks associated with empowering meritocratically chosen bu-

reaucrats. Still, it is worth keeping in mind, as Amartya Sen notes, that "enough has been achieved in the [East Asian] region—both absolutely and in relation to the record of other regions—to make it legitimate to continue to celebrate the economic performance of East Asia over the decades" (Sen, "Human Rights and Economic Achievements," in *The East Asian Challenge for Human Rights* ed. Joanne Bauer and Daniel A. Bell [New York: Cambridge University Press, 1999], 89). Moreover, it is unclear at this stage to what extent "Japanese-style" managers are responsible for the crisis (the fickle nature of international capital, reckless lending by Western banks, and inappropriate policy recommendations by the International Monetary Fund that drove East Asian countries deeper into recession also seem to be responsible). Even if local, meritocratically chosen elites share much of the blame, the reforms of "actually existing" Confucian meritocracy suggested here may help to prevent such "mistakes" in the future.

37. Perhaps the House of Scholars should be limited to 200 or 300 seats, so as to allow for high-quality deliberations.

38. Most democrats would likely favor a House of Scholars that is constitutionally subordinate to the lower democratic house. But even a House of Scholars with minimal constitutional powers could play a politically significant role. Deputies could sit on commissions and independent bodies that evaluate policy and advise the government, and viewpoints by members of the House of Scholars may attract substantial social support in a country with a tradition of respect for a meritocratically chosen political elite.

39. I provide a more detailed defense of the proposal for a House of Scholars in a Chinese context in chap. 5 of my forthcoming book *East Meets West: Human Rights and Democracy in Asia.* (Princeton University Press, Spring 2000), See also my article "A Confucian Democracy for the Twenty-First Century" in *Law in a Changing World: Asian Alternatives,* ed. MORIGIWA Yasutomo, *Archiv Fuer Rechts-Und Sozialphilosophie*, Beiheft 72, 1998, 37–49 (Stuttgart: Franz Steiner Verlag).

40. Some deliberative "experiments" have already taken place, with mixed success. James Fishkin's idea of "deliberative polls" was implemented in January 1996, when about 600 randomly chosen Americans met on the eve of the presidential campaign for the purpose of deliberating about national issues (see Robert Dahl, "On Deliberative Democracy," *Dissent* [Summer 1997]: 57). Fishkin's proposal, however, is expensive to implement, and the recommendations that emerge have no legal or political force (the hope that elected politicians would change their minds regarding particular policy issues in response to the results of deliberative polls has yet to materialize). More seriously, perhaps, there is no reason to expect that ordinary citizens with no special talent, expertise, or experience will come up with particularly good policy recommendations.

In the same vein, David Matthews (a former cabinet secretary in the Ford administration) has experimented with deliberative democracy in Dayton, Ohio, by convening citizen meetings and using the local newspaper to air the views of ordinary Americans concerning the city government's redevelopment plans. According to *The Economist*, however, "it is not clear . . . that the government's redevelopment plans were seriously affected by the forums; despite considerable publicity, an average of only 11 people attended each one." In other sessions, "it turns out that several of the talkers have a professional interest in juvenile violence, as pastors or social workers; and that several others are Kettering employees. The ordinary citizen still seems to have had very little to say for himself" ("Building the Perfect Citizen," *The Economist*, August 22, 1998, 30). Here, too, the problem is that deliberative democrats appear to have invested too much hope in the capacity and the motivation of ordinary citizens. This is not to deny that "populist" deliberations may sometimes be useful to resolve local conflicts, but it is quite unlikely that this approach will be sufficient to resolve complex moral controversies with national (and international) implications.

7

Mutual Respect as a
Device of Exclusion

STANLEY FISH

A good part of the argument of *Democracy and Disagreement* appeared earlier in Gutmann and Thompson's influential essay "Moral Conflict and Political Consensus."[1] That piece begins by observing that "religious controversy has traditionally been regarded as the paradigm of moral conflict that does not belong on the political agenda"[2] (because it is intractable) and fairly quickly turns into a discussion of how to exclude from that agenda policies favoring racial discrimination. The authors think of themselves as going against the grain of Nagel-like appeals to higher-order principle, but in the end (and predictably) they make just such an appeal themselves in the name of "mutual respect."

In the old debate between those who think of liberalism as a device for managing and minimizing conflict and those who think of liberalism as a device for producing a better society populated by better persons, Gutmann and Thompson are clearly on the side of the latter, and that is why they are uneasy with a liberalism that requires of the state only that it be tolerant, neutral, and inactive. The trouble with these principles, they say, is that although they might succeed in keeping divisive issues off the political agenda, they do so in a blanket way that does not allow for the discriminations a state concerned with its own health and the health of its citizens should be making. If the state adopts a posture of "live and let live," refrains from either favoring

88

or disfavoring any moral position, and limits itself to presiding over the fray without trying to influence it in any direction, all controversial positions will be regarded in the same way, either as distractions we would be better off without (let the clergy and the philosophers worry about these questions) or as matters so difficult to adjudicate (there is simply no truth to be discovered at the bottom of such disputes) that they are best left to the marketplace of ideas. As a result, peace, if we achieve it, will have to be bought at the price of future edification, for the citizenry will have been prevented by a strict hands-off policy from engaging in debates that might have led to its moral and political improvement.

Not that Gutmann and Thompson are recommending unrestricted public debate on controversial positions; rather, they wish to limit debate to those positions that speak to a genuine moral question in ways that have the potential, at least, of advancing the conversation. What is required is a means of distinguishing between these bona fide positions and positions whose ascendancy would have the effect of subverting morality altogether. Blanket toleration and neutrality will not be these means, for they set the bar either too high or too low. The bar is set too high by someone like Nagel, who would exclude from public forums beliefs that cannot be justified from "a standpoint that is independent of who we are."[3] By this standard, Gutmann and Thompson complain, "the liberal's belief in human equality" (which Nagel would embrace and want the state to enforce) would fall into the same category as a belief that "sanctions racial discrimination."[4] Neither is independent of "who we are," and so would be excluded, but surely, say Gutmann and Thompson, "they are not equally acceptable (or unacceptable) starting points for public deliberation."[5]

The situation is no better when the bar is set too low and positions, rather than being excluded because they are controversial, are let in because they are controversial. Indiscriminate lumping in either direction brings its dangers; in the case of a policy favoring racial discrimination, the danger is that if the policy becomes a serious contender for state action, it might prevail and we would be headed back in the direction of slavery, whereas if the state washes its hands of the question (because it has been and continues to be disputed) and leaves it to each individual's conscience, citizens will then be "free to discriminate or not according to their religions."[6]

The dilemma is clear (and classic). How does the liberal state deal with doctrines—like racial discrimination or religious intolerance—that are inimical to it and threaten its survival? If such doctrines are welcomed into the conversation, they may shut it down; if the door is closed to them, liberalism will seem to be exercising the peremptory authority it routinely condemns. Long ago Oliver Wendell Holmes declared himself willing to grasp the first handle of this dilemma and take his (or our) chances: "If in the long run the beliefs expressed in proletarian dictatorship are destined to be accepted by the dominant forces of the community, the only meaning of free speech is that they should be given their chance and have their way."[7] Gutmann and Thompson, however, are less libertarian in their sentiments and less willing to trust the matter to fate. They want the state to act positively in the "right" direction, yet they want also to be true to the liberal principle of giving as much scope as possible to moral and intellectual debate.

They get what they want by cutting the Gordian knot and declaring "that the defense of racial discrimination is not a moral position at all,"[8] and because it is not a moral position, keeping it off the political agenda violates no principle of tolerance. This is an amazing statement, but it is no more or less than an up-to-date version of Locke's invocation of the "judgment of all mankind"[9] in justification of his preferred intolerances, and it is no accident that Gutmann and Thompson find their own justification in Locke. They note, correctly, that Locke does not urge "neutrality among all religions . . . only among those religions that accept the voluntary nature of faith."[10] If faith is voluntary, something one can come to only on one's own, it will be both wrong and futile for the state to command it "by the force of its laws because faith cannot by its nature be commanded."[11] This must mean, Gutmann and Thompson conclude, that faith "follows rational persuasion."[12] Of course, what Locke means by rational persuasion—or, as he puts it, "light and evidence"—may not be what Gutmann and Thompson mean.[13] He means the expostulation and remonstration of Christian conversation among brethren. They mean the rule-governed give-and-take of a philosophy seminar. Between these two is a space of equivocation they eagerly enter, and in a flash they declare that the "secular analogue" to Locke's insistence on the voluntary nature of faith is the requirement that "moral judgments by society must be a matter of deliberation,"[14] with deliberation being understood as the formal interplay of assertion, challenge, and the marshaling of evidence. It follows, then, that a position that cannot be deliberated in this way (because it fails to respond to challenges or is buttressed by no evidence) is not a moral position, and, therefore, "racial discrimination is not a moral position," for "no one can claim that . . . it is a position about which reasonable people might morally disagree."[15]

But wait a minute: There are certainly people, even today, who would make that claim and back it up with reasons. Yes, that's true, say Gutmann and Thompson, but their reasons "fail . . . to qualify as moral reasons."[16] Why? Because they "can be shown to be rationalizations," that is, proxies for motives (a desire to oppress, a lust for power) those who give them would be unwilling to acknowledge. And how do you know that? Because, while they offer "evidence," either they refuse to consider "accepted methods of challenging" it or the evidence they offer comes from a source rational beings cannot take seriously, as when they "claim that God speaking literally through the Bible or the laws of nature forbids the mixing of races."[17] Notice that what looks like an argument is really a succession of dismissive gestures designed to deflect objections to a position the authors are unwilling to relinquish or even examine. (Ironically, these gestures are the best example of the closed-mindedness the authors inveigh against.) Anyone who favors racial discrimination is just sick and has no reasons except hate and prejudice; if he has reasons they are unaccompanied by evidence; if he has evidence it is the wrong kind; if he has the right kind, it is not as good as the evidence we have. You know that they could go on forever in this vein because all they are doing is negotiating a very small circle that begins and ends with their own prior conviction and a vocabulary made in its image. The key word in that vocabulary is "reasonable," but all that is meant by the word is what my friends and I take to be so. After all, we are reasonable persons; *we* know that no argument for racial discrimination could have any moral or rational basis; therefore anyone who makes such an argument is unreasonable.

To be sure, there are repeated attempts to present this in-house parochialism as if it were the expression of an impersonal and general rule, as when Gutmann and Thompson describe their position as issuing from "a disinterested perspective that could be adopted by any member of society" and distinguish it from the "implausible beliefs"[18] of those who cite the Bible or the laws of nature. But aren't those for whom the Bible is authoritative members of society, and isn't the fact that these believer-citizens refuse the authors' perspective evidence that it is not disinterested at all (unless believers of a fundamentalist type are regarded as second-class citizens whose views don't count, which is just how they are regarded here)? And isn't "disinterested" one more word—like "impartial" and "reasonable"—that claims the high ground of neutrality while performing exclusionary work?

A little later on, the same work is done by the phrase "disposition toward openness": citizens should be required "to cultivate a disposition toward openness. We should try to break personal and institutional habits that discourage our accepting the position of our opponents at some time in the future."[19] What renders this "requirement" apparently reasonable, even unexceptionable, are the words "personal" and "habits," which together trivialize what some citizens might regard as their beliefs, not beliefs in the sense of opinions—a sense liberalism must assume so that its logic seems obvious—but beliefs in the sense of what one takes, at the very deepest level and on the basis of incontrovertible evidence (empirical, biblical, whatever), to be true. So long as "habit," "personal," and "opinion" are what you are holding onto, resisting the "disposition toward openness" doesn't seem defensible and looks very much like putting one's head in the sand, stubbornly refusing to see the light, and so on. After all, don't you want your opinions to be backed up and confirmed by independent evidence, and in the event that they are not, aren't you better off by having been shown the shakiness of what you had mistakenly held to be firm? The answer is that citizens who hold the doctrine of biblical inerrancy do not accept the category of independent evidence, of evidence to which the words of the Bible must conform if they are to be believed, and, indeed, they will regard the lack of a fit between their own conclusions and the conclusions that might be reached by the "generally accepted methods of inquiry"[20] as the severest judgment possible on the generally accepted methods of inquiry. Gutmann and Thompson in turn will find them unreasonable, insufficiently reflective, and closed-minded, all the while not recognizing how closed their own minds are to systems of belief in the context of which some questions (did Christ die for our sins and is he risen?) are definitively settled, not because believers avert their eyes from new sources of evidence but because, as they see it, all the evidence is already in and proceeds from a source so high that no piling up of arguments on some "other side" could possibly matter.

The issue is not an abstract or theoretical one; it has been joined in a much-discussed case, *Mozert v. Hawkins,* which pits one Vicki Frost, a fundamentalist Christian and the mother of a grade-school daughter, against an educational establishment that would require her child to participate in a program of "critical reading" designed to cultivate the capacity for considering every side of a question—the capacity, in short, of openness of mind. Mrs. Frost and some of her cobelievers objected not because they were upset by a particular doctrine but because they rejected the idea that "exposure to the diversity" of doctrines was a good thing. As far as they were concerned, it was a very bad thing because the materials their children were required to read might very well have the effect of undermining their faith. As Nomi Stolzenberg points out, "The plaintiffs objected to the very principles—tolerance and evenhandedness—traditionally used to justify liberal education."[21]

Predictably, their objection was met by a reinvocation of those same principles in the form of a point made by the superintendent of the Hawkins County school district and accepted by a succession of courts. The plaintiffs, the superintendent declared, misunderstood the fact that "exposure to something does not constitute teaching, indoctrination . . . or promotion of the things exposed,"[22] and in their brief consideration of the case,[23] Gutmann and Thompson echo his judgment. The argument of the fundamentalist parents, they say, "ignores a simple distinction between teaching students about a religion and teaching them to believe in a religion."[24] But what they ignore and (along with the superintendent) fail to understand is that the distinction between "teaching about" and "teaching to believe in"—between exposure and indoctrination—rests on a psychology that is part and parcel of the liberalism Vicki Frost and her friends don't want imposed on their children. In that psychology, the mind remains unaffected by the ideas and doctrines that pass before it, and its job is to weigh and assess those doctrines from a position distanced from and independent of any one of them. (Note how in this picture the mind is a microcosm of the liberal society in which it operates and flourishes.)

However, in another psychology, one undergirded by a conviction of original sin, the mind is not (at least not since Eden) so strongly independent. Rather than standing apart from the range of views that contend for its approval, it is, in its congenital weakness and disposition to be overwhelmed, at the mercy of those views; and accordingly, it behooves the parent or educator to take care lest their charges be influenced in the wrong directions, as they well might be if they were introduced to notions they were ill-equipped to resist. In this psychology (of which there are secular analogues), exposure is not an innocent or healthy experience, but one fraught with dangers. The chief danger is not any particular doctrine to which the children might be exposed but the unannounced yet powerfully assumed doctrine of exposure as a first principle, as a virtual theology. This is where the indoctrination comes in—not at the level of urging this or that belief but at the more subliminal level at which what is urged is that encountering as many ideas as possible and giving each of them a run for its money is an absolutely good thing. What the children are being indoctrinated in is distrust of any belief that has not been arrived at by the exercise of their unaided reason as it surveys all the alternatives before choosing one freely with no guidance from any external authority.

Unaided reason, however—reason freed from the tethering constraints of biblical commands or parental precepts—is what Vicki Frost and her coreligionists distrust; yet they are being told that its imposition will in no way affect their children's moral views and, moreover, that the ideology of preferring no point of view to another is neutral, is, as Nagel would say, a higher-order impartiality. And even if impartiality were the right word and named what resulted from hewing to the distinction between exposure and indoctrination, the plaintiffs would feel no less injured because, as Stolzenberg notes, "on their own terms, the believer's representations of her beliefs are representations of truth, or . . . 'claims on our existence,' that require either affirmation or rejection, but not impartiality."[25] Whereas Vicki Frost and her colleagues pledge allegiance to an authority (God, the church, the Bible) and wish their children to follow it (not critically examine it), public education is informed by an ideology in "perennial protest against all forms of absolute authority," an ideology that everywhere displays "an antipathy to closing ranks around any system of belief."[26] That antipathy rarely announces itself as such but instead wears softer labels—exposure to diverse views, open-mindedness, evenhandedness—that mask the sharp hardness of what is being done.

In Gutmann and Thompson's argument, it is the notion of "mutual respect" (their version of "higher-order impartiality") that does the work of exclusion in the name, supposedly, of generosity. Mutual respect, they say, "manifests a distinctively democratic kind of character—the character of in-dividuals who are morally committed, self-reflective about their commitments, discerning of the difference between respectable and merely tolerable differ-ences of opinion, and open to the possibility of changing their minds or modifying their positions at some time in the future if they confront unan-swerable objections to their present point of view."[27] The idea is simple enough, and as usual it seems unexceptionable: Regard those with whom you disagree not as enemies to the death but as partners in the search for truth, and hold yourself ready to change or modify your point of view if you are unable to refute a reasoned challenge to what you believe. But the imperative will begin to seem less "reasonable" and commonsensical if you ask a simple two-part question: Where do the challenges to your belief come from, and when should you be distressed if you cannot meet them? If the challenges come from within the structure of your belief (since you have already ac-knowledged that all men are created equal, how can you support a policy of racial discrimination?), then the standard to which you are being held is one that you have already acknowledged, and what is being asked of you is, simply, that you be consistent with yourself. If, however, the challenge comes in terms not recognized by the structure of your belief, why should you be the least bit concerned with it, since it rests on notions of evidence and argument to which you are in no way committed?[28] If you tell a serious Christian that no one can walk on water or rise from the dead or feed 5,000 people with two fishes and five loaves, he or she will tell you that the impossibility of those actions for mere men is what makes their performance so powerful a sign of divinity. For one party, the reasoning is "No man can do it and therefore Christ didn't do it"; for the other, the reasoning is "Since no man could do it, he who did it is more than man." For one party, falsification follows from the absence of a plausibly empirical account of how the purported phenomena could have oc-curred; for the other, the absence of a plausibly empirical account is just the point, one that does not challenge the faith but confirms it.

What Gutmann and Thompson will say is that the second party is not really reasoning. This is what they mean when they distinguish between "re-spectable and merely tolerable differences of opinion." A difference of opinion you respect is an opinion held by someone who argues from the same premises and with the same tools you do; an opinion you merely tolerate—although we won't imprison you for holding it, neither will we take any account of it in the process of formulating policy—is an opinion held by someone who argues from premises and with tools you and your friends find provincial at best and dangerous (because fanatical) at worst. It is at this point that you dismiss those premises (i.e., biblical inerrancy) as ones no rational person could subscribe to, whereas in fact what you have done is define "rational" so as to make it congruent with the ways of thinking you and those who agree with you customarily deploy. "Mutual respect" should be renamed "mutual self-congratulation," since it will not be extended beyond the circle of those who already feel comfortable with one another. In the case of Gutmann and Thompson, not surprisingly, the circle of comfort, and therefore the shape of rationality, will be drawn in accordance with the norms of the academy in general and of political science departments in particular, which means that those within the circle will hold their beliefs at arm's length and relate to them in a style marked by diffidence, aversion to strong assertion (except in a very few cases, like that of racial discrimination), and a pervasive, if mild and unaggressive, skepticism. It is not accurate to characterize these men and women as "morally committed," for what they are committed to is not their morality but the deliberative process to which their morality is delivered up on the way, perhaps, to being abandoned. What they are committed to is the deferring of commitment in favor of an ever-attenuated "conversation" whose maintenance is the only value they wholeheartedly embrace.

It is no surprise, then, when those whose relationship to their values is more intimate are read out of a conversation for which they have been rendered unfit (they really *believe* something) by the circumscribing definitions of those who preside over it. Such persons, whether they think that this should be a Christian nation, or a nation where rewards and benefits are distributed by race, or a nation where full legal rights are withheld from homosexuals, are declared not to have a moral position, a judgment supposedly backed up by perspicuous philosophical distinctions and empirical evidence but in fact a judgment informed by nothing more "principled" than a dislike of certain points of view. As card-carrying liberals, Gutmann and Thompson cannot acknowledge dislike of a point of view as a reason for keeping it out of a conversation; after all, the very first premise of their liberalism is that private moral judgments should not be imposed on others in the form of public policy. Therefore, they must find a way of dressing up their personal moral judgments so they will appear to have been generated by a wholly impersonal mechanism.

The result is the sleight of hand of which this sentence is one more example: "Nor has a logically consistent argument been constructed on plausible premises to show that homosexual sex cannot be understood as part of the human condition."[29] The questions suggests themselves immediately: consistent with what (or whose) basic assumptions? Cannot something be understood as part of the human condition and yet also as wrong and worthy of condemnation (murder, child molestation)? Who gets to say what is and is not a plausible premise? And how is it that premises plausible (a real weasel word) to millions of people have been ruled out of court in advance? The answers are obvious and embarrassing because they point to an act of power, of peremptory exclusion and dismissal, that cannot be acknowledged as such lest the liberal program of renouncing power and exclusion be exposed for the fiction it surely is. Those who preach toleration or open-mindedness or mutual respect know that there are some ideas they can't tolerate or be open to or respect, and unless they are willing to follow the fatalism of Holmes, they must find a way of keeping them off the agenda while still proclaiming that they are practicing toleration, open-mindedness, and mutual respect. They find that way, as Locke found it, in the discovery and invocation of exactly the kind of universal—call it the "judgment of all mankind," or a "higher-order rationality"—declared unavailable by the very liberalism they profess.

Moreover, those who perform these self-justifying and piously self-righteous gymnastics are unable to hear a criticism of their performance even when they raise it themselves. Gutmann and Thompson pretend, for a moment, to engage sympathetically with the plaintiffs in *Mozert* when they ask, "What if the parents reject the principle of reciprocity" and "argue that it is biased against fundamentalism, and in favor of religions that conform to deliberative views of civic education and prevailing modes of empirical inquiry?"[30] I couldn't have put it better myself, but when Gutmann and Thompson reply to their own question, it turns out that they missed its force: "But the value of public reason expressed by the deliberative perspective is not just another morality. It is offered as the morally optimal basis on which citizens who disagree about moralities and religions can act collectively to make educational policy."[31]

This is a nice double move: Gutmann and Thompson allow the fundamentalist parents to object that "deliberative views" of civic education are hostage to a special morality (not everyone would accept it), but then they assert that while it may be a morality, it is not "just" another one. Rather, it has the distinguishing (and salvational) characteristic of providing the framework in which all the other, less capacious, moralities can disagree without being unduly unpleasant to one another; it provides a "morally optimal basis."

Yes it does, for those citizens who already identify the moral optimum with the scene of rational reflection and debate. Other citizens—Vicki Frost among them—identify it differently, and if the requirement of deliberative give-and-take is imposed on them, it will not accommodate their disagreement with the liberal mainstream but delegitimize it, as Gutmann and Thompson do when they dismiss the fundamentalist objection as evidence that "those who make it do not take into account the problem of moral disagreement in politics."[32] But for the fundamentalists there is no "problem" of moral disagreement; there is just moral disagreement, a conflict between conceptions of the good. The only "problem" is that at the moment, in a case like *Mozert*, they're not winning the conflict, and they will hardly be comforted by being told that they shouldn't want to, that they are part of a problem. Indeed, if they think about themselves as part of a problem, they will have surrendered to their opponents and become vulnerable to what Gutmann and Thompson consider their strongest point. "Even the objection that reciprocity [mutual respect, giving the other fellow a hearing] is biased must be stated in a form that appeals to a sense of fairness . . . accepted by other citizens."[33] This would be telling were the fundamentalist objection to the doctrine of reciprocity that it is biased; the objection is that it is *wrong*, that the moral optimum is not everyone talking to one another in a decorous deliberative forum but is, rather, everyone allied to and acting in conformity with the Truth and the will of God. Gutmann and Thompson never come close to taking the measure of the arguments that might be made against them, and they continue to try to have it both ways, claiming to be the apostles of respect and the keepers of the open door at the same time that they slam the door shut the moment someone not of their crowd wants to come in.

But, someone might reasonably object, this is hardly helpful. Suppose that you believe (as I in fact do) that policies favoring racial discrimination have no place on the political agenda, and believe too that if a state or the nation should turn in the direction of theocracy, it would be a bad thing. What do you do if, by my arguments at least, there is no principled way—no way not tied to a particular agenda—of lobbying for the exclusion from public deliberation of points of view you consider dangerous? Do you simply allow such points of view to flourish and hope for the best? Or do you do what the theorists discussed here do (although they would no doubt dispute this description): cast about for an abstract formula under whose cover you can exclude things left and right, all the while claiming clean (neutral, impartial, mutually respectful) hands? Is there no alternative?

Gutmann and Thompson actually have an answer to that question, but for reasons that are finally not surprising, they don't see it, even though they provide evidence for it in an observation they rush right past: "A policy favoring racial discrimination, it is now generally agreed, deserves no place on the political agenda. Such a policy is not an option that legislatures or citizens would seriously consider, and if it were to do so, we should expect courts to prevent its adoption."[34] Although over fifteen pages of the essay remain to be written, one wonders why the authors didn't stop here, since it would seem that what they seek—a way of keeping policies favoring racial discrimination off the agenda—has already been found. What's the problem? The problem (they never say this, but it is implied by the fact that the essay continues) is that the solution has been the accomplishment of politics rather than theory. The agreement on which they report has been reached in the course of a history that includes the civil rights struggles of the 1950s and 1960s, the election in 1964 of a president from the South, two speeches by Martin Luther King Jr., the televising of official violence against freedom riders, a Republican president who not only went to China but put in place mandatory programs of affirmative action, the Civil Rights Act of 1964, the Voting Rights Act of 1965, the immense popularity of Alex Haley's *Roots*, the breaking of the color barrier in professional sports. No one of these was either decisive or inevitable, but as a result of their entirely contingent occurrence in an equally contingent sequence, saying certain things—you must keep those people in their place, America belongs to the Americans, you wouldn't want one to marry your sister—became at the least unfashionable and at the most socially and economically disadvantageous, while saying certain other things—people should be judged on the content of their character, not the color of their skins; diversity is a good that should be reflected in the classroom and the workplace; this country is committed to the eradication of racism—became de rigueur and a ticket of entry into public life. This does not mean that the old sentiments were erased from the hearts of those who had previously expressed them or that minds once confused had now been cleared of mistaken notions; rather, it means that one vocabulary fell into favor and disuse, while another stepped into the place it had formerly occupied, and that this new vocabulary was at once a response to shifts in the political wind and an event in those shifts.

The problem is that the political winds may shift again. That is why Gutmann and Thompson are not satisfied with timely and prudential "reasons for rejecting racial discrimination" and require reasons of a "different, stronger kind,"[35] reasons whose force does not vary and/or diminish with circumstances. After all, if policies favoring racial discrimination have been only politically discredited—discredited by contingent events and the ascendency of one rhetoric over another—the same policies could be politically rehabilitated, perhaps through the generation of "scientific evidence" that gives them new justificatory life (witness *The Bell Curve*)[36] or by quantifying their effects and discovering that they promote efficiency and wealth maximization. To be sure, any such rehabilitation seems unlikely, but the fact that it is even possible is enough to make the point that politics can go backward. It is because politics cannot be freeze-framed at the moment its wheel of fortune delivers an outcome you favor that Gutmann and Thompson want to bypass the political process and turn to reasons of "a stronger kind," to principled reasons. These stronger reasons would hover above the political process and intervene whenever it was about to take a wrong turn. In this way, the "hope of liberal theory," the hope that citizens can "agree on principles"[37] that will once and for all circumscribe the political agenda, will have been realized.

But where will these reasons of a stronger kind have come from? Who will have thought them up? The answer is that they will have come from one or another of the viewpoints contending in the political arena. After all, the desire to remove policies favoring racial discrimination from the agenda is not universal; if it were, there would be no problem and the agenda would circumscribe itself. Whatever "principle" one might offer as a device for managing the political process will itself be politically informed, and any agreement it secures will be the result of efforts by one party first to fill the vocabulary of principle with meanings reflecting its agenda and then to present that vocabulary, fashioned as an adjunct to a political program, as the principled, apolitical source of that same program.

I do not mean this as a description of anyone's intention or even as a criticism, as it would be if there were an alternative. There are no cynics in my scenario, only persons whose strongly held beliefs and commitments lead them to understand, and understand sincerely, notions like "equality," "fairness," and "neutrality" in one way rather than another. It is when someone's understanding of these resonant words (which do not interpret themselves) is regnant in the public space that something like an "agreement" has been secured. Once that agreement is in place, some policies will be (at least publicly) unthinkable, and everyone will regularly say of them, "No one would seriously urge . . ."; but in time the unthinkable will be reintroduced in a new guise, and the agreement that once seemed so solid will fall apart preliminary to the fashioning of a new one, no less political, no less precarious.

What this means is that there are no different or stronger reasons than policy reasons and that the announcement of a formula (higher-order impartiality, mutual respect, the judgment of all mankind) that supposedly outflanks politics or limits its sphere by establishing a space free from its incursions will be nothing more or less than politics—here understood not as a pejorative but as the name of the activity by which you publicly urge what you think to be good and true—by another name.

Bonnie Honig makes my general point when she observes that "most political theorists are hostile to the disruptions of politics" and "assume that the task of political theory is . . . to get politics . . . over and done with."[38] The goal is to replace large *P* Politics—the clash between fundamentally incompatible vision and agendas—with small *p* politics—the adjustment through procedural rules of small differences within a field from which the larger substantive differences have been banished. The problem is that the distinction between what is procedural and what is substantive is itself a substantive one, and therefore in whatever form it is enacted, it will engender the very conflicts it was designed to mitigate, as those who would have enacted it differently or not enacted it at all cry foul, or error, or blasphemy. When this happens (as it always will), the would-be engineers of peace and stability always respond in the same way, by calling the malcontents unreasonable, or fanatical, or insufficiently respectful of difference, or some other name that dismisses their concerns by placing them beyond a pale whose boundaries, they continue to claim, have been drawn by nature or by reason. Gutmann and Thompson almost acknowledge as much when they observe that their preferred deliberative perspective "cannot reach those who refuse to express their public claims in terms accessible to their fellow citizens."[39] Rather than seeing this as a limitation on the deliberative project, they immediately see it as a limitation on the citizens that project excludes. "No moral perspective in politics can reach such people," they declare, but what they really mean is that the moral perspective "such people" remain determined to enact is different from the moral perspective Gutmann and Thompson (along with many liberals) assume. And that is finally why "such people" must be left out of the conversation—not because they exhibit a characterological or cognitive flaw but because they don't believe what Gutmann and Thompson believe.

In fact, however, they don't even believe it; that is, their commitment, despite assertions to the contrary, is not to deliberative democracy but—and this is true of everyone and carries with it no blame—to particular outcomes. This is most clearly seen when Gutmann and Thompson take up Carol Moseley-Braun's successful effort to reverse the renewal of a patent on the Confederate flag insignia. Moseley-Braun's performance does not at first glance bear the signs of deliberative reason; it was marked, as Gutmann and Thompson note, by oratory passion, tears, shouts, and threats of a filibuster. Here is their dilemma: They like the outcome but don't want to think it was achieved by inappropriately nondeliberative means. They negotiate the dilemma by transforming Moseley-Braun's tactics into ones that are, if not deliberative themselves, at least productive of deliberation. They do this by transforming Moseley Braun's rhetorically coercive performance into a strategy designed to produce reasoned deliberation, a strategy made necessary by a history in which the concerns Moseley Braun represented had not been taken seriously. "When reasonable perspectives are neglected, there is a strong argument from the premises of deliberative democracy itself to use any legal means necessary to get those views taken seriously."[40] "[E]ven extreme non-deliberative methods may be justified as necessary steps to deliberation."[41]

In other words, when the processes of deliberation do not produce what you think to be the reasonable result, do an end-run around them and pretend that it is still deliberation you are engaged in. The response of Moseley Braun's colleagues on this occasion had nothing to do with argument and everything to do with her success in painting them into an unhappy political corner. The senators simply didn't want to be recorded as persons in favor of the Confederacy at this late date, especially when they were being confronted by the Senate's only black member and one of its relatively few women members. Gutmann and Thompson acknowledge as much when they say of her speech that it "stimulated a debate that changed senators' minds, or at least their positions."[42] That is quite an "or." A change in mind would be precisely the result of the deliberative process Gutmann and Thompson want to favor. A change in position can be, and was in this case, a change to which one is coerced by a strategist who has raised the stakes to a point where you can't stay in the game but have to fold your cards. You can call this any number of things—political maneuvering, intimidation, blackmail; but you can call it deliberation only if you are so committed to the category (and to a particular outcome) that you contrive to blind yourself to the very facts you would honor by that name. Again, I criticize Gutmann and Thompson not for preferring an outcome to deliberation but for claiming to be doing something else and for thinking that there is something else to do.

Notes

1. Amy Gutmann and Dennis Thompson, "Moral Conflict and Political Consensus," *Ethics* 101 (October 1990): 64–88.

2. Ibid., 65.

3. Thomas Nagel, "Moral Conflict and Political Legitimacy," *Philosophy and Public Affairs* (1987): 215, 229.

4. Gutmann and Thompson, "Moral Conflict and Political Consensus," 67.

5. Ibid., 68.

6. Ibid., 69.

7. *Gitlow v. People of New York*, 268 U.S. 652, 45 S. Ct. 625 L.Ed. 1138 (1925).

8. Gutmann and Thompson, "Moral Conflict and Political Consensus," 69.

9. John Locke, *A Letter concerning Toleration* (1689), reprinted in *John Locke: A Letter concerning Toleration*, in *Focus* 8, ed. John Horton and Susan Mendus (1991), 45.

10. Ibid.

11. Ibid., 68.

12. Ibid.

13. Ibid.

14. Gutmann and Thompson, "Moral Conflict and Political Consensus," 68.

15. Ibid., 69–70.

16. Ibid., 70.

17. Ibid., 70.

18. Ibid., 71.

19. Ibid., 80.

20. Ibid., 71.

21. Nomi Stolzenberg, "He Drew a Circle That Shut Me Out: Assimilation, Indoctrination, and the Paradox of a Liberal Education," *Harvard Law Review* 106, no. 3 (January 1993): 591.

22. *Mozert v. Hawkins County Board of Education*, 897 Fed. 2d. 1058, 87, 1063 (6th Cir. 1987).

23. Gutmann and Thompson, *Democracy and Disagreement* (Cambridge: Belknap Press of Harvard University Press, 1996), 63–69.

24. Ibid., 66.

25. Stolzenberg, "He Drew a Circle That Shut Me Out," 630–31.

26. Alan Ryan, "Liberalism," in *A Companion to Contemporary Political Philosophy*, ed. Robert E. Goodin and Philip Petit (Oxford: Blackwell, 1993), 297, 292.

27. Gutmann and Thompson, "Moral Conflict and Political Consensus," 76.

28. This doesn't mean that you cannot slip out of the bonds you have fashioned, only that you will have to do some work, whereas if alien bonds are put on you, you won't even feel them.

29. Gutmann and Thompson, "Moral Conflict and Political Consensus," 75.

30. Gutmann and Thompson, *Democracy and Disagreement*, 67.

31. Ibid.

32. Ibid.

33. Ibid., 67–68.

34. Gutmann and Thompson, "Moral Conflict and Political Consensus," 69.

35. Ibid.

36. Richard J. Herrnstein and Charles Murray, *The Bell Curve: Intelligence and Class Structure in American Life* (New York: Free Press, 1994).

37. Gutmann and Thompson, "Moral Conflict and Political Consensus," 64.

38. Bonnie Honig, *Political Theory and the Displacement of Politics* (Ithaca: Cornell University Press, 1993), 2.

39. Gutmann and Thompson, *Democracy and Disagreement*, 55.

40. Ibid., 136.

41. Ibid., 135.

42. Ibid., 135.

8

Deliberation

Method, Not Theory

RUSSELL HARDIN

*I*n *Democracy and Disagreement*, Amy Gutmann and Dennis Thompson address the centrally most difficult problem of democratic theory and government: how to handle deep disagreements.[1] Their resolution is to plump for deliberative democracy. This has been perhaps the single most popular move of democratic theorists in our time, especially theorists under the sway of Jürgen Habermas. But Gutmann and Thompson are not as abstract and vague as Habermas in his prescriptions, which seem to presuppose that disagreements can commonly be bridged if only we talk enough and hold to the "normative prerequisites of discourse," which sound like rules for parlor or academic discussion rather than rules for the political fray of democratic policymaking.[2] Gutmann and Thompson know that some of our disagreements are real and deep and that, in the face of these, deliberative democracy can be defended primarily not for its effectiveness in bridging all conflicts but for its qualities as a procedure in reaching political decisions.

There is one big issue that I wish to raise with their analysis and with their presumptive prescriptions. This issue is the tendency to blur or ignore the difference between direct moral judgments and the nature of institutions for acting on such judgments. This issue has been a central part of debate in political theory, particularly in utilitarian and Rawlsian political theory. In the wake of Rawlsiana that threatens to swamp all shores, there has been surprisingly little institutional design, although one might think that worry about institutions would be the main focus of that literature.[3] Similarly, Gutmann and Thompson do not do much institutional design. Indeed, they say at the end of their book that they do none (358), but leave that to the future, and perhaps to others. In raising this central issue, my purpose is partly to pose an alternative vision of how to justify government and its policies, and my argument will therefore not primarily be a matter of internal criticism of the arguments of Gutmann and Thompson. Rather, it will be driven by the recognition that our theory of justification must be a two-stage theory.

Much of moral philosophy is essentially direct, not two-stage. Intuitionists, many Kantians, some utilitarians, religious ethicists, conventional advocates of "the moral rules," and many commonsense moralists suppose that the whole or the main story of ethics is to tell individuals how to behave without reference to intervening institutional arrangements.

Political theory for a large, complex society must inherently be two-stage rather than direct because government of such a society requires intervening institutions. Principles for how to reach decisions in one institutional setting need not be the same as those in another setting. For example, we might use popular majoritarian procedures to choose an institution that works without the use of popular majoritarian procedures in handling some range of problems. This might be done, for example, in creating a system of courts and in creating many government agencies that do not use entirely open procedures for reaching decisions. Political theory has long been treated as institutionalist and therefore as indirect or two-stage, as, for example, in the works of Thomas Hobbes, David Hume, Montesquieu, and the less philosophical but more pragmatic James Madison. The entire tradition of contractarianism, despite its devastating incoherence, is grounded in two-stage argument. First we supposedly agree on the idea or the general form of government, and then we let government work its wonders without constantly requiring our agreement on its actions and policies.

Gutmann and Thompson call their account of deliberative democracy a theory. Deliberation seems, rather, to be a method for enhancing the prospects of discovery of facts and of policies to address social issues. Natural scientists deliberate as much as any of us in their goal of doing physics, biology, and so forth. They typically even meet Habermas's normative prerequisites of discourse when they do. The reason is that they seek truths, and deliberation with others enhances their chances of finding them. They would say that deliberation is part of the discovery process, rather than part of the process of justification of their findings or a part of their theories. Similarly, deliberation, or discussion with others, plays an important role in ordinary personal knowledge and understanding. But it is not a theory of such knowledge.

Deliberation in politics has a similar function. It is apt to be quite useful to have input from various people in reaching good decisions. Deliberation in politics commonly has the specific role of helping us understand the interests of others, as well as helping us discover better ways of accomplishing various ends. Hence, it is mostly a pragmatic device, although its use in politics may also benefit us by satisfying those whose policies do not get adopted that at least they have been heard.[4] In this respect, it is not merely part of a discovery process, although it is still not a theory.

Deliberation can be applied to two classes of problems: reaching consensus on values of some kind and reaching effective conclusions on how best to achieve those values. If deliberation is a method, then it can be applied at any point in the chain of political discovery and justification. If it is a theory of government or politics, it cannot be applied at both implementation and institutional design levels. Indeed, if it were a theory, it would lead inexorably to the two-stage account of the problem of democratic governance. Much of the discussion of deliberation, by Habermas, Gutmann and Thompson, and others, clearly casts it as a method of discovery.

In the past, especially in the first half of the twentieth century, it has been moral philosophers who have ignored the distinction between direct and indirect, because institutional, moral assessments. Yet here we have two political philosophers who generally blur it. To make the issue clear, I will pose the structure of Hobbes's vision against theirs. I use Hobbes here not for the content of his theory but for his great originality in seeing the two-level nature of our general problem of political justification. This is an aspect of Hobbes's account that has received inadequate recognition by subsequent thinkers.

I will then briefly discuss the split between individual-level and institutional-level analysis of politics and, as an example of this, Gutmann and Thompson's criticisms of utilitarianism. My purpose is to address the relation of their theory to the institutions that would have to instantiate it. They discuss this issue in ad hoc ways through many examples. What they miss is the two-stage understanding of the relation of institutions to policies, actions, and outcomes. Their focus is almost entirely at the level of policy deliberation, although their discussions also allow for constitutional deliberation over institutional design.

The Hobbesian Structure of Argument

In his theory of politics, Thomas Hobbes put forward a structure of justification of political institutions that may implicitly parallel the background vision of Gutmann and Thompson. Hobbes supposed that the one value that is prior to all others is survival or life, without which we cannot address any other values. He added to this fundamental concern with survival the related concern with general welfare, without which we also cannot do much about achieving any other value. But if we bring welfare into the picture, we necessarily have to make trade-offs between your welfare and mine or even between welfare and other values. Hobbes mostly dodged such problems by supposing that, for causal reasons, the need for order so thoroughly trumps all other considerations that we can concentrate on resolving the problem of order in the confidence that what follows must be radically better than what we would have without order. In coordinating on an order, we seemingly relegate choices over such trade-offs to the system of government we have adopted.[5]

Of course, Hobbes preferred that we adopt a system of, essentially, dictatorship, although he also allowed the possibility of oligarchic or democratic government with great powers, especially if we have already achieved order under one of these, which we should therefore not overthrow out of a concern for merely making things better at the risk of making life insupportable. Hence, he achieved a very nearly determinate resolution of our problems of political choice by first choosing a set of institutional arrangements that then make daily and other policy decisions. He did so by establishing a two-stage theory of government and of justification. At the first stage, we create and justify government. At the second stage, government creates policies.

We may generalize from the Hobbesian structure of argument. That structure is first to claim that some principle or principles are prior, so that politics over other principles is regulated by the resolution of this prior principle. For Gutmann and Thompson and many deliberation theorists, the prior principles are those of deliberative democracy, which will regulate moral and other debates over public issues. This is not always true of Habermas's vision. Often, Habermas implicitly supposes that there is an underlying consensus that deliberation will discover. Insofar as there is a "right answer" out there to be discovered, deliberation is therefore merely a method for its discovery, and not a prior value or even a theory. His stance is therefore coherent— although one might sensibly see it as utterly implausible in contemporary societies, in which deep disagreement, as Gutmann and Thompson say (18– 26), is common and not likely to be bridged by even the best of discourses.

The most striking difference between Hobbes's arguments and those of Gutmann and Thompson is that the latter frequently shift between the institutional and policy levels, giving a single kind of justification for choices at both levels, that is, for choices of institutions and of specific policies. If Hobbes had been pressed to give a justification for a particular policy under a government, he would have had to say merely that it is, after all, what the government has chosen. There is essentially nothing more for him to say. He presumably would not have attempted to say that the argument he used for justifying political order should then also be brought to bear directly on actual policy choices. His political theory is at the level of the structure of the government and not at the level of the actions of the government once it is in place. Hence, his theory might seem to be prima facie objectionable at this level—a point to which I will return below.

Gutmann and Thompson have a very different vision of their enterprise. They can discuss government and specific policies in the same paragraph, as though justifications were the same for both of these. But it is simply in the nature of the case of government in a context in which there is disagreement that this shifting between levels is incoherent for a single justification. If we have institutions, the reason is that *they make a difference in what we do or accomplish*. Therefore, they act in ways that need not fit the normative principle that justifies them. And the agents of institutions need not act according to the normative principles that ground the institutions but need only act according to the roles assigned to them. In particular, they commonly may be motivated strictly by incentives attached to their roles and not directly by the values or purposes that justified the creation of their roles.[6] (This is a seemingly difficult point that I will discuss below.) It is instructive that, as noted further below, Gutmann and Thompson themselves criticize utilitarianism on these implicit grounds when they suppose that utilitarianism is a theory that must yield the same results no matter at which level we apply it but that it cannot coherently do so. Deliberative democracy cannot yield the same results at both levels, therefore we cannot say that it must or should do so.

It is unclear which way Gutmann and Thompson would prefer to go if they were to grant that their *theory* should apply only at one of the levels. I think, however, that their best argument would be that deliberative democracy applies not at either the very general level of choosing institutions for making and implementing policies or at the policymaking level, both of which involve actual decisions, although of quite different kinds. Rather, deliberative democracy applies at the level of formulation and justification of policies and constitutional provisions (constitutional provisions are prior to policies in both a conceptual and, usually, temporal sense). *It informs decisions but is not a procedure for making decisions.* That is, they should take Habermas's sometime position in arguing for deliberation as a discovery process, not as a theory.

Hence, the commitment to deliberative democracy does indeed cut across the two levels, but in a way that is not incoherent because it does not finally determine anything at either level. Its recommendations at one level cannot come into practical conflict with its recommendations at the other level because its recommendations are not determinate at either level—they are not decisions for action. Deliberative democracy is part of a theory of how to carry on public debate and discovery, not a theory of public choice. The discovery goes in at least two directions: from citizens to officials of various kinds and from officials to citizens. In this sense, Hobbes was involved in the practice of deliberative democracy in his effort to analyze the nature of a workable government and to publish his insights to others even though his conclusion at the institutional level was not to use democratic procedures for decision-making.

Hobbes's central value was survival and welfare (survival is clearly a necessary condition for welfare). Government that produces order is a means to these. His judgment of a government therefore would have to depend on whether it produced order. At the policy level and in daily life, we want welfare. Therefore, at the constitutional level we want to create institutions of strong government. Hobbes's political sociology might be bad, but the structure of his argument is right. Gutmann and Thompson want deliberation in all institutions. Let us try to fit this to the two-level structure of government and life. Clearly, our various governmental institutions have varied purposes, such as criminal justice, redistribution, provision of infrastructures, and so on. It seems straightforward that, in determining these purposes, we should democratically deliberate. Once we have done that and once we bring our best political sociology to bear on determining how to achieve one of these democratically determined purposes, we now design particular institutions.

When we do all of this, it is possible, even eminently likely, that we could deliberatively choose to create some institutions that are not themselves deliberative. Gutmann and Thompson say that "deliberative democracy does not divide institutions into those in which deliberation is important and those in which it is not" (358). Immanuel Kant argued that deliberation should often take place outside various institutions but that role holders within them should do what their roles prescribe. They should behave purely "passively."[7] For example, a soldier should generally follow orders, a postal clerk should file the mails properly, and so forth. Once we take seriously the two-level division of democratic choice into constitutional and action levels, we cannot insist that deliberation must rule at both levels, because deliberation at the constitutional level can rule out deliberation at the action level. (I will return to this issue below, under "The Scope of Deliberation in Politics.")

In oral comments, Gutmann and Thompson contend that the real difference between their enterprise and Hobbes's is that he was doing abstract political philosophy, whereas they are doing theory on the ground of actual policymaking. Hence, even to bring Hobbes up misses their point. But the relevance of this discussion of Hobbes is merely to grasp his structural insight that we first create institutions according to how they can accommodate whatever normative principle drives us. And then we let them run. We cannot trivially, without explanation, thereafter make decisions according to our normative principle independently of the institutions we have designed to accommodate them. Our principle does not make decisions for us; our institutions do.

Utilitarian Political Theory

Gutmann and Thompson say that "utilitarianism, libertarianism, and egalitarianism all imply that democratic decisions are justifiable only if they can be shown to be morally correct on principles determined independently of democratic deliberation" (229). Suppose we have set up institutions to achieve deliberation according to their principles or to achieve utilitarian, libertarian, or egalitarian outcomes and that those institutions happen to be democratic. Now suppose the result in some context is repugnant on one of these moral theories. What have we said? We have said, rightly and beyond criticism, that the result in that context is morally wrong according to our theory. It does not follow that we must therefore conclude that we should violate the democratic result. We certainly cannot conclude that our decisions are justifiable only if they are judged, one by one, to be morally correct. Again, our moral principles cannot make decisions. Only actual people or institutional structures with principles to apply can do so.

Why do we need a two-stage account here? In answer, note first that we need a two-stage account even of such simple matters as economic production of complex goods. Each person in an assembly process is to act according to a specified role that requires certain *actions*. The process does not require the person to judge the best overall way to accomplish the organization's production. If everyone acted relatively autonomously according to her own judgment, the result would often be anarchic at worst and sloppily inefficient at best. Government actions are often more complex than those of a firm that produces commodities. The government actions are often subject both to productive, efficiency criteria and to normative criteria. But the individual role holders in various governmental agencies are similar to those in economic organizations. Their task is merely to perform their roles well. Of course, in all kinds of organization, it is possible that people on the line can have ideas for improving what the organization does or how it does what it does and that their advice could improve organizational performance. But to act from my good idea without first getting the organization to accommodate itself to that idea would commonly be harmful to my organization's purpose. And the claim, perhaps true, that the organization would be better off if it did things my way would not justify my independently doing things my way.

In the background of Gutmann and Thompson's criticisms is the dreadful debate over the rightness of utilitarianism that Rawls cogently dissected and dismissed in "Two Concepts of Rules."[8] A standard ploy in the criticism of utilitarianism was (and, alas, still is) to propose such examples as that a utilitarian sheriff should let a mob lynch an innocent, even perhaps help it do so, if that would quiet the mob and stop it from doing even greater harm. Rawls noted simply that it would not be plausible to design the role of sheriff to have the discretion to act to achieve greatest utility in every action rather than to adhere to the role definition. We need the whole set of roles within the institution of justice because only through their use can we do a good utilitarian job of producing good outcomes. We need police, jailers, lawyers, prosecutors, judges, and maybe even executioners. And we need for each of these people to perform their own tasks as defined by their roles, not to try to achieve the best overall outcome according to some moral theory. For example, we do not want the police to become judges who suppress or contrive evidence to reach the supposedly correct verdict.[9] Individual citizens might engage in civil disobedience to make their moral point against some policy. But officials who do so can properly expect to be sanctioned for their actions.

What can we say about the two levels of direct moral assessment and institutional judgment or decision? In utilitarian, libertarian, and some other moral theories, we can deduce (using a lot of social science and factual knowledge) how our institutions should be designed to produce results that are, as nearly as possible, moral in the relevant way or ways. Then, as in Rawls's argument, we may have nothing more to say *politically* when those institutions produce seemingly less than utilitarian, libertarian, or whatever results.[10] Of course, we can say *morally* that they have produced a less-than-moral outcome. The only thing more we might have to say *politically* is that the institutions need revision to make them work better. But we can plump for this only if we think they can in fact be made to work better. In some cases, there may be no ground for such hope. For example, if we have a death (or any other punishment) penalty, we can be sure that it will occasionally be misapplied to innocents. That is a morally bad result, but we cannot create the institution that would be able both to punish some of the guilty and always to avoid punishing the innocent.

Note that utilitarian and egalitarian theories can actually be directed at both the institutional and the policy or outcome levels. For example, strictly utilitarian arguments can be used to design institutions that are expected to have utilitarian outcomes. *The connection between the two levels is causal rather than moral.* What utilitarians want are utilitarian outcomes. To get them requires institutions of certain kinds. Those institutions, again, need not require, and typically would not expect to get, their agents to act as utilitarians but only to follow the rules of their positions in the institutions. In this sense, utilitarianism has been both a personal and an institutional theory through most of its history, although it was ethereally misdirected by G. E. Moore early in the twentieth century in a perversely influential but trivializing work.[11] That is to say, it is both a personal moral theory and a political, institutional theory.[12] But even egalitarianism, which is not generally taken to be a personal moral theory, can be applied as a political theory at both the outcome and the institutional levels through a causal theory of how political institutions can be made to produce egalitarian outcomes.

Gutmann and Thompson have a far less nuanced vision of our political world. They directly judge the morality of institutions. While it would be presumptuous to assert very strongly that this is an impossible trick, it is prima facie such a remarkable move that it wants some argument to justify it. While Gutmann and Thompson present extended discussions of their three principles—reciprocity, publicity, and accountability—they do not address the odd move to direct moral assessment of the institutions independently of what the institutions do other than to follow these procedural principles.

Implicitly, they criticize three standard moral theories—utilitarianism, libertarianism, and egalitarianism—for doing what the theories should do: namely, allow for moral judgments. It is, of course, just such judgments that must play a substantial role in the deliberations of their own morally restricted theory. Indeed, Gutmann and Thompson make extensive use of moral claims, especially of utilitarian and egalitarian theories. Such claims are not the only content of democratic deliberation, but they are evidently a very large part of it in many contemporary societies and in Gutmann and Thompson's view.

Finally, consider a minor but instructive misstatement. Gutmann and Thompson claim that "these perspectives as commonly interpreted imply either that there exists a single correct answer that should . . . trump democratic deliberation, or (when their own theoretical principles are indeterminate) that there is no correct answer at all as far as justice is concerned" (229). Before turning to the central claim here, note that the last fillip is trivially and transparently wrong. We can be indeterminate while not concluding that there is "no correct answer *at all.*" Ordinal utilitarianism and fairness theories commonly lead to assessments that are indeterminate over some restricted range, but the restrictions can be substantial enough to rule out the bulk of all possible resolutions of our problem of the moment.[13]

Now turn to the central claim about how these theories are "commonly interpreted." I do not know what people "commonly" interpret the theories this perverse way, but this is a bad and incoherent interpretation of them. Dennis Thompson's Mill did not think of utilitarian political theory this way.[14] If we start from an equally bad interpretation of deliberative democracy, we will similarly conclude that it is a wasteland. My own preferred theory, utilitarianism, does not entail that there must be a single correct answer. Indeed, utilitarian judgment shares with ordinary pragmatic judgment that it must wait for factual analysis and economic, psychological, and sociological theory before it can commend anything at all in most public policy contexts.[15]

Given the severe constraints of limited knowledge under which we make big decisions, utilitarians must therefore often be far from determinate in their recommendations. Commonly, they must recommend something roughly like deliberation *as a device for the discovery of relevant causal relationships* before they can produce any policy prescription at all.

The Theory of Deliberative Democracy

Other than the literature on distributive justice, which threatens to eat up all the resources we might sooner distribute according to one of the various theories, there may be no recent literature in political philosophy larger than that on deliberative democracy. Despite the vast outpouring of work, however, there is little instruction for the neophyte on just how such a theory works on the ground. When one objects that little deliberation of any rich kind can take place between 200 million adult citizens and their representatives, deliberationists retort that there is a lot of it—in the workplace, over dinner, on the bus, in letters to leaders, in legislatures, and so on. This is, of course, what has gone on more or less always in modern democracies. Yet the message of the deliberationists seems to be that we need to revise our politics to be deliberative or to be more deliberative. This is the plea of Gutmann and Thompson (51). So, one may ask, Which is it? Either we have always been deliberative— although theorists have evidently failed properly to describe or label our politics as deliberative—or we need to become deliberative—in which case, again, the objector wonders how this will work for 200 million American adults or more than 40 million French adults or a similarly large number of some other citizenry.

It is hard to avoid the suspicion that deliberative democracy is the "democracy" of elite intellectuals. They sometimes even approximate the Habermasian moral prerequisites of discourse, although less often than one might wish (at least in political science departments at major universities). It is virtually impossible to avoid the suspicion that deliberation will work, if at all, only in parlor room discourse or in the small salons of academic conferences, not in the normal world of rough-and-tumble politics. Far too much of real politics is about winning and losing for the participants to miss opportunities for scoring against potential opponents. The pragmatic bargaining that Gutmann and Thompson disparage as morally inferior to deliberative democracy is often the main event in politics. The participants in such politics are partisans and—often even by their genuinely moral lights—rightly so.

Against the sanguine vision of deliberative democracy, consider two objections from the side of citizens. First, deliberative democracy clearly has the problem that Oscar Wilde saw in socialism: It would require too many evenings, evenings that are in short supply and that are in demand for other

worthy activities, such as living. The gloriously politicized society of 1989 Czechoslovakia is very nearly the real-world equivalent of the ideal type of deliberative democracy. That was less than a decade ago, but it is gone. Indeed, both 1989 and Czechoslovakia are gone. Is that a grievous loss? No. If 1989 had been kept alive for half a decade, it would have turned into a nightmare of overzealous politics, indeed, of useless politics for the sake of nothing but politics. At some point citizens want to get on with their lives, and their lives are not primarily the lives of citizenship. Anyone looking back over the twentieth century to assess the merits of various political claims for participation must find the sometimes relatively antiparticipatory stances of Hannah Arendt and Albert Camus very appealing. Arendt and Camus seemed to believe that living our lives should be our main concern and should not often be trumped by politics.

Second, the moral constraints of deliberative democracy should rightly apply primarily to *public officials*, not to citizens. Officials should be expected to give reasons for their decisions and judgments, but citizens, who make few decisions other than to vote, should not be expected, or at least should not be required, to give reasons, because, for epistemological reasons, they cannot be expected to do so.[16] Two of the three ground principles—publicity, accountability, and reciprocity—of Gutmann and Thompson's vision apply primarily to officials. Indeed, publicity and accountability are constraints that virtually every standard moral theory would exact of officials. These principles can be inferred from the main classes of moral and political theory in our time: theories based in welfare, fairness, and autonomy. The principles were fundamentally important to John Stuart Mill's more or less utilitarian vision of representative democracy—his discussion of publicity has not been surpassed. It is hard to imagine a theory of democracy, whether one that is deduced from some prior moral theory or one that is merely posited without being grounded in more general moral principles, that would not require accountability and publicity on the part of officials.

Citizens, however, are arguably rightly protected from publicity in their act of voting in nations that have a secret ballot. If so, then they may also be generally freed from any requirement of publicity of their views. And it is very difficult to conceive a serious or formative role for general accountability on the part of citizens. Recall the joke of the bumper sticker in the aftermath of Watergate: "Don't blame me—I'm from Massachusetts." Massachusetts was the only state in which a majority had voted against President Nixon's reelection in 1972. The force of the message of the bumper sticker turns on the implication that the Nixon voters in other states had voted for Watergate and therefore could be blamed for it. Yet, of course, such stalwart Republicans as Barry Goldwater were apparently appalled by Nixon's antics and surely did not vote for Watergate. Some citizens might be held accountable for their racism, bellicose chauvinism, or other supposed moral failings. But these charges would come from some moral theory or principle *outside the democratic system,* a principle that need not be democratic. The constraints of publicity and accountability on public officials are, on the contrary, *inherent in their democratic positions.*

The only one of Gutmann and Thompson's three ground principles that seems to apply to citizens is reciprocity, and even it seems to apply more nearly at the level of groups than of individual citizens. Citizens do not generally make individual requests of government (although in a typical session of the U.S. Congress there are numerous private member's bills to benefit specific, named individuals), and they do not contest with each other over political issues. Rather, they speak as or on behalf of groups. Even for groups, once they are voting, reciprocity has no role. Its role is little more than that of improving open discussion in the debates running up to policy decisions by government and, subsequently, criticizing decisions once they are taken. To use Mill's unfortunate phrase, its role is in the competition of the marketplace of ideas. In that role, even bad ideas are often useful for sparking debate that finally produces better ideas. For citizens, the deliberative theory in deliberative democracy can be little more than Mill's misnamed marketplace of ideas.

Why is "the marketplace of ideas" a bad phrase for what interests us here? There is no analogous role for bad products in the marketplace of products. My bad product is out of the market as soon as your better product displaces it. But bad ideas seem never to leave us, especially bad political ideas. Indeed, it often seems that particularly bad political ideas get transformed into ideologies, which are no longer subject to rational analysis and assessment but simply float above the world they are supposed to affect. Nevertheless, seemingly bad political ideas might eventually be revised or shown to be good ideas. And, at worst, they may be useful as counterpoints to arguments for other ideas. Merely pointing out that certain political moves have tended to lead to fascism, gross inequality, civil war, or other disasters may be a valuable contribution to public debate and eventual understanding.

The Scope of Deliberation in Politics

In oral remarks, Gutmann and Thompson argue that their vision of democratic deliberation is not analogous to participatory democracy in the way suggested above in the mention of 1989 and Czechoslovakia.[17] But if it isn't, then it is hard to see what its force is. Who are the deliberators? And what are the issues over which they are to deliberate? If citizens are the deliberators and if major public initiatives or failures of initiative are the issues, then it is hard to imagine a meaningful deliberative democracy that is not similar to the visions of advocates of participatory democracy. Let us therefore briefly canvass

the role of deliberation in various contexts. Even from the limited survey below, Gutmann and Thompson must assent to giving deliberation roles of varying importance across institutions—perhaps contrary to their claim, cited above, that "deliberative democracy does not divide institutions into those in which deliberation is important and those in which it is not" (358). Let us consider its roles in the central institutions of democratic government.

What democratic institutions should we have, and which of them should be deliberative? Clearly, we need justice, legislative, administrative, and popular or citizenship institutions. In the justice system, juries should be deliberative, but their deliberations arguably should be private and should never be publicized. Courts that are panels of judges can and should be deliberative. After all, the function of both juries and such courts is to assess facts. In much of European practice, such courts do not present their reasons, only their decisions. In higher U.S. courts, reasoned opinions are typically given in support of decisions, even by those who dissent from the majority decision. There are good arguments in favor of either practice. This very fact suggests that general publicity cannot always be democratically desirable. There should even be deliberation among the police and prosecutors, whose task is to discover facts, but this should generally not be public deliberation. Similarly, administrative agencies should often recur to deliberation as they attempt to assess facts and to establish rules. But justice and administration are not the main focus of a theory of deliberative democracy. That focus is legislative and popular deliberation.

Legislatures might well be deliberative on occasion, but at least the American Congress has seen deliberation displaced by public posturing in recent times, in part because statements in Congress are now part of the degrading permanent campaign of American politics. Deliberation often takes place off to the side of the congressional main stage, in staff meetings and in expert panels convened to discover various things and to invent policy options. It is a subordinate activity and an activity that might take place as much in a nondemocratic polity in which the search for good policy is taken seriously.

It is interesting that the decline of deliberation within Congress, if there was much before, is largely a response to the demands of electoral politics, or popular democracy. *Popular democracy in a large society with representative government subverts deliberation.* In the United States, the subversion results from two related facts. First, posturing is virtually demanded by the effort to reach a large public audience who, rightly, have other things to occupy their time and thoughts and who deal with politics more through catchphrases and slogans than through analysis. It is analysis that requires deliberation. Being mobilized in support of a candidate or a policy requires no analysis. Second, posturing is an inherent part of the unquenchable demand for money for American electoral politics. For raising money from large public interest groups such as those that support or oppose abortion or immigration, this follows from the nature of mass politics. But even for raising money from concentrated special interests, posturing is often necessary to protect against attacks from larger publics.

Because of the sheer size of the polity, citizens have little interest in participating and, given this fact, even less interest in being well enough informed to participate well.[18] Joseph Schumpeter's strictures on democracy are devastating for any claim that citizens should deliberate or enter into deliberative discussions.[19] This is not merely a matter of Wilde's complaint against socialism or the implausibility of the continuation of Czech politics much beyond 1989 but also of the intellectual demands that deliberation exacts. Most people cannot be strongly motivated to understand something that they cannot affect or make use of in their lives, especially something as complex and variegated as public policy over most matters.

In sum, we might hope that jurors and many others with more formal roles within the government deliberate, and we might wish that legislators would deliberate more than they seemingly do. But to hope, expect, or wish for citizens to do much deliberating is unreasonable and forlorn. Yet if citizens are not chief among the deliberators, how can we speak of deliberative *democracy*? Deliberation is very important in politics, but it cannot typically be very democratic. Indeed, if deliberation is primarily within government or within smaller critical communities that might be taken as advisory to government, it can serve as well in a nondemocratic society, as Kant firmly argued in the case of Frederick the Great, his own enlightened monarch.[20]

Concluding Remarks

The Hobbesian stipulation that we must first survive and then moralize is compelling. It is essentially a pragmatic claim for political order, almost even a conceptual claim. If we want anything, we must have survival. If we want survival, we must have political order. Hence, almost by syllogism, if we want anything, material or moral, we must have political order. The things we might want to secure under government therefore do not trade off against having government. One might argue that there are flaws or objectionable claims in the pieces of Hobbes's argument, but its structure makes political order almost strictly prior to all else. He leaves us a method for governing.

Gutmann and Thompson make a very different move, although it may appear superficially to be structurally similar. They essentially stipulate that we must first meet the standards of deliberative democracy and then moralize over other matters according to those standards. Their grounding of deliberative democracy is, of course, moral rather than pragmatic. But this means that, if I have moral objections to what the polity chooses to do, I can compellingly argue that my moral concern trumps the morality of deliberative democracy. There is no higher or prior morality or any other consideration in deliberative democracy to shield it from such a claim. Deliberation is not even so much as a method for governing but only a method for discovery and, sometimes but not always, a method for mollifying losers by giving them the sense of at least being heard. These are good things, but they fall far short of being a general theory of democratic politics. They are not even a central part of what makes democracy distinctive.

Deliberative democracy sounds wonderful. But it is a method, and methods are fallible. If it elevates a Hitler to rule in my society, revolution and guns might then seem to be even better methods of achieving our ends. A consequentialist—for example, either a utilitarian or a fairness theorist—might add that what we want in politics are specific outcomes or types of outcome. Procedures and institutions are chosen contingently according to how well they produce those outcomes. They are what we use to get to outcomes, but they do not have either conceptual or moral priority over outcomes. They have merely temporal and causal priority.

The failure to distinguish between institutional design for deliberative inputs to political decisions and the moral assessment of those decisions or the morality of their purpose suggests an oddly apolitical view of the world. We apply an odd kind of morality by brute force to the way we decide, as though we were a wielding a crowbar to achieve an immediate outcome. But what we must surely do is design our institutions to accommodate our moral theories. We must then rely on these institutions for achieving actual outcomes in various policy realms. This is the striking difference between morality for an individual and political theory for a society. When they have criticized moral theories, Gutmann and Thompson have fallen prey to the fallacy, which Rawls demolished, of ignoring the necessary role of institutions, especially in their chapter-length criticism of utilitarianism (165–98). Then they have fallen prey to an oddly contrary fallacy of supposing they can judge the morality of institutions directly, as though without attention to the trumping concern of what the institutions actually do.

Political theory cannot be reduced to individual-level moral theory, and political institutions cannot be evaluated or morally judged by brute application of some moral principle to their structure. This is true already for merely causal reasons: Institutions can help us to do things we could not do without them. Indeed, one can argue that institutions, or at least very many of them, are inherently consequentialist in that they are designed to cause or accomplish something. If so, then one must argue backward from their purpose to their structure, and this yields their justification. If an institution's purpose is moral and if it does not violate morality in accomplishing that purpose, then the institution is morally justified. For many of the most important decision-making institutions in a democracy, it is incoherent to suppose we need an institution to accomplish some purpose and then to argue as though we could reach direct judgments of the rightness or wrongness of particular institutional actions independently of their fit with the institution's structure. If we need the institution to enable us to make relevant decisions, that is because we cannot make those decisions as well directly.

Gutmann and Thompson implicitly hold deliberative democracy to be a prior value that *politically* trumps moral values of other kinds. They are most explicit on this point in their chapter on utilitarianism as a public political theory. Making deliberation a political trump may seem analogous to John Locke's argument that toleration must politically trump religious values.[21] But Locke's argument was framed as a causal claim that, without toleration, those with variant religious views could not even fulfill them, so that intolerance was harmful to their own religious views. The most compelling causal claim for deliberation must be that it leads to better results in the sense of helping to discover relevant facts and policies. But this leaves open to analysis whether we should always want deliberation and, at least for citizens, whether it is even possible.

Perhaps a better analog of the role of deliberative democracy is James Madison's more general and more nearly contemporary variant of Locke's view of toleration. In *Federalist* 49, Madison says, "It is the reason, alone, of the public, that ought to control and regulate the government. The passions ought to be controlled and regulated by the government." Deliberation has its proper role when it is on the side of reason and reasoning about government—about its institutions and its actions. Its greatest value is to help us understand institutions, and its further value is sometimes, but not pervasively, to help institutions and their role holders understand their workings.

Notes

An earlier version of this essay was presented at the meetings of the Pacific Division of the American Philosophical Association, Berkeley, Calif., April 28, 1997, in a session on Amy Gutmann and Dennis Thompson, *Democracy and Disagreement* (Cambridge: Belknap Press of Harvard University Press, 1996). I am grateful to other participants in that session, especially Gutmann and Thompson, for comments on the essay.

1. I will give page references to this book in parentheses in the text.

2. In Jürgen Habermas, *The Theory of Communicative Action*, vol. 1: *Reason and the Rationalization of Society*, trans. Thomas McCarthy (Boston: Beacon, 1984).

3. Among the few works that do this is Charles Beitz, *Political Equality* (Princeton: Princeton University Press, 1989).

4. It would be interesting to understand just how being heard is more satisfying than merely being counted, but that is not part of our discussion here.

5. Russell Hardin, "Hobbesian Political Order," *Political Theory* 19 (May 1991): 156–80.

6. See, further, Russell Hardin, "Institutional Morality," in *The Theory of Institutional Design*, ed. Geoffrey Brennan and Robert E. Goodin (Cambridge: Cambridge University Press, 1995), 126–53; and "Institutional Commitment: Values or Incentives?" in *Economics, Values, and Organization*, ed. Avner Ben Ner and Louis Putterman (Cambridge: Cambridge University Press, 1998), 419–33.

7. Immanuel Kant, "An Answer to the Question: 'What Is Enlightenment?,' " in *Kant's Political Writings*, ed. Hans Reiss (Cambridge: Cambridge University Press, 1970; original essay from 1784), 54–60, esp. 56–57.

8. John Rawls, "Two Concepts of Rules," *Philosophical Review* 64 (1955): 3–32. See, further, Russell Hardin, *Morality within the Limits of Reason* (Chicago: University of Chicago Press, 1988), 100–105.

9. See Russell Hardin, "The Artificial Duties of Contemporary Professionals," *Social Service Review* 64 (December 1991): 528–41.

10. For example, in *Political Equality* Beitz concludes, rightly, that if we do our best to set up a fair electoral procedure that gives every voter equal input and that procedure systematically undervalues your vote, we have nothing more to say, within the theory and its institution.

11. G. E. Moore, *Principia Ethica* (Cambridge: Cambridge University Press, 1903).

12. For an account of institutional utilitarianism, see Hardin, *Morality within the Limits of Reason*, chaps. 3 and 4.

13. In a question-begging passage, Gutmann and Thompson grant that "deliberative democracy is also indeterminate . . . but . . . for good nonutilitarian reasons" (196).

14. Dennis Thompson, *John Stuart Mill and Representative Government* (Princeton: Princeton University Press, 1976).

15. Even game theory is indeterminate because strategic interaction, which is a central and pervasive part of social order and disorder, and causal understandings are indeterminate. Every theory is necessarily indeterminate. See Russell Hardin, "Determinacy and Rational Choice," in *Rational Interaction: Essays in Honor of John C. Harsanyi*, ed. Reinhard Selten (Berlin: Springer-Verlag, 1992), 191–200.

16. See, further, Russell Hardin, "Democratic Epistemology and Accountability," *Social Philosophy and Policy* (forthcoming).

17. These remarks were made at the American Philosophical Association session in Berkeley for which this essay was originally written.

18. See, further, Russell Hardin, *Liberalism, Constitutionalism, and Democracy* (Oxford: Oxford University Press, forthcoming), chap. 4; and Hardin, "Democratic Epistemology and Accountability."

19. Joseph A. Schumpeter, *Capitalism, Socialism, and Democracy* 3d ed. (New York: Harper, 1950), 261–63.

20. Kant, "What Is Enlightenment?," 58–60.

21. John Locke, *A Letter concerning Toleration* (1689; reprint, Indianapolis: Bobbs-Merrill, 1950).

PART II

Expanding the Limits of Deliberative Democracy

9

Agreement without Theory

CASS R. SUNSTEIN

My principal goal in this essay is to extend a particular insight in *Democracy and Disagreement* and to suggest that on multimember bodies, especially courts, it is possible to achieve agreements on particular judgments without achieving agreement on the theoretical commitments that underlie those judgments. My discussion of the uses of incompletely theorized agreements, as a central part of a well-functioning deliberative democracy, is very much in the spirit of the Gutmann/Thompson approach. I conclude, however, with two questions or reservations about that approach. First, I suggest that sometimes it is legitimate for participants in politics to raise the political or moral stakes and to make claims that are gratuitous, in the sense that they are not indispensable to resolution of the dispute at hand. Second, I suggest that deliberative democracy comes with its own distinctive and internal constitutional preconditions; Gutmann and Thompson build into that ideal certain constitution-like principles that seem to me external to, and independent of, deliberative democracy itself.

One of the most important ideas in *Democracy and Disagreement* is that of *economizing on moral disagreement*. Gutmann and Thompson urge that participants in political life ought not to take on one another's deepest moral convictions when it is unnecessary for them to do so. I think that this claim is largely correct, and here I want to develop it in somewhat more detail, with particular reference to the performance of collective institutions, above all the judiciary. How might a multimember body—a legislature, a club, a set of citizens comprising a nation, especially a court—proceed in the face of conflict and disagreement on fundamental matters?

My basic suggestion is that well-functioning courts try to solve problems through *incompletely theorized agreements*. Sometimes these agreements involve abstractions, accepted amid severe disagreements on particular cases. Thus, people who disagree on pornography and hate speech can accept a general free-speech principle, and those who argue about homosexuality and disability can accept an abstract antidiscrimination principle. This is an important phenomenon in both law and politics. But sometimes incompletely theorized agreements involve concrete outcomes rather than abstractions, and because of the close relationship between judicial reasoning and judgments about particulars, this is what I will be emphasizing here.

When people (and here we may speak of individual agents as well as of collective institutions) are uncertain about an abstraction—is equality more important than liberty? does free will exist?—they can move to a level of greater particularity. This phenomenon has an especially notable feature: It enlists silence, on certain basic questions, as a device for producing convergence despite disagreement, uncertainty, limits of time and capacity, and heterogeneity. Incompletely theorized agreements are a key to legal and political reasoning in particular and practical reason in general. They are an important source of social stability and an important way for people to demonstrate mutual respect.

Consider some examples from ordinary politics. People may believe that it is important to protect endangered species, while having quite diverse theories about why this is so. Some people may stress what they see as human obligations to species or nature as such; others may point to the role of endangered species in producing ecological stability; still others may emphasize the possibility that obscure species can provide valuable medicines for human beings. Similarly, people may invoke many different grounds for their shared belief that the law should protect labor unions against certain kinds of employer coercion. Some people may emphasize the democratic functions of unions; others may think that unions are necessary for industrial peace; others may believe that unions protect basic rights. So, too, people may favor a rule of strict liability for certain torts from multiple diverse starting-points— though some people will root their judgments in economic efficiency, others in distributive goals, still others in conceptions of basic rights.

The agreement on particulars is incompletely theorized in the sense that the relevant participants are clear on the result without agreeing on the most general theory that accounts for it. (As we shall soon see, I understand the term "general" in a relative sense, with the thought that people try to reach agreement at a more particular level than the level at which they disagree.) Often they can agree on a rationale offering low-level or midlevel principles. They may agree that a rule—reducing water pollution, allowing workers to unionize—makes sense without entirely agreeing on the foundations of their belief. They may accept an outcome—reaffirming the right to have an abortion, protecting sexually explicit art—without understanding or converging on an ultimate ground for that acceptance. What accounts for the outcome, in terms of a full-scale theory of the right or the good, is left unexplained.

There is a limiting case of incomplete theorization: *full particularity*. This phenomenon occurs when people agree on a result without agreeing on any kind of supporting rationale. Any rationale—any reason—is by definition more abstract than the result that it supports. Sometimes people do not offer any reasons at all, because they do not know what those reasons are, or because they fear that the reasons that they have would turn out, on reflection, to be inadequate and hence to be misused in the future. This is a common phenomenon in law. Thus, juries usually do not offer reasons for outcomes, and negotiators sometimes conclude that something should happen without concluding why it should happen. I will not emphasize this limiting case here; I shall focus instead on outcomes accompanied by low-level or midlevel principles.

My emphasis on incompletely theorized agreements is intended partly as descriptive. These agreements are a pervasive phenomenon in ordinary human reasoning and in politics and especially law. But my goal is not simply descriptive. As Gutmann and Thompson emphasize, there are special virtues to avoiding large-scale theoretical conflicts. Incompletely theorized agreements can operate as foundations for both rules and analogies, and such agreements are especially well suited to the institutional limits of many collective institutions, including courts.

In social life, people reason in ways that grow out of the particular role in which they find themselves. They know what actions are permissible, and what actions are off-limits, only because of their role. As practical reasoners, people take their roles for granted and live accordingly. Consider the close relationship between reasoning and role for such diverse figures as parents, students, waiters, doctors, employees, consumers, and automobile drivers. Any particular role is accompanied by a set of relevant and irrelevant considerations. The particular social role of judges fits especially well with incompletely theorized agreements.

How People Converge

It seems clear that people may agree on a *correct* outcome even though they do not have a theory to account for their judgments. Jones may know that dropped objects fall, that bee stings hurt, that hot air rises, and that snow melts, without knowing exactly why these facts are true. The same is true for morality. Johnson may know that slavery is wrong, that government may not stop political protests, that every person should have just one vote, and that it is bad for government to take property unless it pays for it, without knowing exactly or entirely why these things are so. Moral judgments may be right or true even if they are reached by people who lack a full account of those judgments (though moral reasoners may do better if they try to offer such an account, a point to which I will return). The same is very much true for law. Judge Thompson may know that if you steal someone's property, you must return it, without having a full account of why this principle has been enacted into law. We may thus offer an epistemological point: People can know *that* x is true without entirely knowing *why* x is true.

There is a political point as well. Sometimes people can agree on individual judgments even if they disagree on general theory. In American law, for example, diverse judges may agree that *Roe v. Wade*,[1] protecting the right to choose abortion, should not be overruled, though the reasons that lead each of them to that conclusion sharply diverge. Some people think that the Court should respect its own precedents; others think that *Roe* was rightly decided as a way of protecting women's equality; others think that the decision reflects an appropriate judgment about the social role of religion; still others think that restrictions on abortion are unlikely to protect fetuses in the world, so the decision is good for pragmatic reasons. We can find incompletely theorized political agreements on particular outcomes in many areas of law and politics—on both sides of racial discrimination controversies, both sides of disputes over criminal justice, both sides of disputes over health care.

Rules and Analogies

Rules and analogies are the two most important methods for resolving disputes without obtaining agreement on first principles. Both of these devices attempt to promote what deliberative democrats emphasize is a major goal of a heterogeneous society: *to make it possible to obtain agreement where agreement is necessary, and to make it unnecessary to obtain agreement where agreement is impossible.* People can often agree on what rules mean even when they agree on very little else. And in the face of persistent disagreement or uncertainty about what morality requires, people can reason about particular cases by reference to analogies. They point to cases in which their judgments are firm. They proceed from those firm judgments to the more difficult ones. This is how ordinary people tend to think.

We might consider in this regard American Supreme Court Justice Stephen Breyer's discussion of one of the key compromises reached by the seven members of the United States Sentencing Commission.[2] As Breyer describes it, a central issue was how to proceed in the face of highly disparate philosophical premises about the goals of criminal punishment. Some people asked the commission to follow an approach to punishment based on "just deserts"—an approach that would rank criminal conduct in terms of severity. But different commissioners had very different views about how different crimes should be ranked. In these circumstances, there could be an odd form of deliberation in which criminal punishments became ever more, and more irrationally, severe, because some commissioners would insist that the crime under consideration was worse than the previously ranked crimes. In any case, agreement on a rational system would be unlikely to follow from efforts by the seven commissioners to rank crimes in terms of severity.

Other people urged the commission to use a model of deterrence. There were, however, major problems with this approach. We lack empirical evidence that could link detailed variations in punishment to prevention of crime, and the seven members of the commission were highly unlikely to agree that deterrence provides a full account of the aims of criminal sentencing. An approach based on deterrence seemed no better than an approach based on just deserts.

In these circumstances, what route did the commission follow? In fact, the commission abandoned large theories altogether. It adopted no general view about the appropriate aims of criminal sentencing. Instead the commission abandoned high theory and adopted a rule—one founded on precedent: "It decided to base the Guidelines primarily upon typical, or average, actual past practice." Consciously articulated explanations, not based on high theory, were used to support particular departures from the past.

Justice Breyer sees this effort as a necessary means of obtaining agreement and rationality within a multimember body charged with avoiding unjustifiably wide variations in sentencing. Thus his more colorful oral presentation: "Why didn't the Commission sit down and really go and rationalize this thing and not just take history? The short answer to that is: we couldn't. We couldn't because there are such good arguments all over the place pointing in opposite directions. . . . Try listing all the crimes that there are in rank order of punishable merit. . . . Then collect results from your friends and see if they all match. I will tell you they don't."[3]

The example suggests a more general point. Through both analogies and rules, it is often possible for practical reasoners to converge on particular outcomes without resolving large-scale issues of the right or the good. People can decide what to do when they disagree on exactly how to think.

Agreements and Justice

The fact that people can obtain an agreement of this sort—about the value and meaning of a rule or about the existence of a sound analogy—is no guarantee of a good outcome, whatever our criteria for deciding whether an outcome is good. Perhaps the Sentencing Commission incorporated judgments that were based on ignorance, confusion, or prejudice. Some of the same things can be said about analogies. People in positions of authority may agree that a ban on same-sex marriages is acceptable because it is analogous to a ban on marriages between uncles and nieces; but the analogy may be misconceived, because there are relevant differences between the two cases, and because the similarities are far from decisive. The fact that people agree that case A is analogous to case B does not mean that case A *or* case B is rightly decided. Perhaps case A should not be taken for granted. Perhaps case A should not be selected as the relevant foundation for analogical thinking; perhaps case Z is more pertinent. Perhaps case B is not really like case A. Problems with analogies and low-level thinking might lead us to be more ambitious. We may well be pushed in the direction of general theory—and toward broader and perhaps more controversial claims—precisely because analogical reasoners offer an inadequate and incompletely theorized account of relevant similarities or relevant differences.

All this should be sufficient to show that the virtues of decisions by rule and by analogy are partial. But no system of politics and law is likely to be either just or efficient if it dispenses with rules and analogies. In fact, it is not likely even to be feasible.

Constitutions, Cases, and Incompletely Theorized Agreements

Incompletely theorized agreements play a pervasive role in law and society. It is quite rare for a person or group completely to theorize any subject, that is, to accept both a general theory and a series of steps connecting that theory to concrete conclusions. Thus, we often have an *incompletely theorized agreement on a general principle*—incompletely theorized in the sense that people who accept the principle need not agree on what it entails in particular cases. This is the sense emphasized by American Supreme Court Justice Oliver Wendell Holmes in his great aphorism "General principles do not decide concrete cases."[4] The agreement is incompletely theorized in the sense that it is *incompletely specified*. Much of the key work must be done by others, often through casuistical judgments, specifying the abstraction at the point of application.

Sometimes constitution-making becomes possible through this form of incompletely theorized agreement. Many constitutions contain incompletely specified standards and avoid rules, at least when it comes to the description of basic rights. Consider the cases of Eastern Europe and South Africa, where constitutional provisions include many abstract provisions on whose concrete specification there has been sharp dispute. Abstract provisions protect "freedom of speech," "religious liberty," and "equality under the law," and citizens agree on those abstractions in the midst of sharp dispute about what these provisions really entail. Much lawmaking also becomes possible only because of this phenomenon.

Let us turn to a second phenomenon. Sometimes people agree on a mid-level principle but disagree about both more general theory and particular cases. People may believe, for example, that government cannot discriminate on the basis of race, without having a large-scale theory of equality, and also without agreeing whether government may enact affirmative action programs, or segregate prisons when racial tensions are severe. People may think that government may not regulate speech unless it can show a clear and present danger—but disagree about whether this principle is founded in utilitarian or Kantian considerations and about whether the principle allows government to regulate a particular speech by members of the Ku Klux Klan.

My particular interest here is in a third kind of phenomenon, of special interest for practical reason: incompletely theorized agreements on particular outcomes, accompanied by agreements on the narrow or low-level principles that account for them. There is no algorithm by which to distinguish between a high-level theory and one that operates at an intermediate or lower level. We might consider, as conspicuous examples of high-level theories, Kantian-ism and utilitarianism, and see illustrations in the many distinguished (aca-demic) efforts to understand such areas as tort law, contract law, free speech, and the law of equality as undergirded by highly abstract theories of the right or the good. By contrast, we might think of low-level principles as including most of the ordinary material of low-level justification or legal "doctrine"— the general class of principles and justifications that are not said to derive from any particular large theories of the right or the good, that have ambiguous relations to large theories, and that are compatible with more than one such theory.

By the term "low-level principles," I refer to something relative, not ab-solute; I mean to do the same thing by the terms "theories" and "abstrac-tions" (which I use interchangeably). In this setting, the notions "low-level," "high," and "abstract" are best understood in comparative terms, like the terms "big" and "old" and "unusual." Thus, the "clear and present danger" standard for regulation of speech is a relative abstraction when compared with the claim that members of the Nazi Party may march in Skokie, Illinois. But the "clear and present danger" idea is relatively partic-ular when compared with the claim that nations should adopt the consti-tutional abstraction "freedom of speech." The term "freedom of speech" is a relative abstraction when measured against the claim that campaign fi-nance laws are acceptable, but the same term is less abstract than the grounds that justify free speech, as in, for example, the principle of personal autonomy. What I am emphasizing here is that when people diverge on some (relatively) high-level proposition, they might be able to agree when they lower the level of abstraction.

In analogical reasoning, this phenomenon occurs all the time. People might think that A is like B, and is covered by the same low-level principle, without agreeing on a deep theory to explain why the low-level principle is sound. They agree on the matter of similarity, without agreeing on a large-scale account of what makes the two things similar. In the law of discrimination, for example, many people think that sex discrimination is "like" race discrimination and should be treated similarly, even if they lack or cannot agree on a general theory of when discrimination is unacceptable. In the law of free speech, many people agree that a ban on speech by a communist is "like" a ban on speech by a member of the Ku Klux Klan and should be treated similarly, even if they lack or cannot agree on a general theory about the foundations of the free-speech principle.

Incomplete Theorization and the Constructive Uses of Silence

What might be said on behalf of incompletely theorized agreements, or incompletely theorized judgments, about particular cases? Some people think of incomplete theorization as quite unfortunate—as embarrassing or reflective of some important problem or defect. When people theorize, by raising the level of abstraction, they do so to reveal bias, or confusion, or inconsistency. Surely participants in politics and law should not abandon this effort.

There is some truth in these usual thoughts. But they are not the whole story. On the contrary, incompletely theorized judgments are an important and valuable part of both private and public life. They help make politics and law possible; they even help make life possible. Most of their virtues involve *the constructive uses of silence*, an exceedingly important social and legal phenomenon. Silence—on something that may prove false, obtuse, or excessively contentious—can help minimize conflict, allow the present to learn from the future, and save a great deal of time and expense. What is said and resolved is no more important than what is left out.

My principal concern in this section is the question of how judges on a multimember body should justify their opinions in public; the argument therefore has a great deal to do with the problem of collective choice. But some of the relevant points bear on other issues as well. They have implications for the question of how an individual judge not faced with the problem of producing a majority opinion—a judge on trial court, for example—might write; they bear on the question of how a single judge, whether or not a member of a collective body, might think in private; and they relate to appropriate methods of both thought and justification wholly outside of the adjudication and even outside of law. Thus, we might understand the term "judge" to refer not only to those who are technically judges but also to many other agents attempting to use practical reason to settle their problems.

Begin with the special problem of public justification on a multimember body. The first and most obvious point is that incompletely theorized agreements are well suited to a world—especially a legal world—containing social dissensus on large-scale issues. By definition, such agreements have the large advantage of allowing a convergence on particular outcomes by people unable to reach anything like an accord on general principles. This advantage is associated not only with the simple need to decide cases but also with social stability, which could not exist if fundamental disagreements broke out in every case of public or private dispute.

Second, incompletely theorized agreements can promote two goals of a liberal democracy and a liberal legal system: to enable people to live together, and to permit them to show each other a measure of reciprocity and mutual respect. The use of low-level principles or rules allows judges on multimember bodies and hence citizens generally to find commonality and thus a common way of life without producing unnecessary antagonism. Both rules and low-level principles make it unnecessary to reach areas in which disagreement is fundamental.

Perhaps even more important, incompletely theorized agreements allow people to show each other a high degree of mutual respect, or civility, or reciprocity—a value particularly emphasized by Gutmann and Thompson. Frequently, ordinary people disagree in some deep way on an issue—pornography, or homosexual marriages, or what to do in the Middle East—and sometimes they agree not to discuss that issue much, as a way of deferring to each other's strong convictions and showing a measure of reciprocity and respect (even if they do not at all respect the particular conviction that is at stake). If reciprocity and mutual respect are desirable, it follows that public officials or judges, perhaps even more than ordinary people, should not challenge their fellow citizens' deepest and most defining commitments, at least if those commitments are reasonable and if there is no need for them to do so.

To be sure, some fundamental commitments might appropriately be challenged in the legal system or within other multimember bodies. Some such commitments are ruled off-limits by the authoritative legal materials. Many provisions involving basic rights have this function. Of course, it is not always disrespectful to disagree with someone in a fundamental way; on the contrary, such disagreements may sometimes reflect profound respect. When defining commitments are based on demonstrable errors of fact or logic, it is appropriate to contest them. So, too, when those commitments are rooted in a rejection of the basic dignity of all human beings, or when it is necessary to undertake the contest to resolve a genuine problem. But many cases can be resolved in an incompletely theorized way, and that is all I am suggesting here.

Turn now to reasons that call for incompletely theorized agreements whether or not we are dealing with a multimember body. The first consideration here is that for arbiters of social controversies, incompletely theorized agreements have the crucial function of reducing the political cost of enduring disagreements. If judges disavow large-scale theories, then losers in particular cases lose much less. They lose a decision, but not the world. They may win on another occasion. Their own theory has not been rejected or ruled inadmissible. When the authoritative rationale for the result is disconnected from abstract theories of the good or the right, the losers can submit to legal obligations, even if reluctantly, without being forced to renounce their largest ideals.

The second point is that incompletely theorized agreements are valuable when we seek moral evolution over time. Consider the area of equality, where considerable change has occurred in the past and will inevitably occur in the future. A completely theorized judgment would be unable to accommodate changes in facts or values. If a culture really did attain a theoretical end-state, it would become too rigid and calcified; we would know what we thought about everything. This would disserve posterity. Hence, incompletely theorized agreements are a key to debates over equality, with issues being raised about whether gender, sexual orientation, age, disability, and other factors are analogous to race; such agreements have the important advantage of allowing a large degree of openness to new facts and perspectives. At one point, we might think that homosexual relations are akin to incest; at another point, we might find the analogy bizarre. Of course, a completely theorized judgment would have many virtues if it is correct. But at any particular moment in time, this is an unlikely prospect for human beings, not excluding judges.

Compare practical reasoning in ordinary life. At a certain time, you may well refuse to make decisions that seem foundational in character—about, for example, whether to get married within the next year, or whether to have two, three, or four children, or whether to live in San Francisco or New York. Part of the reason for this refusal is knowledge that your understandings of both facts and values may well change. Indeed, your identity may itself change in important and relevant ways, and for this reason a set of commitments in advance—something like a fully theorized conception of your life course—would make no sense. Legal systems and nations are not very different.

The third point is practical. Incompletely theorized agreements may be the best approach that is available for people of limited time and capacities. A single judge (or ordinary agent) faces this problem as much as a member of a multimember panel. Here, too, the rule of precedent is crucial; attention to precedent is liberating, not merely confining, since it frees busy people to deal with a restricted range of problems. Incompletely theorized agreements have the related advantage, for ordinary lawyers and judges, of humility and modesty. To engage in analogical reasoning, for example, one ordinarily need not take a stand on large, contested issues of social life, some of which can be resolved only on what will seem to many a sectarian basis.

Fourth, incompletely theorized agreements are well adapted to a system that should or must take precedents as fixed points. This is a large advantage over more ambitious methods, since ambitious thinkers, in order to reach horizontal and vertical coherence, will probably be forced to disregard many decided cases. In light of the sheer number of decided cases and adjudicative officials, law, for example, cannot speak with one voice; full coherence in principle is unlikely in the extreme.

Here, too, we can find many analogies in ordinary life. A parent's practices with his children may not fully cohere. Precedents with respect to bedtime, eating, homework, and much else are unlikely to be susceptible to systematization under a single principle. Of course parents do not seek to be inconsistent; of course a child may justly feel aggrieved if a sibling is permitted to watch more hours of television for no apparent reason; but full coherence would be a lot to ask. The problem of reaching full consistency is all the more severe in politics and law, where so many people have decided so many things, and where disagreements on large principles lurk in the background.

Overlapping Consensus and Incomplete Theorization

There is a relationship between the notion of incompletely theorized agreements and the well-known idea of an "overlapping consensus," set out by John Rawls.[5] Rawls urges that a society might seek a reasonable overlapping consensus on certain basic political principles—allowing people, from their own diverse foundations, to agree on those principles. The idea of an overlapping consensus, like the notion of incompletely theorized agreement, attempts to bring about stability and social agreement in the face of diverse "comprehensive views."

But the two ideas are far from the same. I have emphasized that when we disagree on the relatively abstract, we can often find agreement by moving to lower levels of generality. Rawls is more interested in the opposite possibility— that people who disagree on much else can agree on political abstractions and can use that agreement for political purposes. Rawls emphasizes that when we find disagreement or confusion, or when "our shared political understandings . . . break down," we move toward political philosophy and become more abstract.[6] Thus Rawls writes that abstraction "is a way of continuing public discussion when shared understandings of lesser generality have broken down. We should be prepared to find that the deeper the conflict, the higher the level of abstraction to which we must ascend to get a clear and uncluttered view of its roots."[7] Of course what Rawls says may be true: People can be moved toward greater abstraction by their disagreement on particulars. But people may have trouble with abstraction. A special goal of the incompletely theorized agreement on particulars is to obtain a consensus on a concrete outcome among people who do not want to decide questions in political philosophy. They may be uncertain about how to choose among different forms of liberalism, or about whether to select liberalism or a certain alternative.

One of the basic aspirations of Rawls's approach is to avoid certain abstract debates in philosophy generally. Rawls wants to enable people to agree on political principles when they are uncertain how to think about many questions of philosophy or metaphysics. Thus, Rawls seeks to ensure a political approach that "leaves philosophy as it is."[8] But if what I have said is right, judgments in law and politics sometimes bear the same relation to political philosophy as do (on Rawls's view) judgments in political philosophy to questions in general philosophy and metaphysics. The political philosopher may attempt not to take a stand on large philosophical or metaphysical questions; so, too, the lawyer, the judge, or the political participant may urge outcomes that make it unnecessary to solve large questions in political philosophy. Because of their limited role, judges, legislators, and citizens may very much want to leave political philosophy "as it is."

Of course, some background abstractions should limit the permissible set of incompletely theorized agreements. Otherwise there is no assurance that an incompletely theorized agreement is just, and we should design our legal and political systems so as to counteract the risk of unjust agreement. If we want to limit the category of incompletely theorized agreements so as to ensure that they are defensible and not mere accident, we may have to move toward more ambitious ways of thinking. But if an incompletely theorized judgment does command agreement—and if one correct account of justice calls for it—nothing should be amiss.[9]

Analogies in General

I turn now to analogical thinking, an important mechanism by which people reach incompletely theorized agreements. For present purposes, we can put to one side the formal dimensions of analogical reasoning[10] and suggest more simply that as I understand it here, analogical reasoning has four different but overlapping features. These features are *principled consistency; a focus on particulars; incompletely theorized judgments; and principles operating at a low or intermediate level of abstraction.* Taken in concert, these features produce both the virtues and the vices of analogical reasoning in law. Here are some brief remarks on each of these features.

First, and most obviously, judgments about specific cases must be made consistent with one another. A requirement of principled consistency is a hallmark of analogical reasoning (as it is of practical reasoning of almost all sorts). It follows that in producing the necessary consistency, some principle, harmonizing seemingly disparate outcomes, will be invoked to explain the cases. The principle must of course be more general than the outcome for which it is designed.

Second, analogical reasoning is focused on particulars, and it develops from concrete controversies. The great Supreme Court justice Oliver Wendell Holmes put the point in this suggestive if somewhat misleading way: A common law court "decides the case first and determines the principle afterwards."[11] Holmes's suggestion is misleading, since in order to decide the case at all, one has to have the principle in some sense in mind; there can be no sequential operation of quite the kind Holmes describes. But Holmes is right to say that ideas are developed with close reference to the details, rather than imposed on them from above. In this sense, analogical reasoning, as a species of casuistry, is a form of "bottom-up" thinking.

Despite the analogizer's focus on particulars, any description of a particular holding inevitably has some more general components. We cannot know anything about case X if we do not know something about the reasons that count in its favor. We cannot say whether case X has anything to do with case Y unless we are able to abstract, a bit, from the facts and holding of case X. In this sense the form of thinking I am describing rejects the understanding, rooted in Aristotle, that practical reasoners can move "from particular to particular." There is no such movement; principles must be developed to unite the particulars. The key point is that analogical reasoning involves a process in which principles are developed from, and with constant reference to, particular cases.

Third, analogical reasoning in law operates without anything like a deep or comprehensive theory that would account for the particular outcomes it yields. The judgments that underlie convictions about the relevant case are incompletely theorized. Of course, there is a continuum from the most particularistic and low-level principles to the deepest and most general. I suggest only that analogizers avoid those approaches that come close to the deeply theorized or the foundational. In this way, analogical thinkers do not attempt to reach reflective equilibrium. Their way of proceeding involves little in the way of width or breadth. They do not compare cases with all possible cases; they do not try to develop deep theories. Along these dimensions, analogical reasoners are far less ambitious than those who seek reflective equilibrium.

There is another, related difference between analogical thinking and the search for reflective equilibrium. In that search, all judgments are, in principle, subject to revision if they conflict with some other judgment that is general, particular, or somewhere in between. But in many domains, analogical reasoners must take certain particular judgments as rigidly fixed points. Certainly this is true for practical reason in law. It is often true for practical reason in politics as well. The fact that some particular points are fixed makes it unlikely that analogical reasoners can reach reflective equilibrium, since several of those particular points might seem to those reasoners to be wrong. Hence, analogical reasoners aspire only to local and partial coherence.

Fourth, and finally, analogical reasoning produces principles that operate at a low or intermediate level of abstraction. If we say that an employer may not fire an employee for accepting jury duty, we might mean (for example) that an employer cannot require an employee to commit a crime. This is a standard, perhaps even a rule, and it does involve a degree of abstraction from the particular case; but it does not entail any high-level theory about labor markets, or about the appropriate relationship between employers and employees. If we say that a communist march cannot be banned, we might mean that political speech cannot be stopped without a showing of clear and immediate harm; but in so saying, we do not invoke any large theory about the purposes of the free-speech guarantee, or about the relation between the citizen and the state. People can converge on the low-level principle from various foundations, or without well-understood foundations at all.

The Common Law, the Constitution, and Rules

Common law judges decide particular controversies by exploring how previous cases have been resolved. This is a familiar point; participants in common law are insistently analogical and tend to avoid abstractions. It is less often emphasized that analogical reasoning is crucial in constitutional cases. This is so in a wide range of nations, including America, Israel, Germany, Canada, Australia, and Hungary. Indeed, American constitutional law is often constructed from analogies—not from text or history, not from moral theory, and not from existing social consensus. Much of the meaning of the American Constitution comes via analogies.

In cases decided *under rules*, people also engage, much of the time, in a form of analogical reasoning. This is a counterintuitive claim. Interpretation of rules is often said to be at an opposite pole from analogical reasoning. But the opposition is far too simple. Often interpretation of rules involves analogy, too.[12] In so saying we can vindicate Justice Holmes's striking suggestion that rules should be interpreted through examination of "the picture" that the words "evoke in the common mind."[13]

Some intriguing work in cognitive science and psychology supports Holmes's view. Because of how human beings think, rules and categories are defined by reference to characteristic instances. Suppose, for example, that we are investigating a single class of things—birds, or vehicles, or nations, or works of art, or mammals. How do we know whether members of any such class are alike or different? It turns out that people have a mental picture of a model or typical example of the category, and they reason analogically, asking whether a member of the class is "like" or "unlike" that typical example. Thus, people tend to think that a canary is more "bird" than a penguin, though both are birds; a truck is more "vehicle" than an elevator; an apple is more "fruit" than a coconut.[14] Experiments show "the robust psychological reality of the typicality of a single exemplar of a given class. . . . The typicality of an exemplar is then routinely measured by the distance between the exemplar and the class as a whole."[15]

What these experiments reveal is that categories receive their meaning by reference to typical instances. When we are asked whether a particular thing falls within a general category, we examine whether that thing is like or unlike the typical or defining instances. Very much the same is true in the interpretation of rules.

Consider these cases:

1. A statute enacted in 1920 forbids people to "sell babies." In 1993, Mr. and Ms. Jones hire Ms. Andrea Smith to be a surrogate mother. Does the contract violate the statute?[16]

2. A statute makes it a crime, with a thirty-year mandatory minimum, for someone to "use a firearm in connection with a sale of an unlawful substance." Smith sells a firearm in return for cocaine, an unlawful substance. Has Smith violated the statute?[17]

3. In 1964, Congress enacted a law forbidding any employer from "discriminating on the basis of race." Bennett Industries has an affirmative action program, offering preferential treatment to African American applicants. Does Bennett Industries discriminate on the basis of race, in violation of the 1964 statute?[18]

Here we have three cases involving the meaning of rules. All of them produced divided courts. It would be especially good to be able to decide such cases without invoking large-scale theories of the good or the right. If judges, to decide such cases, must develop a deep account of what lies behind the ban on discrimination, or the prohibition on baby-selling, or the ban on the use of guns in connection with drug transactions, things will become very difficult very quickly. But there is a feasible alternative, and it is roughly the same for all three cases, which should therefore be seen as variations on a single theme.

For the dissenting judge, the first case was especially easy. The statute forbids "baby-selling." Smith sold her baby to the Jones couple. No controversial claim is necessary in order for us to see that a baby has been sold. We do not need analogies at all. Much less do we need deep theories of any kind. Here is a simple case of rule-following.

But things cannot proceed so quickly. Has Smith really sold "her" baby? How do we know whether it was ever hers? Mr. and Ms. Jones say that they are simply purchasing what might be called gestational services, and not a baby at all. In this way, they say, the case is quite different from one in which a parent sells a born child who is unquestionably hers. To be sure, it may seem natural to think that Smith's biological connection to the baby gives her ownership rights—whether whole or partial—in the child she has brought to term. But property rights do not come from the sky or even from nature; property rights as we understand them have legal sources. The claim that "X has a property right" means that X has a *legal* right of some sort to the interest in question. The problem for the court is that when the case arose, the legal system had made no antecedent decision at all on the subject of ownership of the baby. The legal system had not allocated the child to Smith, or, for that matter, to Mr. and Ms. Jones. It follows that we do not really know whether we have a sale of a baby. Staring at the language of the statute will not be enough.

In deciding the case, the majority of the court acknowledged that the text was not simple as applied to the situation of surrogacy. Instead the court asked: Is a surrogacy arrangement relevantly similar to or relevantly different from the sale of a baby? The court therefore reasoned analogically. It held that the surrogacy arrangement was lawful. Its argument took the following form. There is at least a plausible difference between a surrogacy arrangement and the sale of a born child. In the former case, the child would not exist but for the arrangement. A ban on the sale of an existing child causes special risks for the child and for poor parents in general, who might be put under particular pressure to sell their children. The surrogacy situation is factually different on both of these counts. The child would not exist without the arrangement and may face lower risks from any deal, and the surrogate mother is in quite a different situation from parents who sell a born child. (Despite the bow in the direction of literalism, the dissenting judges used a similar method. They reasoned analogically and found the analogy apposite.)

In any case, the legislature that outlawed baby-selling made no specific, considered judgment to ban surrogacy. The court thought that it ought not to take the language of the statute to foreclose a voluntary arrangement for which the legislature had made no considered judgment, at least where there is a plausible difference between that situation and the obvious or defining cases.

Does this approach take a theoretical stand? Does it offer an account of why baby-selling is banned? In a sense the answer to both questions is yes. To reason analogically, the court had to decide whether the sale of a baby is relevantly similar to or relevantly different from a surrogacy arrangement, and to make that decision, it had to come up with an account of why the sale of a baby is banned. But notice the special form of the argument. There was no deep theoretical claim about the limits of the marketplace or about the sale of human beings. The court described the justification behind the ban at a relatively low, commonsensical level of abstraction. Moreover, the court did not say that a surrogacy arrangement was, in terms of basic principle, really different from a ban on baby-selling. It said only that there were differences that might be thought relevant.

Much of the court's decision involved the use of *default rules,*[19] motivated by the goal of easing the decision and obtaining an appropriate allocation of authority between courts and legislatures. In the court's view, a broadly worded criminal statute should not be applied to a controversial situation not within the contemplation of the enacting legislature, and plausibly different from the "picture" that inspired the legislation—unless and until there has been democratic deliberation on that question.

The use of the resulting default rule much simplified the exercise of practical reason in the case. In this way the decision can be seen as one of a large class of cases in which a default rule operates to simplify and constrain the operation of practical reason. This is an especially important and underanalyzed phenomenon. It occurs when agents identify a principle (itself likely to be incompletely theorized) by which to settle cases that are otherwise close to equipoise. Default rules are a standard part of practical reason, whether or not they are visible to the relevant agents.[20]

Now turn to the second case. In one understanding of the word "use," Smith has certainly "used" a firearm in connection with the sale of drugs. The gun was part of the transaction. But there is another linguistically possible conception of the word "use," one suggesting that if we read the law in its context, Smith has not really violated the statute. Perhaps someone "uses" a gun only if he uses it as a weapon. Smith did no such thing.

The Supreme Court held that Smith violated the statute. The Court did not really pretend that the words of the statute were clear. Instead, it reasoned partly in this way: We know that a gun may not be used as a weapon in connection with the sale of drugs. Is the use of a gun as an object of barter relevantly similar? The Court said that it was. It said that Smith's own use of a gun, as an item of barter, poses serious risks to life and limb, since that very use puts a gun into the stream of commerce with people engaged in unlawful activity. Notice here that the Court did generate an account of what lay behind the ban on use of guns, but the account was quite commonsensical and low-level, and it worked by analogy.

Writing in dissent, Justice Scalia was incredulous. In part he relied on what he took to be the ordinary meaning of the word "use." But in part he too relied on an argument from analogy. In his view, Smith's conduct was different from that contemplated by the statute. Smith did not threaten to shoot anyone. He should therefore be treated differently from people whom Congress specifically sought to punish.

Now let us go to the third case. The antidiscrimination law prohibits "discrimination on the basis of race." But is an affirmative action program "discrimination on the basis of race"? If we consult any good dictionary, we will find that the word "discrimination" is ambiguous on the point, and in any case there are real hazards in relying on dictionaries. The word "discrimination" could be interpreted so as to forbid any form of differentiation and hence any racial differentiation—but it could also be interpreted to include invidious discrimination, or distinctions based on prejudice and hostility, in which case affirmative action programs might be unobjectionable.

Seeing the case like the majority in the surrogacy dispute and like Justice Scalia in *Smith*, the majority of the Supreme Court treated the words of the civil rights statute as ambiguous in their context. Instead of relying on a "plain" text, it proceeded roughly in the following way. We know that discrimination against members of racial minorities is unlawful. Is discrimination against whites similar or different? The Court said that it could be seen as relevantly different. The purpose and effect of the antidiscrimination law were to eliminate second-class citizenship for blacks, not to perpetuate it. The Court appeared to be arguing that the controversial issue of affirmative action should not be resolved through the broad interpretation of an ambiguous term, if that issue had never been squarely faced by the enacting legislature.

The three cases are hard, and they could be analyzed in many different ways. I believe that in each of them, the statutory barrier should have been found inapplicable. This is not for deeply theoretical reasons but because of institutional concerns justifying a default rule: If it is reasonable to see a relevant difference between the obvious instances covered by the statute and the case at hand, if application to the case at hand would outlaw a voluntary social practice, and if there is good reason to doubt that the case at hand was or would have been within the contemplation of the enacting legislature, courts should not apply the statutory term.

Whether or not we think these cases were rightly decided, they support a simple point. Sometimes a rule is ambiguous. For the practical reasoner, the unambiguous applications serve as fixed points. The judge cannot question those applications. The applications operate very much like holdings in decided cases, or like precedents. But on the question at hand, there is no rule at all. This is a pervasive phenomenon in the interpretation of rules. It is pervasive not only in law but also in everyday life, whenever the meaning of rules becomes unclear.

Conceptual Ascent?

Borrowing from Henry Sidgwick's writings on ethical method,[21] an enthusiast for ambitious thinking might respond to analogical argument and for incompletely theorized agreements in the following way. There is often good reason for practical reasoners to raise the level of abstraction and ultimately to resort to large-scale theory. As a practical matter, concrete judgments about particular cases will prove inadequate for morality or law. Sometimes people do not have clear intuitions about how cases should come out; sometimes seemingly similar cases provoke different reactions and it is necessary to raise the level of theoretical ambition to explain whether those different reactions are justified, or to show that the seemingly similar cases are different after all. Sometimes people simply disagree. By looking at broader principles, we may be able to mediate the disagreement. In any case, there is a problem of explaining our considered judgments about particular cases, in order to see whether they are not just a product of accident, and at some point it is important to offer that explanation. When our modest judge joins an opinion that is incompletely theorized, he has to rely on a reason or a principle, justifying one outcome rather than another. The opinion must itself refer to a reason or principle; it cannot just announce a victor. Perhaps the low-level principle is wrong, because it fails to fit with other cases or because it is not defensible as a matter of (legally relevant) political morality.

In short, the incompletely theorized agreement may be nothing to celebrate. It may be wrong or unreliable. Thus, if a judge is reasoning well, she should have before her a range of other cases, C through Z, in which the principle is tested against others and refined. At least if she is a distinguished judge, she will experience a kind of "conceptual ascent," in which the more or less isolated and small low-level principle is finally made part of a more general theory. Perhaps this would be a paralyzing task, and perhaps our judge need not often attempt it. But it is an appropriate model for understanding law and an appropriate aspiration for evaluating judicial and political outcomes.

There is some truth in this response. At least if they have time, moral reasoners should try to achieve vertical and horizontal consistency, not just the local pockets of coherence offered by incompletely theorized agreements. In democratic processes, it is appropriate and sometimes indispensable to challenge existing practice in abstract terms. But the response ignores some of the distinctive characteristics of the arena in which real-world judges must do their work. Some of these limits involve bounded rationality and thus what should happen in a world in which all of us face various constraints; but some of them involve limits of role morality in a world in which judges (now using the term technically) are mere actors in a complex system and in which people legitimately disagree on first principles. In light of these limits, incompletely theorized agreements have the many virtues described above, including the facilitation of convergence, the reduction of costs of disagreement, and the demonstration of humility and mutual respect.

As I have noted, incompletely theorized agreements are especially well adapted to a system that must take precedents as fixed points; practical reasoners could not try to reach reflective equilibrium without severely compromising the system of precedent. Usually local coherence is the most to which lawyers and judges may aspire. Just as legislation cannot be understood as if it came from a single mind, so precedents, compiled by many people responding to different problems in many different periods, will not reflect a single authorial voice.

There are many lurking questions. How we do know whether moral or political judgments are right? What is the relation between provisional or considered judgments about particulars and corresponding judgments about abstractions?[22] Sometimes people interested in practical reason write as if abstract theoretical judgments, or abstract theories, have a kind of reality and hardness that particular judgments lack, or if as abstract theories provide the answers to examination questions that particular judgments, frail as they are, may pass or fail. On this view, theories are searchlights that illuminate particular judgments and show them for what they really are. But we might think instead that there is no special magic in theories or abstractions, and that theories are simply the (humanly constructed) means by which people make sense of the judgments that constitute their ethical and political worlds. The abstract deserves no priority over the particular; neither should be treated as foundational. A (poor or crude) abstract theory may simply be a confused way of trying to make sense of our considered judgments about particular cases, which may be much better than the theory. In fact, it is possible that moral judgments are best described not as an emanation of a broad theory but instead as a reflection of prototypical cases, or "precedents," from which moral thinkers—ordinary citizens and experts—work.

Is Analogical Reasoning Conservative?

A separate challenge, traceable to Jeremy Bentham, is that the method of analogy and incompletely theorized agreement is insufficiently scientific, unduly tied to existing intuitions, and, partly for these reasons, static or celebratory of existing social practice. On this view, analogical reasoning is particularly problematic, since it works so modestly from existing holdings and convictions. It needs to be replaced by something like a general theory. For the critics, analogizers are Burkeans, and their approach suffers from all the flaws associated with Edmund Burke's celebration of the English common law. It is too insistently backward-looking, too skeptical of theory, too lacking in criteria by which to assess legal practices critically.

At first glance, the claim seems mysterious. Analogical reasoning cannot work without criteria. Whether analogical reasoning calls for the continuation of existing practice turns on the convictions or holdings from which analogical reasoning takes place. Without identifying those convictions or holdings, we cannot say whether existing practices will be celebrated. The process of testing initial judgments by reference to analogies can produce sharp criticism of many social practices and, eventually, can yield reform. Judgments or holdings that are critical of some social practices can turn out, through analogy, to be critical of other practices as well.

In fact, analogical thinking has often produced large-scale change. In American law, *Brown v. Board of Education* invalidated racial segregation in education. By analogy to *Brown*, American courts invalidated racial segregation elsewhere too. Even more than that, they reformed prisons and mental institutions; struck down many racial classifications, including affirmative action programs; invalidated sex discrimination; and prevented states from discriminating on the basis of alienage and legitimacy. The analogical process has hardly run its course. Whether analogical reasoning is conservative or not depends not on the fact that it is analogical but on the nature of the principles brought to bear on disputed cases.[23]

Of course, a full theory of practical reasoning should make it possible to say which holdings are wrong and which particular judgments or "holdings" should be rejected because they are wrong. Analogical reasoning, at least as thus far described, is unhelpful here. But sometimes reasoning by analogy does help to reveal mistakes. Reference to other cases helps show us that our initial judgments are inconsistent with what we actually think. Of course, every system must make many decisions on how to weigh the interest in stability against the interest in getting things right (with the acknowledgment that what is now thought to be right might not in fact be right).

Judges, Theory, and the Rule of Law

At this point we might make distinctions between the role of high theory within the courtroom and the role of high theory in the political branches of government. To be sure, incompletely theorized agreements play a role in democratic arenas; consider laws protecting endangered species or granting unions a right to organize. But in democratic arenas, there is no general taboo, presumptive or otherwise, on invoking high-level theories of the good or the right. On the contrary, such theories have played a key role in many social movements with defining effects on American constitutionalism, including the

Civil War, the New Deal, the women's movement, and the environmental movement. Abstract, high-level ideas are an important part of democratic discussion, and sometimes they are ratified publicly and placed in a constitution.

By contrast, development of large-scale theories by ordinary courts is problematic and usually understood as such within the judiciary. The skepticism about large-scale theories is partly a result of the fact that such theories may require large-scale social reforms, and courts have enormous difficulties in implementing such reforms.[24] When courts invoke a large-scale theory as a reason for social change, they may well fail, simply because they lack the tools to bring about change on their own. An important reason for judicial incapacity is that courts must decide on the legitimacy of rules that are aspects of complex systems. In invalidating or changing a single rule, courts may not do what they seek to do. They may produce unfortunate systemic effects, with unanticipated bad consequences that are not visible to them at the time of decision and that may be impossible for them to correct thereafter.[25] Legislatures are in a much better position on this score. To say this is not to say that judge-initiated changes are always bad. But it is to say that the piecemeal quality of such changes is a reason for caution.

More fundamentally, it is in the absence of a democratic pedigree that the system of precedent, analogy, and incompletely theorized agreement has such an important place. The need to discipline judicial judgment arises from the courts' complex and modest place in any well-functioning constitutional system. To be sure, judges have, in some societies, a duty to interpret the constitution, and sometimes that duty authorizes them to invoke relatively large-scale principles, seen as part and parcel of the constitution as democratically ratified. Many people think that judicial activity is best characterized by reference to use of such principles. Certainly there are occasions on which this practice is legitimate and even glorious.

To identify those occasions, it would be necessary to develop a full theory of legal interpretation. For present purposes we can say something more modest. Most of judicial activity does not involve constitutional interpretation, and the ordinary work of common law decision and statutory interpretation calls for low-level principles on which agreements are possible. Indeed, constitutional argument is itself based largely on low-level principles, not on high theory, except on those rare occasions when more ambitious thinking becomes necessary to resolve a case, or when the case for the ambitious theory is so insistent that a range of judges converge on it. And there are good reasons for the presumption in favor of low-level principles—reasons having to do with the limited capacities of judges, the need to develop principles over time, the failure of monistic theories of the law, and the other considerations traced above.

Incompletely Theorized Agreements and Disagreement

Incompletely theorized agreements have virtues, but their virtues are partial. Stability, for example, is brought about by such agreements, and stability is usually desirable; but a system that is stable and unjust should probably be made less stable. In this section I offer some qualifications to what has been said thus far. Some cases cannot be decided *at all* without introducing a fair amount in the way of theory. Moreover, some cases cannot be decided *well* without introducing theory. If a good theory is available, and if judges can be persuaded that the theory is good, there should be no taboo on its judicial acceptance. The claims on behalf of incompletely theorized agreements are presumptive rather than conclusive.

What of disagreement? The discussion thus far has focused on the need for convergence. There is indeed such a need, but it is only part of the picture. In law, as in politics, disagreement can be a productive and creative force, revealing error, showing gaps, moving discussion and results in good directions. The American political order has placed a high premium on "government by discussion," and when the process is working well, this is true for the judiciary as well as for other institutions. Agreements may be a product of coercion, subtle or not, or of a failure of imagination.

Legal disagreements have many legitimate sources. Two of these sources are especially important. First, people may share general commitments but disagree on particular outcomes. Second, people's disagreements on general principles may produce disagreement over particular outcomes and low-level propositions as well. People who think that an autonomy principle accounts for freedom of speech may also think that the government cannot regulate truthful, nondeceptive commercial advertising—whereas people who think that freedom of speech is basically a democratic idea and is focused on political speech may have no interest in protecting commercial advertising at all. Academic theorizing can have a salutary function in part because it tests low-level principles by reference to more ambitious claims. Disagreements can be productive by virtue of this process of testing.

Certainly if everyone who has a reasonable general view converges on a particular (by hypothesis reasonable) judgment, nothing is amiss. But if an agreement is incompletely theorized, there is a risk that everyone who participates in the agreement is mistaken and, hence, that the outcome is mistaken. There is also a risk that someone who is reasonable has not participated and that if that person were included, the agreement would break down. Over time, incompletely theorized agreements should be subject to scrutiny and critique. That process may result in more ambitious thinking than law ordinarily entails.

Nor is social consensus a consideration that outweighs everything else. Usually it would be much better to have a just outcome, rejected by many people, than an unjust outcome with which all or most agree. Consensus or agreement is important largely because of its connection with stability, itself a valuable but far from overriding social goal. As Thomas Jefferson wrote, a degree of turbulence is productive in a democracy.[26] We have seen that incompletely theorized agreements, even if stable and broadly supported, may conceal or reflect injustice. Certainly agreements should be more fully theorized when the relevant theory is plainly right and people can be shown that it is right, or when the invocation of the theory is necessary to decide cases. None of this is inconsistent with what I have claimed here.

It would be foolish to say that no general theory can produce agreement, even more foolish to deny that some general theories deserve support, and most foolish of all to say that incompletely theorized agreements warrant respect whatever their content. What seems plausible is something more modest: Except in unusual situations, and for multiple reasons, general theories are an unlikely foundation for law and politics, and caution and humility about general theory are appropriate, at least when multiple theories can lead in the same direction. This more modest set of claims helps us to characterize incompletely theorized agreements as important phenomena with their own special virtues. The argument on behalf of incompletely theorized agreements is ultimately part of a theory of just institutions in general and deliberative democracy in particular, with a claim that basic social principles are best developed politically rather than judicially. And whether or not this is so, incompletely theorized agreements play a fundamental role in practical reasoning, especially but not only in the public domain.

Incompletely Theorized Agreements, Gratuitous Arguments, Democracy

My argument here has focused on legal reasoning, which is related to, but of course narrower than, the general topic of democratic discussion. Is it always, or generally, appropriate for participants in democracy to economize on moral disagreement? As I have suggested, this is an independent question. I think Gutmann and Thompson are correct to suggest that there is something like a presumption against gratuitous challenges to the deepest convictions of one's fellow citizens, a presumption rooted in the notion of reciprocity; but I wonder if there are not circumstances in which the presumption is rebutted. Sometimes mutual respect is entirely consistent with calling one's fellow citizens to account for their deepest convictions. Indeed, some of the most glorious moments in democratic deliberation occur when a firm, even immodest moral position is placed on the table, with great clarity and a sense of urgency—

whether or not it is, strictly speaking, necessary to defend a judgment about a particular issue.

There are many examples in America and elsewhere. Martin Luther King Jr. did not always economize on moral disagreement. The same is true of (for example) James Madison, Abraham Lincoln, and Franklin Delano Roosevelt; each of them refused, at times, to participate in incompletely theorized agreements and sought to declare deeper theoretical ground for their sometimes unnecessarily contentious claims. This was a large part of their basic project. Indeed, constitutional aspirations are sometimes rooted in (unnecessarily) contentious moral positions, and such aspirations can be a salutary basis, and object, of political deliberation. Properly understood, the ideal of reciprocity seems to impose no irrebuttable taboo, in democratic politics, against (gratuitous) claims about moral requirements, certainly if the speaker has good grounds for making the relevant argument, or if the claims are made in the face of pervasive or serious injustice. In this way there are substantial differences between deliberation on a court and deliberation in politics generally. The argument I have sketched here has everything to do with role-related constraints on judicial behavior. In politics, citizens occupy a distinctive role, and while it is generally good for them to economize on moral disagreement, there is nothing like a rule to this effect.

Deliberative Democracy and Constitutional Preconditions

Does deliberative democracy come with its own constitutional preconditions? At first glance, the ideal does seem to impose constitution-like constraints on democratic politics. The connection between the ideal and any particular set of constitutional limits is extremely complex,[27] but some points do seem clear. The notion of deliberative democracy requires, for example, freedom of political speech, the right to assemble, and the right to vote. It also implies a principle of political (not economic) equality, by which each person counts as no more and no less than one. It may well require a republican form of government, if that form of government is seen to require reasons for the imposition of burdens or the denial of benefits. In this way, republican government is opposed to authoritarian government and also to outcomes that rest on preferences rather than reasons. Most generally, the notions of deliberation and democracy imply a kind of internal morality for democracy, and that internal morality may well be inconsistent with many things that a majority might wish to do. From those notions, it would likely be possible to obtain a robust set of constitutional constraints.

To say this is not, however, to endorse the particular arguments made by Gutmann and Thompson with respect to the constitution of deliberative democracy. What is the connection between deliberative democracy and the three Gutmann/Thompson principles of basic liberty, basic opportunity, and fair opportunity? I wonder whether as they understand these principles, there is much of a connection with deliberative democracy itself. To be sure, the internal morality of democratic deliberation does have something to say about both liberty and opportunity, insofar as certain understandings of these goods are genuine prerequisites for a well-functioning democracy. But the dispute between paternalists and (certain kinds of) Millians raises independent questions; so do debates about welfare policy and affirmative action. Those who seek to qualify as deliberative democrats can disagree about these issues without the least disqualification.

I wonder as well whether the authors' fair-minded and insightful discussion of various issues of policy and principle is not, in the end, a contribution to, and an example of, democratic deliberation, rather than a statement of a principle that is constitution-like in character, that forms part of the constitution of deliberative democracy, or that is internal to the ideal of democratic deliberation. In my view, the constitution of deliberative democracy is best taken to involve those principles and procedures without which deliberative democracy is not possible. The resulting set of principles and procedures is not modest, and it is important to develop them with great care; for deliberative democrats, this is an insufficiently explored question. But it seems clear that a well-functioning deliberative democracy can accommodate a wide range of positions on such issues as paternalism, affirmative action, and welfare policy. The debate among the competing views is not, for the most part, a constitutional, or constitution-like, matter.

Notes

Some aspects of this essay, designed for a legal audience, appear in "Incompletely Theorized Agreements," *Harvard Law Review* 108 (1995): 1733; a general treatment appears in Cass R. Sunstein, *Legal Reasoning and Political Conflict* (New York: Oxford University Press, 1996).

1. *Roe v. Wade*, 410 U.S. 113 (1973). On the refusal to overrule *Roe*, see *Planned Parenthood v. Casey*, 112 S.Ct. 2791 (1992).

2. Stephen Breyer, "The Federal Sentencing Guidelines and the Key Compromises upon Which They Rest," *Hofstra Law Review* 17 (1988): 1, 14–19.

3. As quoted in the *New Republic*, June 6, 1994, p. 12.

4. *Lochner v. New York*, 198 U.S. 48, 69 (1908) (J. Holmes, dissenting).

5. John Rawls, *Political Liberalism* (1993; reprint, New York: Columbia University Press, 1996), 133–72. See also John Rawls, "Reply to Habermas," *Journal of Philosophy* 92 (1995): 132–58.

6. Rawls, "Reply to Habermas," 43–45.

7. Ibid., 46.

8. Ibid., 134.

9. I am grateful to Yael Tamir for helpful discussion of the points in this paragraph.

10. These are discussed in my *Legal Reasoning and Political Conflict*, chap. 3.

11. Oliver Wendell Holmes, "Codes and the Arrangements of Law," *Harvard Law Review* 44 (1931): 725, reprinted from *American Law Review* 5 (1870): 11.

12. Cf. Ludwig Wittgenstein, *Philosophical Investigations 83* (New York: Macmillan, 1953): "But if a person has not yet got the concepts, I shall teach him to use the words by means of examples and by practice.—And when I do this I do not communicate less to him than I know myself."

13. *McBoyle v. United States*, 283 U.S. 25, 28 (1931).

14. See Paul Churchland, *The Engine of Reason, the Seat of the Soul* (Cambridge: MIT Press, 1995); Massimo Piattelli-Palmarini, *Inevitable Illusions: How Mistakes of Reason Rule Our Minds* (New York: Wiley, 1994).

15. Piattelli-Palmarini, *Inevitable Illusions*, 152.

16. *Surrogate Parenting Association v. Kentucky*, 704 S.W.2d 209 (1986).

17. *Smith v. United States*, 113 S.Ct. 2050 (1993).

18. *United Steelworkers v. Kaiser Aluminum*, 443 U.S. 193 (1979).

19. See Edna Ullmann-Margalit, "On Presumption," *Journal of Philosophy* 80 (1983): 143, 154–62.

20. These points, together with others made in the text, point the way toward a criticism of the illuminating picture of legal reasoning in Ronald Dworkin, *Law's Empire* (Cambridge: Harvard University Press, 1986). Dworkin's account sees the judge as developing the "best constructive interpretation" of a practice, often by developing deeply theorized understandings of certain areas of law. But judges often find this task too difficult or hubristic. Like other people engaged in practical reason, they attempt instead to use low-level principles and default rules on which diverse people can converge. See my *Legal Reasoning and Political Conflict*, chap. 2, for a more detailed discussion.

21. See Henry Sidgwick, *The Methods of Ethics*, 7th ed. (New York: Dover Publications, 1966), 96–104.

22. In Rawls's understanding of the search for reflective equilibrium, we consult "our considered convictions at all levels of generality; no one level, say that of abstract principle or that of particular judgments in particular cases, is viewed as foundational. They all may have an initial credibility." Rawls, *Political Liberalism*, 8.

23. Joseph Raz, in *The Authority of Law: Essays on Law and Morality* (Oxford: Oxford University Press, 1979), defends analogical thinking as a response to the problem of "partial reform," that is, the risk that piecemeal reforms will fail to serve their own purposes, because public or private actors will adapt (as in the idea that the minimum wage decreases employment). In Raz's view, analogical thinking responds to this risk by ensuring that any "new rule is a conservative one, that it does not introduce new discordant and conflicting purposes or value into the law, that its purpose and the values it promotes are already served by existing rules" (204). There is truth in this claim, but if the purpose or values are described in

certain ways, the analogical process may lead in highly nonconservative directions, with no abuse to analogies themselves.

24. See Gerald N. Rosenberg, *The Hollow Hope: Can Courts Bring About Social Change* (Chicago: University of Chicago Press, 1991).

25. Examples are offered in R. Shep Melnick, *Regulation and the Courts: The Case of the Clean Air Act* (Washington: Brookings Institution, 1983), and Donald Horowitz, *The Courts and Social Policy* (Washington: Brookings Institution, 1977). The point is described from the theoretical point of view in Lon Fuller, "The Forms and Limits of Adjudication," *Harvard Law Review* 92 (1978): 353, and Joseph Raz, "The Inner Logic of the Law," in *Ethics in the Public Domain* (New York: Oxford University Press, 1994), 224.

26. Thus, Jefferson said that turbulence is "productive of good. It prevents the degeneracy of government, and nourishes a general attention to . . . public affairs. I hold . . . that a little rebellion now and then is a good thing." Letter to Madison (January 30, 1798), reprinted in *The Portable Thomas Jefferson*, ed. Merrill D. Peterson (New York: Viking Press, 1975).

27. For discussion, see Jürgen Habermas, *Between Facts and Norms* (Cambridge: MIT Press, 1996), and Cass R. Sunstein, *The Partial Constitution* (Cambridge: Harvard University Press, 1993), chap. 5.

10

Justice, Inclusion, and Deliberative Democracy

IRIS MARION YOUNG

In Democracy and Disagreement *Amy Gutmann and Dennis Thompson offer the most complete theory of deliberative democracy yet developed. They specify six principles that define the norms of deliberative democracy, and they elaborate the meaning and implications of each. Moreover, they use these principles to analyze recent political discussion in the United States, more extensively and in greater detail than any other recent writing on deliberative democracy.

I endorse the basic project of *Democracy and Disagreement.* With Gutmann and Thompson, I wish to contribute to developing a theory and practice of democratic process that challenges the commonly held view that democratic politics consists in the competition of diverse and selfish interests over power and resources. I too believe that democracy should be understood and practiced as involving moral commitments and the discussion and adjudication of moral claims, particularly claims about justice. Gutmann and Thompson have made significant strides toward such a conception of deliberative democracy. I will argue in this essay, however, that their articulation of this conception is too broad in one respect and too narrow in another.

I will argue that Gutmann and Thompson's specification of substantive principles of basic opportunity and equal opportunity as part of a theory of democracy wrongly collapses the value of justice into the value of democracy.

I will argue, further, that the principles they propose to govern the organization and conduct of deliberation—reciprocity, publicity, and accountability—should be supplemented by a principle of inclusion. A conception of deliberative democracy revised in this way puts more robust constraints on the process of deliberative democracy at the same time that it does less to remove subjects and opinions from the deliberative table.

Democracy and Justice

Gutmann and Thompson define three principles that together constitute the disposition to seek mutually justifiable reasons in a process of deliberation: reciprocity, publicity, and accountability. These principles shape discourse aiming to give reasons in a cooperative political context, as well as the nature of the fora in which claims and arguments should be made. The reciprocity principle requires participants in discussion to appeal to reasons and principles that others in the discussion are able to accept. The publicity principles says that political deliberations should be open to view and that deliberators must offer only those claims and reasons that can be uttered in public. The accountability principle requires that deliberators and decision-makers must be prepared to justify their positions and decisions before others.

Three additional principles ought to govern the content of political discussion in a deliberative democracy, according to Gutmann and Thompson: basic liberty, basic opportunity, and equal opportunity. In the principle of basic liberty, they include the usual political and civil liberties of speech, assembly, due process, movement, and so on. The principle of basic opportunity says that everyone in the society should be guaranteed a minimum of goods and education to make a decent life possible. The fair opportunity principle, finally, says that everyone should have an equal opportunity to compete for high-income or high-status positions.

I agree that all six of these principles are sound principles of political morality. I join with Gutmann and Thompson in wishing to persuade everyone to accept them. I conceive the second three principles, however, as principles that help define a conception of *justice* rather than a conception of democracy. In my view, ideal democratic norms are not identical to norms of social justice, and we should not make democracy conditional upon justice. Democracy does, of course, entail some basic liberties, such as those of speech, assembly, association, and movement. Without the guarantee of these liberties, there simply are no deliberative fora. That democracy itself entails personal and civil liberties like freedom of cultural expression or freedom of religion, however, is more controversial, though I have no doubt that they are required by justice. I wish to focus here, however, on the principle of basic opportunity. Gutmann and Thompson claim that the norms of deliberative democracy include a guarantee for everyone of a minimum of goods and education necessary to make a decent life possible. Constraining democratic deliberations by such a principle of social and economic justice, however, removes from the deliberative table some of the most common and serious issues of moral and political disagreement expressed in liberal democracies today.

It appears that Gutmann and Thompson do aim to limit the deliberative agenda in this way. They assert, for example, that a deliberative forum can rule out of order a claim by relatively well-off citizens that a tax to pay for health care for the working poor wrongly violates their liberty (210). More generally, they claim that legislators who fail to consider raising taxes in order to guarantee basic opportunity are violating norms of deliberative democracy (223).

Let me be clear. I am not arguing that justice is less important than democracy. Nor do I deny a connection between democracy and justice. The connection is more one of means to end, however, than that democracy is identical to or presupposes justice. Even in the best democracies, reasonable and accountable people disagree about what justice requires, both in principle and in practice. Specifying in advance what justice requires in a theory of democracy detaches that theory from debates about justice, which one hopes a deliberative conception of democracy will help clarify.

Gutmann and Thompson have plausible reasons for specifying social and economic justice as a condition of deliberative democracy. They are mindful of the fact that economic deprivation and inequality produce serious departures from the political equality that deliberative democracy requires. Too often the rich can direct the political process to serve their interests, while poor and working people have little effective political voice. Privileges of wealth, status, and family background pave the road to political power, while disadvantages of class, gender, and race erect hurdles on the path to much more modest success. If social and economic inequality in this way produce political inequality, which is to say, a departure from democratic norms, then it would seem to follow that real democracy presupposes social and economic justice.

At one level, I cannot disagree that the most extensive realization of principles of reciprocity, publicity, accountability, and, I will shortly add, inclusion probably requires more social support and economic equality than currently exists in many democracies. If we specify a particular conception of social justice as a condition of democratic legitimacy or a constraint on deliberative reasons, however, then it seems to me that we foreclose the question of how to bring about greater justice. Assuming we live in a society with unjust inequalities and wrongful socially caused constraints on many people's lives, how do we propose to change this, if not by democratic means? Surely it is possible to institutionalize rough political equality even under conditions of economic injustice, to the extent that justice can be debated and pursued by democratic means; we should not have to wait for a societywide commitment to basic opportunity in order to have a degree of deliberative democracy that can give moral legitimacy to many political outcomes.

A major argument for instituting more democratic practices that encourage reciprocity, publicity, and accountability should be that doing so is likely to yield more just policies and institutional relations. Several of Gutmann and Thompson's extended examples of deliberative democracy in action illustrate how limiting the norms of deliberative democracy to these principles alone can go a long way toward promoting political equality even under conditions of serious social and economic inequality. Because norms of deliberation constrain political participants to make moral appeals and not simply to assert their interests and preferences, "deliberation offers a better chance of overcoming the influence of status on the political process" (133). If instituting constraints on the nature of claims and reasons and the nature of the fora in which they are made in this way makes socially unequal deliberators more politically equal, then greater justice is more likely to come about. Citizens will be better able to get their political opinions and perspectives into the discussion and hold one another more completely accountable for justifying their proposals as in the interests of justice.

Deliberative Inclusion

Gutmann and Thompson's principles of reciprocity, publicity, and accountability, combined with political liberties of speech, assembly, association, and so on, are themselves almost sufficient for a theory of democratic process the outcome of which can claim normative legitimacy. The principles of reciprocity, publicity, and accountability themselves tend to constrain the sorts of claims and reasons that can be made in a deliberative democracy to those that appeal to justice. These principles alone rule out assertions of mere self-interest or preference as acceptable claims in legitimate public discourse. While deliberatively democratic institutions should not determine in advance what counts as social justice, either in general or for a particular political dispute, they should require that deliberators seek justice and voice their disagreements in terms of justice. Democratic processes so constrained do not guarantee that decisions will increase social justice, but they are more likely to do so than those that allow or encourage the expression of self-interest primarily and permit the more powerful interests to determine public policy.

Thus, I believe that principles of deliberative democracy should be limited to Gutmann and Thompson's first three principles governing the form and fora of deliberative expression, along with those political and civil liberties necessary to enact those principles. The additional principles of basic and fair opportunity, however, along with several types of liberty, should be thought of as principles of justice rather than democracy. To fashion this thinner conception of deliberative democracy in a way that stimulates fair discussion of what justice requires, however, one additional principle is needed: inclusion.

A principle of inclusion says that a deliberative procedure is legitimate only if all interests, opinions, and perspectives present in the polity are included in the deliberations, provided they are compatible with the reciprocity principle. I have no doubt that Gutmann and Thompson would endorse this principle. It can be argued that such a principle of inclusion is presupposed by or embedded in their principles of reciprocity, publicity, and accountability. Several of their case narratives illustrate, among other things, the value of including diverse or marginalized voices in deliberation. It is important to make inclusion an explicit principle in a normative theory of deliberative democracy, however, for several reasons.

First, inclusion is not directly implied by these three principles. A deliberative forum can abide by the principles of reciprocity, publicity, and accountability without being inclusive. Indeed, it might be easier for a homogeneous body of gentlemen to abide by them than for a public differentiated by, for example, class or gender.

Second, while inclusion may be implicit in other principles governing deliberation, inclusion is significantly different in form from any of the six principles Gutmann and Thompson promote. Their first three principles refer to the form of discourse in deliberation and the nature of the forum in which they are uttered; the second three refer to the content of discussion. By contrast, a principle of inclusion raises the question of who has the opportunity to make claims to a deliberative public and who is there to listen and hold claimants accountable. It makes a significant difference in political discussion if those who make proposals have real reason to believe that the public includes *everyone* who might be affected by decisions and that *anyone* so affected is able to hold them accountable for their opinions and actions.

Third, it is important to make a principle of inclusion explicit because contemporary liberal democracies often do so badly on this score. Passive or active exclusions are an important means of preserving power and privilege, without impeding the operation of formal democracy. In principle, inclusion ensures that every potentially affected agent has the opportunity to influence deliberative processes and outcomes. In a mass, mediated, and representative democracy, in practice inclusion means that all the structural social groups, perspectives, interest groups, at least somewhat widely held opinions, and culturally affiliated people have effective opportunity to have their views on issues represented and that others are held to account in their face of their perspectives. According to such a principle, all contemporary liberal democracies exhibit varying degrees and kinds of exclusion from deliberation. Political elites or media moguls too frequently set the deliberative agenda, even when the subsequent discussion is more inclusive. As already mentioned, power and money often allow some structural or interest groups to dominate discussion, crowding out weaker voices. Stereotypes about some who claim to speak, or prejudicial reactions to their persons or manner, prevent their being taken seriously. As long as these and other processes of exclusion from discussion persist, the relatively privileged and powerful can make policy from their point of view without even being seriously and publicly challenged.

The final reason to make a principle of inclusion explicit, then, is to bring out the fact that most democracies must take positive action to promote the inclusion of people and perspectives when some segments of the polity might profitably exclude or marginalize them. Democrats frequently act as though one can promote inclusion simply by forbidding active and explicit exclusion. More is needed, however, to counteract the "passive" exclusions that often occur in contemporary democracies. Designers of deliberative processes should worry about the timing, location, and structure of deliberative events with an eye to maximizing social voices. In some cases they need to encourage relatively unorganized constituencies to organize themselves, and in others they should worry about the narrow social experience represented in their legislatures, boards, and commissions. These worries already appear to some extent in most liberal democracies, and a theory of deliberative democracy should systematize and extend the norms on which these practices are based.

Application: Deliberations about Welfare Reform

While its theory can apply to many times and places, some parts of the text of *Democracy and Disagreement* are very specific to the time and place of its appearance. Thus, Gutmann and Thompson devote an entire chapter to discussing the obligations of welfare, in the context of the work requirements and removal of welfare entitlement passed by the United States Congress in 1996. They argue for a general obligation of citizens to work, but only if government provides child care and ensures that work is available and that it pays a decent income. They also argue that poor people should be involved in debates about welfare reform and should participate in the administration of welfare programs. This latter argument, however, gets much less attention than evaluation of the content of welfare provision. I will conclude this comment by analyzing what difference attention to a principle of inclusion makes in studying the recent welfare reform debate in the United States.

As I argued above, a theory of democracy in itself should have little to say about the substance of welfare policy but should have a great deal to say about the institutions, practices, and procedures for deliberating about and deciding on welfare policy. The critical difference concerns a distinction between judgments of justice and judgments of legitimacy. We should evaluate the justice of policies according to substantive principles of liberty, fairness, and well-being. A policy can be democratically legitimate, however, even if it is unjust or thought unjust by a large number of people. I construe a theory of deliberative democracy as a test of the legitimacy of decisions rather than their justice. A law, policy, or state action is legitimate to the extent that it can be shown to be the result of public deliberations instantiating principles of reciprocity, accountability, and inclusion. The principle of inclusion holds that a policy outcome of a democratic process is legitimate only if all those affected by the policy have had effective opportunity to participate in the deliberations that led to it. By such a standard of evaluation, I suggest, the policy result of U.S. welfare reform debates was illegitimate, and it would have been illegitimate even if there had been different results.

In a mass, mediated, representative democracy, how do we know whether some people have been excluded from participation in public deliberations? There are a number of ways to observe exclusion, but I suggest the following as one important test that is relevant to the welfare reform debate. If a public debate usually refers to a social segment in the third person, if that social segment rarely if ever appears as a group to whom deliberators appeal, and if there are few signs that public participants in deliberation believe themselves accountable to that social segment, among others, then that social segment has almost certainly been excluded from deliberations.

I suggest that the welfare reform debate of 1992–96 fails this test of inclusion and that public discussions of welfare reform largely remain exclusionary in this sense. Lower-income people, and in particular lower-income single mothers—the social segment arguably the most directly affected by the reforms—on the whole have not been included as participants in the deliberations. In this debate, lower-income single mothers have not been treated as equal citizens with opinions and perspectives that deserve to be taken into account in making just and wise decisions about public assistance. Instead, they have been treated almost entirely as the *objects* of the debate—there has been a great deal of talk about lower-income single mothers, especially those on welfare, as a *problem,* and many experts have analyzed the sources of this problem and made predictions about how policy will produce behavioral change in this problem group. The actual voices, evaluations, and reasons of lower-income people have rarely been heard in the public debate; when they are invited to speak, it is usually not to say what they think but to provide an "object lesson" about the difficulty of living, or the possibilities of change, to support one side or another in the debate. Nor have lower-income single mothers had very much in the way of representatives or advocates for their points of view. As the 1996 debate came to a head, the Children's Defense Fund came out as a strong advocate for considering the effects of welfare reform on children but did not speak for mothers.

If lower-income single mothers had been considered participants in the welfare reform debate, then a congressman would not have been able to show a sign saying "Don't Feed the Alligators" on the floor of the House at one point in that debate. Is there any reason to think that the congressman felt obliged to justify his views to *everyone?* Could he have used the House floor for the act if he had sensed that a significant number of others there considered the congressional debate accountable to lower-income single mothers, as well as others? Inclusion is thus an important principle of deliberative democracy because it expands the meaning of reciprocity and accountability in public. It is not simply that deliberators should have reasons that others can accept but that they must both explicitly *address* the others whom they aim to persuade, and listen to their claims.

I am not suggesting that if lower-income single mothers had been properly included in the welfare reform debate, they would have argued for keeping welfare as we knew it. Far from it. I am saying, however, that it would have been more difficult for some of the things claimed in the debate about the laziness and irresponsibility of poor people to carry weight and that the punitive and disciplinary aspects of the current reforms that are premised on such disrespect for fellow citizens would have been less likely to hold the center of the legislation.

Since June 1996, public discussions of welfare policy have given some minimal forum to the voices of those mothers whose futures are at stake in these changes. Rarely, however, are these women asked to say what they think the policies should be, what is really needed to make them just. Instead, they are usually treated once again as objects of observation: Here's what I used to be doing, and here's what I am doing now. In my experience, most low-income single mothers need little prodding to express savvy analysis of the system and ideas about what would improve it and their lives. To the extent that their opinions and reasons have not been factored into deliberations and continue to be excluded, the outcome of the deliberations cannot be morally legitimate.

Moral legitimacy converges with justice in a deliberative democracy, I have argued, when deliberations instantiate principles of reciprocity, publicity, accountability, and inclusion to the greatest degree. Nevertheless, theory should not build a particular conception of justice into a conception of ideal democracy or suggest that democracy does not exist in the absense of social justice. Doing so, I have suggested, weakens the contribution that evaluations of the legitimacy of a democratic process can make to motivating procedural and participation reforms that might sharpen political debates about justice.

11

Constitutionalism and Deliberative Democracy

JACK KNIGHT

*T*he contemporary debate about deliberative democracy often has a rather utopian quality. Advocates of deliberation regularly take it as self-evident truth that deliberation is a superior form of democratic decision-making. Similarly, many maintain the view that the only things that prevent deliberation from producing a consensus on complex social questions are constraints on time, energy, and resources. In addition, a positive and reciprocal relationship between individual attitudes and collective deliberation is assumed: On the one hand, deliberation requires a certain open and generous stance of mutual respect on the part of the participants, while on the other hand, we are assured that participation in the deliberative process will develop such an individual perspective. And, perhaps most important, the primary focus of the debate remains on abstract conceptions of deliberation, without much attention to how deliberative democracy can actually be institutionalized and maintained. In *Democracy and Disagreement*, Amy Gutmann and Dennis Thompson interject a significant dose of realism into the debate over the value of deliberation for democratic decision-making.[1] They should be commended for advancing this debate on several fronts.

First and foremost, they explicitly address the need for an argument that explains why deliberation is an important and necessary part of any adequate account of democratic legitimacy. While many of us may think that this is so, the case for deliberative democracy will be best furthered by offering a systematic account of why deliberation is valuable and how we can actually institutionalize it in a complex and culturally diverse society. One of the most significant contributions of Gutmann and Thompson's book is their effort to provide such an account by way of a critical comparison of deliberation with other competing conceptions of democracy.

The ambitious agenda that Gutmann and Thompson set for themselves is characterized by a welcome and admirable sense of the practical. We can see this in both their substantive and theoretical concerns. Substantively, they want to develop a theory of deliberative democracy that accommodates the problems of representative accountability and, more important, moral disagreement. They acknowledge the necessity of representative institutions and conceive of a process of deliberation that enhances the accountability of representatives. They acknowledge that deliberation will often result in disagreement, that the conditions of modern society produce many sources of moral disagreement. Especially significant for contemporary debates is their emphasis on the effects of incompatible values and incomplete understanding on the prospects for deliberative agreement. If we do in fact live in a socially diverse world in which agreement about substantive values is unattainable, we must focus our attention on how people with conflicting value systems can live together in peaceful and cooperative ways.

Theoretically, they base their argument on the idea that the benefits of a theory of deliberative democracy are realized in actual social interactions and not as a premise for hypothetical thought-experiments about the types of policies to which the participants would, under the appropriate conditions, freely and voluntarily agree. This distinction highlights a basic problem in the literature on democratic deliberation. It is often unclear whether a theory is intended as a framework for actual social deliberation or merely as a premise for a though-experiment as to what policies *would* be accepted if we *were* to undertake public deliberation. On this latter interpretation, deliberation establishes the terms of "reasonable agreement" that justify claims about the substantive content of basic institutions of society.[2] Rawls, of course, provides a classic example of such an approach.[3] One of the implications of this approach to deliberation is that little attention is paid to the real problems of establishing and maintaining the institutions that would foster such reasonable agreement. By insisting on a focus on actual deliberative interactions, Gutmann and Thompson emphasize the need for assessing the institutional implications of any conception of deliberation. As they readily admit, they do not undertake anything approaching a full investigation of the issues of institutionalization, but they emphasize the importance of such considerations and begin such an assessment in one especially important area: the interpretation of constitutional constraints on deliberation.

In doing so, I will argue, they identify implications for theories of deliberative democracy that extend beyond those that they themselves explicitly embrace. For their consideration of the consequences of institutionalizing deliberation in actual social interactions highlights the fundamental importance of politics in our attempts to implement and sustain deliberation. It may seem odd to suggest that politics has been left out of the debates over deliberative democracy, but it is hard to resist this conclusion. The realities of political conflict are central to any effort to justify deliberative democracy, but they are in fact lacking from most such accounts. While Gutmann and Thompson admirably insist that we have to take such conflict seriously, their own account stops short, I think, of the appropriate integration of politics into our theories of deliberation and democracy. This becomes most clear when we consider what is at stake when we attempt to incorporate constitutional constraints on the process of deliberation. By reviewing the effort by Gutmann and Thompson to establish substantive constraints on deliberative outcomes, we can see not only how political conflict is basic to the process of institutionalizing deliberation in a constitutional democracy but also how such conflict extends beyond the initial establishment of constitutional constraints to the subsequent process of interpreting such constraints. Here Gutmann and Thompson highlight a very important set of issues involving the interplay among deliberative democracy, constitutionalism, and the rule of law.

Gutmann and Thompson develop their argument by contrasting deliberation with what they take to be the two best alternative conceptions, the procedural and the constitutional. On their account, moral deliberation is inevitably a part of democratic discourse. They argue that despite the claims of their respective advocates to the contrary, both procedural and constitutional democracy presuppose moral deliberation about fundamental issues. Thus, any adequate conception of democracy must accommodate moral argument. The thrust of their argument is that democratic deliberation, as they conceive of it, does a better job of dealing with moral deliberation than do procedural or constitutional democracy. They set out four reasons why deliberative democracy best handles fundamental moral disagreement: Deliberation "contributes to the legitimacy of decisions made under conditions of scarcity"; encourages citizens "to take a broader perspective on questions of public policy than they might otherwise take"; clarifies "the nature of a moral conflict, helping to distinguish among the moral, the amoral, and the immoral, and between compatible and incompatible values"; and, "compared to other methods of decisionmaking[,] . . . increases the chances of arriving at justifiable policies" (41–43).

They offer the following statement of their view of deliberative democracy: "The conception consists of three principles—reciprocity, publicity, and accountability—that regulate the process of politics, and three others—basic liberty, basic opportunity, and fair opportunity—that govern the content of policies. It would promote extensive moral argument about the merits of public policies in public forums, with the aim of reaching provisional moral agreement and maintaining mutual respect among citizens" (12). The emphasis on publicity justifies their insistence that a theory of deliberative democracy entails an actual rather than a hypothetical exercise: "To fulfill the purposes of deliberation in a democracy, it is not enough that the policy could be justified. The political process of justification itself shapes in several ways the nature and validity of the reasons that officials give. . . . In a deliberative democracy . . . the principle of publicity requires that government adopt only those policies for which officials and citizens give public justification" (100–101).

Gutmann and Thompson have developed a conception of deliberation that incorporates what they take to be the best features of other approaches to democracy. As they interpret it, they combine the procedural preconditions for legitimate deliberation with the substantive rights advocated by constitutionalists. Democratic legitimacy, on their account, derives from the mutual effects of the process and content constraints. To better see what they take to be distinctive about their conception, it is helpful to contrast their version of constitutional deliberative democracy with other variants of deliberation that rest democratic legitimacy on the deliberative process alone. Here they take Habermas as the defining case.[4]

They attempt to distinguish themselves from his account through their respective treatments of liberty and opportunity. Habermas treats the guarantees of liberty and opportunity as part of the preconditions of democratic deliberation. The legitimacy of collective decisions is derived, on his account, from a process of deliberation that satisfies this ideal set of preconditions. I will say more about this approach in a moment. For now, it is sufficient to see why Gutmann and Thompson reject this conception. They argue that it fails to give adequate weight to liberty and opportunity: "This understanding still does not capture the value of basic rights. Citizens value basic liberty and opportunity, and their mutual recognition by fellow citizens, for reasons other than the role of these values in democratic deliberation. As we shall suggest, even in deliberative democracy, deliberation does not have priority over liberty and opportunity" (17). On the Gutmann/Thompson account, legitimacy rests on the reciprocal effects of deliberation and the moral constraints of liberty and opportunity. That is, a collective decision of a deliberative process is legitimate only if it also satisfies the content constraints of liberty and opportunity.

This incorporation of substantive constraints on deliberation raises a number of important questions for democratic theory and for our theories about constitutionalism and the rule of law. Here it serves to emphasize the complex question of the sources of normative legitimacy in a constitutional democracy. And it demonstrates the fundamental importance of politics in justifying constitutional and democratic institutions. We can see this by considering two questions about the Gutmann/Thompson account. First, how do these constitutional constraints actually work, and how are they justified? Second, do Gutmann and Thompson really accomplish what they claim?—do they offer an account superior to procedural conceptions of deliberative democracy that does not give priority to deliberation?

Standard accounts of democratic decision-making generally distinguish between procedural and substantive constraints. Procedural constraints are justified by the dictates of the democratic process itself, while substantive constraints are justified by some criterion other than the requirements of democracy. In regard to their conditions and content constraints, Gutmann and Thompson resist this distinction and assert that "the principles that constitute a deliberative perspective are not properly considered exclusively substantive or procedural" (229). This leaves us with the question of how they justify deliberation's content constraints regarding liberty and opportunity.

Consider three alternative ways of incorporating the substantive force of the liberty and opportunity constraints into an institutional framework for deliberation. First, we could argue that substantive requirements affecting liberty and opportunity are in fact derivative of the procedural requirements. This is Habermas's strategy in incorporating substantive constraints on deliberation in his list of the preconditions of legitimate discourse. This is also the approach adopted by myself and others who seek to justify rules and policies which guarantee that the social and economic inequalities that characterize society do not adversely affect the deliberative process.[5] On this account, the substantive constraints on deliberation are treated as preconditions implied by the procedural dictates of the democratic process. As I have previously explained, Gutmann and Thompson claim to reject this approach to justifying liberty and opportunity: "The deliberative perspective we develop here, then, explicitly rejects the idea, sometimes identified with deliberative democracy, that deliberation under the right conditions—real discourses in the ideal speech situation—is sufficient to legitimate laws and public policies. We open the door to constitutional principles that both inform and constrain the content of what democratic deliberators can legitimately legislate" (200). But I will return in a moment to the question of whether or not they in fact sustain this rejection.

The second way of incorporating the substantive constraints would, following Rawls, place constraints on the types of arguments that are legitimate to offer in the deliberative process.[6] Rawls is concerned about the reasonableness of the reasons offered in support of the alternatives under consideration by a deliberative body. On his account, the substantive constraints could serve as prohibitions on arguments that endorse policies that infringe on the rights of liberty and opportunity. There are passages in the Gutmann and Thompson book that, at the very least, imply that this is what they have in mind: "In deliberative democracy, by contrast, the search for justifiable answers takes place through arguments constrained by constitutional principles, which are in turn themselves developed through deliberation" (229).

The third approach to the incorporation of liberty and opportunity constraints is to treat them as substantive constraints on the outcomes of the deliberative process. This is the approach most commonly associated with constitutional democracies, and the approach that Gutmann and Thompson most consistently associate with their own account: "Likewise, the principles that constitute the content of deliberative democracy play a role much like the fundamental rights that constitutionalists stress" (49–50).

For Gutmann and Thompson to sustain their claim about the superiority of their conception, they have to show that it is based on a justifiable constraint on reasons or outcomes. If it is justified as a constraint implied by procedures, then their approach is merely a different version of the procedural conception of deliberation. For reasons that I have presented elsewhere, constraints on reasons, the second approach, is inconsistent with the best arguments that we can offer about the benefits of the deliberative process.[7] As Gutmann and Thompson themselves emphasize, deliberation is a process by which reasons are assessed and tested as a way of arriving at the best grounds of collective decision-making: "The self-correcting character of deliberation—its capacity to encourage citizens and officials to change their minds—would be undermined if reasons for policies could not be openly discussed" (101). To put it simply, deliberation should produce reasonableness and legitimacy; it should not be achieved as a predeliberative constraint on what democracy should consider. Thus, I will focus here on the case that Gutmann and Thompson make to justify substantive constraints on outcomes.

One of the problems in assessing their argument is that their justification often seems to invoke the procedural conditions. Gutmann and Thompson argue that their invocation of liberty and opportunity is not contingent on the procedural preconditions of legitimate deliberation. But the argument remains somewhat ambiguous. On the one hand, they argue for a substantive guarantee for opportunity that exceeds what would necessarily be justified by the procedural requirements of deliberation: "A deliberative perspective on opportunity consists of two principles that govern opportunities. The first, which we call the basic opportunity principle, obligates government to ensure that all citizens may secure the resources they need to live a decent life and enjoy other (non-basic) opportunities in our society. The second principle, which we call the fair opportunity principle, governs the distribution of highly valued goods that society legitimately takes an interest in distributing fairly among individuals" (217).

On the other hand, they often link the substantive guarantees to the reciprocity condition, implying that the justification is in fact related to the procedural requirements: "A reciprocal perspective for resolving moral conflicts must make room for moral judgments not only of procedures but also of their results. Constitutional democrats are therefore right to broaden the search for substantive values that can resolve moral disagreements in politics" (34).[8] So there is reason to question whether the best justification they offer is not the one regarding the implications of procedures. But for the sake of argument, I will set this concern aside and assess whether they make a persuasive case for substantive constraints on outcomes. It is on this point that they rest their case that deliberation does not have priority over the substantive values.

To adequately make the case for the incorporation of the substantive constraints, we would expect an argument that provides a justification that is separate from that of deliberation and that gives real content to the constraints on outcomes. But Gutmann and Thompson fail to provide such an argument. At times they argue as if these constraints are universal values, but this argument runs counter to one of their fundamental assumptions: the inevitability of conflict over basic moral values. Instead, they opt to treat liberty and opportunity as general parameters and argue that the substantive content of these constraints must be left to the interpretation and implementation of citizens in an analogous process of deliberation: "In keeping with the spirit of a deliberative constitution, we argue that citizens and public officials are responsible for setting limits to the liberty and opportunity principles, and they should do so through a deliberative process that satisfies the conditions of reciprocity, publicity, and accountability" (200–201).[9]

This treatment of the constitutional constraints on deliberative democracy seems right to me. Instead of positing a theory of constitutional interpretation that asserts the rigidity of these principles, Gutmann and Thompson acknowledge the dynamic nature of this process. But this creates problems for their account, because the content of the liberty and opportunity constraints is determined by deliberation itself. This undermines the claim that on their conception, deliberation does not have priority over these constitutional rights. It seems clear on their own argument that deliberation is the source of the legitimacy of collective decisions. Thus, it is hard to see how their conception would, in the end, fundamentally differ from other variants of deliberation that rest legitimacy on the satisfaction of the preconditions of deliberation.

Now, Gutmann and Thompson might respond here by suggesting that I have mischaracterized their project. Consider the following self-description:

> We developed a principle of basic liberty that can embrace the legitimate claims of both moralists and paternalists. We presented a principle of

fair opportunity that merges the legitimate claims of liberals and egalitarians, and helps reconcile their respective policies of nondiscrimination and preferential hiring. The theoretical aim was to develop the content of a deliberative perspective that can stand the test of its conditions. This is also the practical aim of the actual democratic process that a deliberative perspective recommends. (355–56)

But we might reasonably ask what kind of argument they are making here. If they are offering an argument about the proper content of liberty and opportunity, an argument that could be offered by participants in an actual process of deliberation, then they must accept the possibility that their specific argument might not be part of a functioning constitutional deliberative democracy. This follows from the fact that it is an argument that might be rejected by the others with whom they deliberate. This interpretation of their argument does not support the strength of their basic claim that the content constraints are a *necessary* feature of an adequate account of deliberation. If, on the other hand, they are offering an argument that alleges that their own valuation of liberty and opportunity is one that would be mutually accepted by participants motivated by personal integrity and mutual respect (and thus one that could not be rejected unless the participant rejected either personal integrity or mutual respect), then they are engaged in the type of thought-experiment that they claim fails to adequately capture the basic purpose of deliberative democracy.

And here it is revealing to consider what makes the thought-experiment compelling. As I understand their argument, the only thing that might really guarantee that the rights of liberty and opportunity will constrain the outcomes of deliberation in the ways that they suggest is the set of procedural preconditions that create a process in which citizens make decisions based on free and voluntary participation. They seek substantive constraints that "stand the test of its conditions." But these are the very procedures that allow them to say with confidence that their proposed constraints would be accepted by the participants. The conflict over the substantive content of these constitutional constraints could lead to many possible outcomes, and the purpose of the procedural constraints on this conflict is to increase the probability that the resulting outcome will be the product of the free and voluntary assent of the citizens. Thus, the procedural preconditions of deliberation have priority in the establishment of the legitimacy of these outcomes.

More generally, the use of the deliberative framework as a thought-experiment masks how complicated the process of achieving reasonable agreement might be. Many of the benefits of democratic deliberation rest on the idea that we would be better off sharing our ideas and beliefs because a collective body of available knowledge will be superior to the best ideas and intentions of any particular individual in society. That is, as the examples offered by Gutmann and Thompson well illustrate, the complexity of the problems facing most modern societies is best tackled by our collective deliberations rather than by individual reasoning. But the process of collective deliberation comes with costs. The possibility of conflict arises at every stage of the deliberative process, no matter how well meaning the participants are. This raises the following question for the literature on democratic deliberation: How can an analytical thought-experiment, no matter how well specified, adequately capture the political process by which socially heterogeneous societies would arrive at basic principles of governance?

In the end, Gutmann and Thompson fail to sustain the case that they set for themselves. In assessing what will be necessary for a conception of deliberative democracy that is adequate to the challenge of moral disagreement, they assert: "Critical to finding this common ground is acknowledging the equal status of both the conditions and the content of deliberative democracy. Neither the conditions nor the content should be permitted to have the priority that their proceduralist or constitutionalist friends respectively claim for them" (49). For the reasons that I have offered, they are unable to sustain a conception that does not give priority to the preconditions of deliberation. What they are able to do is to provide new and forceful evidence of how crucial these preconditions are for democratic legitimacy. And this may be all that we can do, but it may be enough, for, as I have also suggested, a procedural conception of deliberation can go a long way toward guaranteeing the substantive values of liberty and opportunity that Gutmann and Thompson seek to secure.

If we choose to ground the legitimacy of constitutional constraints in our commitments to freedom and equality, we should accept the fact that the social and institutional preconditions of democratic deliberation are what is really doing the work here. The argument offered by Gutmann and Thompson derives its plausibility from the fact that it is grounded in our beliefs about the normative legitimacy of democratic decision-making. This suggests that if we are concerned about constitutional constraints on deliberative outcomes, then we should channel our primary energies into establishing and maintaining the preconditions of free and equal participation in the democratic process. This will not be any easy task, for as I have argued elsewhere, establishing these preconditions entails much more than guaranteeing mere formal opportunities to participate.[10] They require us to undertake the policies necessary to guarantee real and substantial participation for every citizen. But beyond this, we should acknowledge the inevitable political nature of these questions and let the people work out the details for themselves.[11] From this perspective, the establishment of the social and political institutions necessary to guarantee that debates about moral and political issues are undertaken on fair and equal terms becomes our fundamental task.

But even such procedural guarantees will not avoid the difficult constitutional and legal issues that Gutmann and Thompson so intelligently highlight. In their effort to integrate constitutional concerns into the debate over deliberative democracy, they demonstrate how the process of constitutional interpretation entails an even greater role for deliberation than most previous theories have envisioned: "Citizens and officials have to interpret and apply the principles of basic liberty, basic opportunity, and fair opportunity—in a process governed by the conditions of deliberation" (229). As I interpret their account, deliberation is not only the source of legitimacy for collective decisions; it is also the source of the legitimacy of the subsequent efforts to interpret and implement those same decisions. They focus on the implications for the substantive rights that might be embodied in a constitution. However, the same issues arise in thinking about how we can institutionalize the procedural preconditions of deliberation. Such complex procedural rights will require a process of interpretation and implementation similar to that envisioned by Gutmann and Thompson.[12] This pervasive role of democratic deliberation in the interpretive process challenges some of our fundamental ideas about constitutionalism and the rule of law. Here, as in other areas, we see the value of the realism inherent in Gutmann and Thompson's account. By encouraging us to consider how deliberation should actually deal with real instances of moral and political conflict, they have significantly clarified (and, in this last instance, expanded) the agenda for advocates of deliberative democracy.

Notes

1. Amy Gutmann and Dennis Thompson, *Democracy and Disagreement* (Cambridge: Belknap Press of Harvard University Press, 1996). All citations to this volume are included in parentheses in the text.

2. One of the main features of such theories is that they generally restrict the range of arguments that are acceptable for consideration to *impartial* or *reasonable* ones. This restriction follows from the view that the only reasons that would be accepted in a properly constructed deliberation would be impartial ones. The problem with such theories is that they confuse what should be the product of the deliberative process with a procedural precondition of that same process. I will say more about this below.

3. John Rawls, *Political Liberalism* (New York: Columbia University Press, 1993). For a critique of this use of analytical thought-experiments in the literature on theories of justice, see Jack Knight, "Justice and Fairness," in *Annual Review of Political Science*, vol. 1, ed. Nelson Polsby (Palo Alto, CA: Annual Reviews Inc., 1998).

4. For the most comprehensive statement of Habermas's theory of deliberation, see Jürgen Habermas, *Between Facts and Norms* (Cambridge: MIT Press, 1996).

5. See, for example, James Bohman, *Public Deliberation* (Cambridge: MIT Press, 1996); Joshua Cohen, "Deliberation and Democratic Legitimacy," in *The Good Polity*, ed. Alan Hamlin and Philip Pettit (New York: Blackwell, 1989); Jack Knight and James Johnson, "Aggregation and Deliberation: On the Possibility of Democratic Legitimacy," *Political Theory* 22 (1994): 277–96; Jack Knight and James Johnson, "What Sort of Political Equality Does Democratic Deliberation Require?," *Deliberative Democracy*, ed. James Bohman and William Rehg (Cambridge: MIT Press, 1997).

6. Rawls, *Political Liberalism.*

7. Knight and Johnson, "What Sort of Political Equality Does Democratic Deliberation Require?"

8. Also consider these representative passages. "Whether or not religious freedom, for example, is necessary for a fair democratic process, it remains a basic liberty of individuals and therefore a moral constraint on majority rule. Procedure and substance are too intertwined here to mark a clear distinction between constraints on majority rule that should be part of a reciprocal perspective and those that should not" (31). "The problem, then, is not merely that utilitarianism expresses citizens' claims in terms that they may not accept, but that the terms neglect basic values, such as liberty, that any reciprocal perspective should recognize" (186).

9. In the following passages Gutmann and Thompson explicitly argue that the content of these substantive constraints will be determined through a process of deliberation. "What counts as a basic opportunity—both the scope and the level at which it is funded—is to be determined through democratic deliberation. A standard for basic opportunities must be publicly defended on moral grounds, consistent with the requirement of reciprocity among citizens" (219). "What the principles of liberty and opportunity require depends in two ways on deliberation. First, the content of the principles themselves is partly shaped by moral discussion in the political process" (223–24).

10. Jack Knight and James Johnson, "The Political Consequences of Pragmatism," *Political Theory* 24, no. 1 (1996): 68–96; Knight and Johnson, "What Sort of Political Equality Does Democratic Deliberation Require?"

11. See Ian Shapiro, *Democracy's Place* (Ithaca: Cornell University press, 1996), and Jack Knight, "Justice and Fairness," for further elaborations of this argument.

12. For a general discussion of these issues as they apply to procedural matters, see Knight and Johnson, "What Sort of Political Equality Does Democratic Deliberation Require?"

12

Internal Disagreements

Deliberation and Abortion

ALAN WERTHEIMER

*A*my Gutmann and Dennis Thompson's *Democracy and Disagreement* is a major contribution to liberal egalitarian democratic theory. Unlike many works in democratic theory, the book does not speak to institutions or voting schemes. It goes to the moral spirit of interpersonal relations among citizens and their representatives. The core idea of the book is allegedly "simple": "When citizens or their representatives disagree morally, they should continue to reason together to reach mutually acceptable decisions" (1). But just as the "one very simple principle" of Mill's *On Liberty* turns out to be more than one principle, none of which are very simple, the authors' core idea is rich and complex. And like Mill's harm principle, their core idea gives rise to questions and difficulties for those, like myself, who are genuinely sympathetic with the project. In what follows, I want to discuss four issues that are internal to their theory. First, I want to ask what it means to seek "mutually acceptable decisions." Second, I suggest that they do not do as much to accommodate those with whom they disagree as their theory suggests that they should. Third, I suggest that the authors' account of the principles that should constrain the deliberative process may provide less space for genuine disagreement and democratic choice than a robust theory of democracy should permit. Fourth, I shall examine how their theory might approach the way in which citizens and representatives should view the results of a voting process. I probe these issues in the spirit of the book, as part of a deliberative process about (deliberative) democracy itself.

Mutually Acceptable Decisions

According to Gutmann and Thompson, when citizens or their representatives disagree morally, they should "continue to reason together to reach mutually acceptable decisions" (1). They suggest that "in deliberative disagreement . . . citizens should try to accommodate the moral convictions of their opponents to the greatest extent possible, without compromising their own moral convictions" (3). In this section, I shall suggest that the authors underemphasize the distinction between deliberation and accommodation and that each entails a different focus of respect.

Deliberation and Accommodation

In general, we deliberate with each other when we think that (1) there is a right answer to an issue and (2) discussion will move us closer to that answer. We may seek to accommodate each other when we believe that there is no right answer to an issue or that continued deliberation will not likely resolve the dispute (even if there is a right answer).

A jury deliberates about its verdict in a criminal case. Its job is to reach the right answer to the question "Is the defendant guilty?" The members deliberate about the evidence to move themselves closer to the truth. If a jury is divided as to whether a defendant is guilty of first-degree murder, it would be appropriate for its members to continue to deliberate, but it would not be appropriate for them to accommodate each other, say, by agreeing on a compromise verdict that the defendant is guilty of manslaughter.

When the tenured members of my department consider whether someone should be recommended for tenure, we hope that discussion will help each of us to more accurately decide whether the candidate meets our criteria for tenure. We seek not to accommodate each other but to answer the question that motivates our discussion. Because we must reach a decision, we may eventually decide by majority rule. But we assume that the deliberation produces a more informed and accurate vote than would have occurred in its absence, or we would move straight to a vote without bothering to deliberate.

By contrast, consider the case in which my wife and I must decide where to take our summer vacation. Bracketing the extent to which our utility functions are interdependent, suppose that my wife prefers to go to the ocean, whereas I prefer to go to a city. Because we do not think that there is an independent right answer to the question of where we should vacation (at least we do not say this!), we do not deliberate. But we do seek to accommodate each other. We may deliberate about how to accommodate our different preferences for there may be a right answer to that second-order question, but the point is to find a "mutually acceptable" accommodation of our views, not to deliberate about the right answer to the first-order question.

Both deliberation and accommodation have their rightful place in a fully developed deliberative democracy. The parties should deliberate about moral issues insofar as deliberation is likely to lead them to agree on what they think is a better or more correct answer, although they may reasonably want to circumscribe that process, since deliberation has its own costs (in time, energy, divisiveness). In other cases, the participants may conclude that the dispute cannot be resolved, either because "the best moral understanding that citizens can muster does not show them which position should be rejected" or because the competing moral claims are, in fact, "inherently incompatible" (73). If and when the parties see that deliberation is not likely to resolve a dispute, then they need to find a way to reach a decision they can all *accept*.[1] Again, they might deliberate on the second-order question of how to accommodate the fact of their disagreement, for there might be a right answer to that question, but at some point they see that it is mutual acceptability and not correctness that they seek.

Respect for Positions and Persons

Let us now consider respect. When it is said that "reasonable persons can disagree" about some matter, we might mean one of several things. First, this statement may be understood as a claim about the general psychological or intellectual capacities of the persons who are disagreeing—that they are "reasonable persons." On this view, reasonable people can hold completely unreasonable positions about empirical and moral matters. Thus, reasonable people believe in astrology or creationism or that aliens from space have visited Earth or that O. J. Simpson was innocent or that homosexuality is seriously wrong.

By contrast, "reasonable persons can disagree" may refer not to the person but to the positions that those persons hold or defend. We may mean that the parties all have appropriate sorts of reasons for their positions, perhaps that they are not arbitrary preferences or prejudices. These reasons may be quite wrong or much less persuasive than reasons on the other side. But the reasons at least have the right *form*. Less minimally, we may mean that there are *good* reasons on more than one side. We may believe that there are stronger reasons on one side than another, but we may also believe (as Gutmann and Thompson think about the abortion debate) that "neither side has yet refuted its rival" (75) or, as Mill put it, that there are no considerations "capable of determining the intellect" on the issue.[2] Finally, we might mean that the reasons on two or more sides are roughly in equipoise, that no position is stronger than at least one other position.

Now the distinction between reasonable persons and reasonable positions cannot be pressed too far. At some level, the evaluation of a person's "reasonableness" must be based on the *general* character of his beliefs and reasons. We would not believe that someone was a reasonable person if she held unreasonable positions on most matters or based her positions on the wrong sorts of reasons. Still, the distinction is important. We can believe that someone is a reasonable person while thinking that his position on any particular matter is entirely unreasonable.

When we are engaged in a disagreement on some matter, we may respect the other person(s) or their position(s) or both. Gutmann and Thompson argue that "citizens who reason reciprocally can recognize that *a position* is worthy of moral respect even when they think it morally wrong" (2–3, emphasis added). Similarly, they say that in a deliberative democracy, "citizens remain open to the possibility of respecting *reasonable positions* with which they disagree" (354, emphasis added). But they also say that when we are guided by the principle of reciprocity, we "recognize and respect *one another as moral agents*" (14, emphasis added).

On my reading, Gutmann and Thompson think that other persons *and* their positions are worthy of moral respect if and only if their positions are genuine *moral* positions. In a "deliberative disagreement," one believes that while the positions held by others may be "morally wrong," they may also be "worthy of moral respect" (2) because those beliefs adopt the moral point of view rather than a "purely strategic, political, or economic view" (83). And the parties to a deliberative disagreement should "try to accommodate the moral convictions of their opponents to the greatest extent possible" (3). By contrast, in a "nondeliberative disagreement," one believes that the positions held by others do not qualify as genuine moral positions. Consequently, one has no obligation of "mutual respect" toward the position or their advocates. On their view, abortion and capital punishment exemplify deliberative disagreement, whereas racial discrimination exemplifies nondeliberative disagreement. They claim that liberals who oppose capital punishment and a legal ban on abortion are more inclined to respect those who favor capital punishment and a ban on abortion than to respect those who favor racial discrimination, even if they think that capital punishment and a ban on abortion are "just as wrong" as racial discrimination (79).[3]

It would seem that the following are among the possible views we might have about respect for positions and persons.

1. One can respect a moral *position* that one believes to be wrong as a plausible moral position.
2. One can respect—as a *moral* position—a position with which one disagrees and which one believes to be entirely implausible.

3. One can fail to respect—as a *moral* position—a position that does not pass certain minimum moral criteria.
4. One can respect—as a moral *agent*—a person who holds positions that fit the description of either (1) or (2).
5. One can fail to respect—as a moral *agent*—person who holds positions that do not qualify as *moral* positions as in (3).

Given this, what attitude should one adopt toward the moral *positions* that one believes to be wrong (as in (1)) or implausible (as in (2))? Consider the issue of abortion once again. I think the view that the fetus is a person at the moment of conception or at very early stages is implausible. I think it is an example of (2) and not (1), but I do not think it is an example of (3).[4] I respect those who advance this position as moral agents because I respect the moral commitments that motivate their view (although this respect may be tempered by a lack of respect for the intellectual rigidity that prevents them from considering the possibility that they are wrong). But regardless of how I think about pro-life advocates as persons, it seems that it is one thing to acknowledge that another position is a moral position (that is, that it is not a case of (3)) and another thing to acknowledge that it is a *plausible* moral position (an example of (1) rather than (2)).

It is worth stopping to observe that this suggests that there are at least two ways in which the grounds of reasonable disagreement may be larger than Gutmann and Thompson seem to anticipate, for people may reasonably disagree about both the *plausibility* and the *moral status* of a position. Even among those who believe that the claim that "the fetus is a person" is incorrect, some think it is a plausible position, whereas others think it is an implausible position. In other words, reasonable people can disagree as to whether reasonable people can disagree.[5] Similarly, there are some positions that clearly qualify as genuine moral positions even if wrong (as in (1)) and other positions that clearly do not (as in (3)). But reasonable people could disagree as to whether a position falls into category (1) and (3) and whether the position or its advocates are worthy of respect.

Deliberation and Mutual Accommodation

Let us bring together the two distinctions we have just considered. What sort of "metaview" should good deliberative democrats take toward the positions of others with whom they disagree? What sort of view should they take toward the agents themselves? When we find ourselves thinking that other positions are implausible or do not qualify as moral positions, neither deliberation nor accommodation seems to be in the cards, although we may try to persuade the other party that he is wrong. When we find ourselves thinking that other positions are plausible, then continued deliberation is fitting and possible. We can continue the search for the right answer so long as the disagreement does not seem irresolvable. But when we find ourselves thinking that other positions are plausible but the disagreement seems irresolvable, then I think that deliberation as such has run out and we are into the territory of accommodation.

Would we be accommodating positions or persons or both? I suppose that both sides may compromise on a position that both sides think is wrong in order to reduce the magnitude of potential moral error in one direction or the other. But I am not sure that this is the most perspicuous description of accommodation. For the most part, we deliberate over positions but accommodate others as persons. For the most part, I cannot see why one should want to accommodate a position that strikes one as clearly wrong (even if it meets the standard of minimal plausibility), but I can fully understand why one should want to accommodate the person who holds that view. Given a mutual desire not only to have the best policies but to live with each other in peace and mutual respect, one may be motivated to give ground, and this without sacrificing one's principles, because one's principles may (nay, should) include the desirability of living in peace and with mutual respect with others.

How Much Accommodation?

So much for distinctions. Let us now return to the argument itself. Despite their commitment to accommodation, it is less clear to what extent Gutmann and Thompson think citizens really should accommodate those who hold views that strike them as wrong or unjust or rights-violating. Consider, once again, the issue of abortion, which Gutmann and Thompson regard as the paradigm of a deliberative disagreement. Assume that there are three possible public policies:

(1) Abortion is prohibited.
(2) Abortion is permitted but not publicly subsidized.
(3) Abortion is permitted and publicly subsidized.

George Sher has proposed that those who believe that (1) or (3) is correct might compromise on (2) on the grounds that it constitutes a genuine moral compromise: The pro-life advocates are asked to give up their more extreme responses to abortion, whereas pro-choice advocates are asked to give up policies that would increase the number of abortions and that ask pro-life advocates to fund a policy that they (plausibly) regard as murder.[6] It is important to emphasize that he proposes (2) not as the policy for which there are the strongest independent reasons but as the policy for which there may be the strongest reasons all things considered—given that among the reasons to be considered is the desire to find a mutually acceptable policy among persons who deserve each other's moral respect.

Gutmann and Thompson argue that Sher's proposal is "not warranted" because he wrongly assumes that the "failure to subsidize abortion violates no one's rights" (88). But this points to a deep worry about the extent to which the authors are actually prepared to accommodate those who hold the pro-life position, given *their* view that the pro-life position is plausible. They may well be right that "permit but do not fund" violates the rights of women who want but cannot afford an abortion. But surely whether a policy violates rights is a question about which reasonable people can disagree. It is not as if there is reasonable disagreement about non-rights-violating matters but no reasonable disagreement about rights-violating matters. After all, on the authors' own analysis, some people plausibly believe that abortion violates the rights of the fetus, whereas others do not think a fetus could have rights. If these are matters about which reasonable people can disagree, then even if Sher is wrong to think that not funding abortion does not violate the rights of indigent women, his proposal for a compromise may go through as a form of accommodation given reasonable disagreement about rights.

Gutmann and Thompson's position is particularly puzzling for another reason to which Sher refers. If we assume that the view that the fetus is a (constitutional) person is a plausible view, then we must consider how we should deal with a disagreement when the moral costs of being wrong are grossly asymmetrical, as they may be in this case. If the pro-life position on the fetus is correct, then the moral wrongness of abortion (killing unborn children) is arguably much greater than the moral wrongness of not allowing women to have abortions if the pro-choice position is correct.[7] So if liberal accommodationists grant that the pro-life position is a plausible position, then this is an argument for asking them to do more to accommodate the pro-life view than they can reasonably ask of their opponents. At a minimum, it is an argument for accommodation that they must take seriously.

The litmus test for accommodation is the extent to which one is prepared to deviate from one's preferred policy position—even on matters of rights or justice—in the interest of seeking mutual acceptability, given reasonable disagreement about rights and justice. On a remarkably wide range of concrete public policy issues, Gutmann and Thompson defend the view that they find most persuasive and that appears to them to be most consistent with their principles of deliberative democracy, but it is less clear how far they think we should be prepared to go toward accommodating those who disagree.

Democratic Space

And this gives rise to the third issue I want to explore: How much space does *Democracy and Disagreement* actually allow for what we might call simple democratic choice? Gutmann and Thompson argue that democratic deliberation should be governed by two sets of principles. The first set of principles— reciprocity, publicity, and accountability—is meant to constrain the *process* by which a polity deliberates on the content. The second set of principles—basic liberty, basic opportunity, and fair opportunity—is meant to define the *content* of deliberative democracy, its "constitution," as it were. These substantive or constitutional constraints are not defended solely on the grounds that they are prerequisites for the democratic process itself, although that may give them considerable support. They are defended as independent moral criteria that any legitimate democratic government must attempt to fulfill. It is a crucial feature of Gutmann and Thompson's view that these constitutional constraints operate *within* the normal political process, that is, on the decision processes of citizens and their representatives, and are not assigned to an external "non-political" institution (such as the Supreme Court) (48). There is no division of moral labor with respect to the principles of deliberative democracy. The same principles constrain all.

Of course, even if we accept the view that democratic deliberation should be constrained by *some* constitutional principles, reasonable people could disagree about what they are and what relative weight they possess, even at a high level of abstraction. There may be communitarian and perfectionist versions of deliberative democracy that are simply not compatible with the emphasis that the authors place on basic liberty, and there may be quasi-libertarian versions of deliberative democracy that would reject out of hand the authors' claim that "governments are not morally free to neglect health care, education, security, and other basic opportunity goods" (216).[8] And there may be utilitarian or consequentialist versions of deliberative democracy that would reject the view that *any* particular value (other than utility) has priority over the general welfare. I do not see how any of these views could simply be rejected out of hand.

Here I shall assume that Gutmann and Thompson's principles are roughly right and ask whether a strong commitment to these principles permits democratic deliberation to take its course in interpreting and applying these principles. It is, after all, a necessary feature of any robust view of democracy that the people or their representatives get to decide on a nontrivial range of public policy matters even if they decide wrongly and that it is morally valuable that they make such decisions, even if they decide wrongly.

Consider the case of Dianna Brown, a forty-three-year-old indigent woman who suffered from terminal liver disease and who died shortly after the Arizona legislature eliminated public funding for liver and heart transplants on the grounds that its limited resources would be better spent on prenatal and pediatric care (201). Gutmann and Thompson argue that "it is *plausible* to claim that the chance to live a normal life by having access to organ transplants is a basic opportunity, provided that their funding is compatible with securing other basic liberties and opportunities of individuals" (30, emphasis added). I agree that it is plausible to make such a claim. But I think it is also plausible to deny this claim or, perhaps more accurately, to deny that the need to provide people with basic opportunities—at least when doing so is extremely expensive—should trump other governmental or nongovernmental uses of resources, even when the decision to fund would not compromise other basic liberties or basic opportunities.

Gutmann and Thompson say that the Arizona legislators who voted for defunding organ transplants "could not justify their decision to citizens like Dianna Brown, whose opportunity to have normal life chances they were denying" (225). I am not so sure. I suppose that we could not reasonably expect Dianna Brown to *accept* a justification were it to be offered, but even so, it does not follow that a plausible or even a persuasive justification could not be given. It might, for example, be argued that from behind a veil of ignorance, people would not want to fund such expensive procedures out of public resources, full well knowing that they might die as a result of such policies. They might prefer that the government spend its resources on other medical and nonmedical needs, such as higher education. In addition, given the potentially staggering cost of providing life-saving medical technologies to all who could benefit from them, they might simply prefer to leave more resources in private hands for individual consumption, and this without endorsing the libertarian claim that the right to keep one's property is a "basic liberty" that acts as a general constraint on the ability of government to tax some citizens to provide for others. It might be argued that there is little difference between the decision not to fund life-saving medical procedures out of public resources and a decision not to subsidize safer (or bigger) cars for all drivers because people prefer to spend their resources on other things. It might also be argued that the subsidization of liver transplants and other medical procedures may give rise to significant moral hazard problems, as citizens are less likely to adopt healthy lifestyles. It might be argued that the taxes required to subsidize expensive medical procedures or other basic opportunity goods have significant negative macroeconomic consequences. Indeed, it might be argued that a political/economic system in which the state refuses to provide directly for many basic opportunities may better provide for such opportunities indirectly and in the long run because a more limited state generates much greater economic *capacity* to provide for such opportunities.

Gutmann and Thompson might reply that these objections to the provision of liver transplants cannot be sustained on their merits. And they might well be correct. But I do not see how they can argue that these positions are implausible or that they do not deserve to be treated with respect. If they *can* argue this, then their constitutional principles do not actually "leave a lot of democratic discretion unconstrained." If they cannot argue this, then they cannot assume that "if legislators can raise taxes, they are obligated to provide the funds for liver transplants," or, perhaps more accurately, although they can *argue* that the legislators are morally obligated to raise taxes to provide for liver transplants, they must be prepared to allow that democratic deliberation about the interpretation and application of the basic opportunity principle might reject the view that the legislators have this obligation (222).

Consider the authors' discussion of commercial surrogacy, an issue that they use to examine how the principle of basic liberty might be understood and applied. They first consider the standard argument that the principle of basic liberty would preclude a ban on commercial surrogacy on the grounds that it interferes with a woman's freedom to sell her labor. They also consider seriously the argument that this principle might require the prohibition of commercial surrogacy arrangements on the grounds that the surrogate "is not free, once she enters the contract, to develop an autonomous perspective on her relationship with her child."[9] The authors maintain that neither argument carries the day, that "neither critics nor advocates of legalization have arguments capable of establishing beyond a deliberative doubt a constitutional right grounded in basic liberty" (247). So they conclude that the "balance of reasons, as best one can now judge," favors a policy under which a woman would be permitted to enter into a commercial surrogacy arrangement but could not bind herself to relinquish the child if she should subsequently change her mind.

As an argument for their preferred policy, this is fair enough. But Gutmann and Thompson imply that a policy of allowing women to enter into *enforceable* surrogacy arrangements is beyond deliberative disagreement, that the real choice is between prohibition and permission without enforceability. They say that criticisms of contract parenting do not provide "sure grounds" for prohibiting such arrangements but that they "supply a strong reason for the surrogate mother to object to the contract, and therefore a strong reason for public policy to ensure that she has a way to act on her objection" (259). Even if we were to accept that there are "strong reasons" to think public policy should not allow for enforceable surrogacy contracts, I believe there are plausible arguments in defense of such a policy, not the least of which is that there is (in general) a basic liberty to bind oneself and also because some important arguments against specific performance contracts do not apply to commercial surrogacy.[10] I do not say that such arguments win the day. But I certainly think they are moral arguments that belong on the agenda of the deliberative discussion.

Now the authors may not dispute my analysis of these two public policy issues. They may grant that reasonable people could disagree about whether a commitment to basic opportunity requires that liver transplants be funded and whether a commitment to basic liberty precludes enforceable surrogacy contracts. If they are not prepared to grant that reasonable people could disagree about these issues, then their constitutional principles would seem to unduly narrow the range of democratic deliberation. If their analyses are intended only as examples of the sorts of arguments that can and should occur *within* a deliberative democracy, then it is possible that deliberative disagreement will often fail to produce mutually acceptable decisions. What should citizens or their representatives do then?

Voting

The standard answer is that they should vote. At some level, the standard answer must be right. In one sense, it is a curious feature of a book on democracy that there is little discussion of voting as a procedure for the resolution of disputes.[11] In another sense, this is not surprising. A major aim of *Democracy and Disagreement* is to emphasize dimensions of a democratic polity that are *not* to be equated with voting and elections: "Voting en masse is no substitute for deliberating in forums that permit representatives to challenge and respond to the views expressed by citizens and allow citizens to engage with representatives and with one another" (142).

But while voting cannot substitute for deliberation, it is also true that deliberation cannot substitute for voting. There is, after all, no reason to think that deliberation or accommodation will typically produce mutually acceptable decisions, and decisions have to be made by some procedure or another. The authors hope that their approach can break the deadlock or defuse the dichotomy between procedural democrats, who stress the importance of a fair process for resolving controversial moral issues, and "constitutionalists," who maintain that substantive values such as justice and rights have priority over the results of a procedure (26–27). But I do not think that the deadlock is so easily broken or that the dichotomy between procedures and outcomes is so easily defused.

Because constitutionalists will disagree about the interpretation and application of the substantive values that allegedly have priority over procedure, there needs to be a procedure for resolving these disagreements.[12] So the question then arises as to how deliberative democrats should think about the process of resolving disputes by voting. I say the question is how deliberative democrats should *think* about voting. The question is not whether some electoral mechanism is necessary. Obviously, it is. But just as Gutmann and Thompson are at great pains to explore the moral spirit of deliberation, we need to inquire into the moral perspective with which we should view the results of a voting process. The issue raised here is analogous but not equivalent to the problem of political obligation. For the question here is not whether citizens are *obligated to obey the law*, but the moral weight or moral legitimacy that they should attribute to a policy that results from an electoral process. The issue is not what the citizen should do but how much moral weight should be attributed to the results of a voting procedure.

If voting follows rather than replaces a deliberative process, there are two reasons for affording the results greater moral value than they might otherwise have. First, to the extent that moral controversies have right answers, we should expect that the deliberative process would increase the probability that electoral results will reflect the right answer and that we may thus have some reason to lower the subjective probability that we assign to our belief that the results are wrong.[13] Second, if votes reflect the constitutional principles that constrain deliberative discussion, there is less reason to think that our commitment to those principles overrides the results of the vote. If votes simply aggregate individual preferences, then we may have reason to discount the moral weight of a vote. But if votes reflect each person's (or many or most persons') understanding of the constitutional values, then these constraints are built into the voting process itself and give it additional weight.[14]

How should one think about the results of a vote when one thinks that the majority is wrong? Here we need to introduce the distinction between the claim that a decision has moral value because it is substantively *justified* and the claim that a decision has moral value because it is *legitimate*. That the majority votes in favor of some policy gives me no reason to think it is the correct policy, but it may give me both good reason to think that it should be the *community*'s policy and, as a citizen, good reason (although not necessarily conclusive reason) to defer to that policy.

Gutmann and Thompson write that "a majority vote alone cannot legitimate an outcome when the basic liberties or opportunities of an individual are at stake" (30). They are right, but we must be careful. It is clear that a majority vote alone cannot *justify* a decision as being substantively correct. Indeed, a majority vote—alone or together with deliberation—may do precious little to justify a decision as substantively correct. But while a majority vote *alone* may be unable to (fully) *legitimate* a decision, it does not follow that it does *nothing* to legitimate a decision. And if the majority vote comes on the heels of a deliberative discussion, it may do a *lot* to legitimate a decision—whether or not basic liberties or opportunities are at stake.

Gutmann and Thompson seem to agree. They do not reject majority rule as the ultimate decision-making rule, but they do argue that it has legitimacy only when it follows a genuinely deliberative consideration of the issues and, in particular, a conscientious consideration of the constitutional values of deliberative democracy. But here a problem of deliberative democracy turns in on itself once again. For just as reasonable people can disagree about general matters of policy, and just as reasonable people can disagree about the constitutional values that guide and constrain policy decisions, reasonable people can also disagree about whether they have done enough deliberation and whether it has been done with appropriate attention to the relevant values. There may be reasonable disagreement all the way down.

Notes

I wish to thank Amy Gutmann and Dennis Thompson for their responses to an earlier version of these remarks. I also thank Patrick Neal for his comments and for convincing me (albeit unintentionally) that my views are closer to the authors' than I was inclined to think.

1. Interestingly, Gutmann and Thompson use the phrase "deliberative disagreement" to refer to the irresolvable disagreements. Yet when the parties have a "deliberative disagreement," their first-order moral disagreement is, by definition, no longer amenable to deliberative resolution.

2. John Stuart Mill, *Utilitarianism*, chap. 1.

3. I am less sure than they that liberals who hold such a view really do think capital punishment and a ban on abortion are "just as wrong" as racial discrimination, but their basic point still holds.

4. I share Ronald Dworkin's view that many of those who say they believe that the fetus is a person do not really believe that this is so. For example, some who claim that abortion is murder would oppose a ban on abortion in case of rape, a view that is hard to defend if one accepts the premise that the fetus is a person. After all, why should an innocent unborn child be killed just because the mother has been victimized? See *Life's Dominion* (New York: Alfred A. Knopf, 1993), 32.

5. Gutmann, Thompson, and I all believe that an early fetus is not a person. But whereas they believe that the claim that the fetus is a person is not implausible, I believe that it is implausible. Unless they want to insist that I am being unreasonable (which is entirely possible!), then reasonable people may disagree as to whether an issue falls into the category of one in which there is a "deliberative disagreement."

6. George Sher, "Subsidized Abortion: Moral Rights and Moral Compromise," *Philosophy & Public Affairs* 10 (1981): 361–72.

7. To represent the point in quantitative terms, let us assume that the probability that the fetus is a person is .10 and the probability that the fetus is not a person is .90. In other words, we shall assume that the pro-choice view is probably correct. Let us also assume that the wrongness of allowing abortion if the fetus is a person is 1,000 and the wrongness of not allowing abortion if the fetus is not a

person is 100. Then the expected disvalue of allowing abortion is 100 (.10 × 1,000), and the expected disvalue of not allowing abortion is 90 (.90 × 100). So the expected disvalue of allowing abortion is greater than the expected disvalue of prohibiting abortion, even if the pro-choice position is more likely to be correct.

8. I say "quasi-libertarian" because the view I have in mind does not *prohibit* a community from providing such goods; it only permits them *not* to provide them if such a decision is the result of a deliberative and democratic process.

9. See Elizabeth Anderson, "Is Women's Labor a Commodity?," *Philosophy & Public Affairs* 19 (1990): 71–92.

10. Unlike the specific performance of a labor contract, which typically requires someone to *do* something and which is difficult to enforce for that reason, an enforceable surrogacy contract would not require that the surrogate do anything after the child is born. It would simply require that the child be awarded to the adoptive parents.

11. The words "voting" and "election" do not appear as index headings, although there are several references to "majority rule."

12. Even if the interpretation of those substantive values is removed to some nonmajoritarian institution, such as the Supreme Court, that institution must make a decision by some procedure such as majority rule, so even there, procedure has its day.

13. Here the Condorcet theorem might seem to rear its head, although I am not sure how far. The Condorcet theorem states that if the probability that any voter is correct is greater than .5, then the probability that the majority of that group is correct approaches certainty as group size increases or as the probability that each individual is correct increases. But the Condorcet theorem assumes that each individual's judgment is independent of the others, and the deliberative process will surely lead to a violation of that condition. Still, it is distinctly possible that deliberation will have some such effect on the quality of the majority's judgment, even if it is impossible to determine how much. To the extent that each voter has reason to think that the results of a majority vote are more likely to be right than the judgment of any particular individual, then one who is on the losing side has good reason to accept the results of the majoritarian process.

14. See Jeremy Waldron, "Rights and Majorities: Rousseau Revisited," in *Nomos XXXII: Majorities and Minorities*, ed. John W. Chapman and Alan Wertheimer (New York: New York University Press, 1990).

13

Democracy and Moral Disagreement

Reciprocity, Slavery, and Abortion

ROBERT P. GEORGE

One hears much these days about the decline of civility, decorum, and respect among adversaries in public discourse and civic affairs in the United States and elsewhere. Some find the possibility of a palliative in variously articulated notions of why it is important, on many morally divisive issues, to "agree to disagree." Many of these notions tend in the direction of skepticism about the possibility of objective truth, practical consensus, or both on such issues. Others tend toward the formal exclusion of substantive moral debate from the realm of politics, lest the passions inevitably unleashed in morally charged political disputation jeopardize social stability. A different tendency is evident, however, in *Democracy and Disagreement: Why Moral Conflict Cannot Be Avoided in Politics, and What Should Be Done about It*, by political philosophers Amy Gutmann and Dennis Thompson. These authors eschew both skepticism and the exclusion of moral ideals from political debate. They offer thoughtful reflections on the implications of moral disagreement for the conduct of civic life and measured advice about how our polity can best cope with deeply entrenched moral disagreement.

Rawls and the Fact of Reasonable Disagreement

Anyone who has ever attended a cocktail party or taught a college course in ethics or political theory is likely to be familiar with the following line of argument: People in our society disagree about the morality of, for example, abortion, pornography, or homosexual conduct. The fact of moral disagreement shows that that there is no objective moral truth about these matters; there is merely subjective opinion. Further, no one has a right to impose his merely subjective moral opinions on those who happen not to share them. Therefore, laws prohibiting, discouraging, or even disfavoring abortion, pornography, or homosexual acts unjustifiably violate people's freedom.

A moment's reflection, however, brings to light a host of fallacies in this line of reasoning. Perhaps the most damning is its illicit inference of an absence of objective moral truth from the existence of moral disagreement. If Alex claims that slavery, for example, is morally wrong, and Bertha disagrees, then the fact of Bertha's disagreement does not mean that Alex's claim is false. True, Alex might be mistaken about the moral wrongness of slavery, but the mere fact of Bertha's disagreement is not a sufficient reason for thinking that he is mistaken. After all, Bertha also might be mistaken. If Charles comes along, not yet having formed his own opinion about slavery but wishing to form a sound opinion, he will want to consider Alex's arguments for slavery's immorality, together with Bertha's counterarguments, before reaching a judgment. Charles could not reasonably conclude from the sheer fact of disagreement between Alex and Bertha that the matter admits of no objective moral truth. Moreover, such a conclusion remains unreasonable if Alex and Bertha shift from debating slavery to arguing about abortion, homosexual conduct, pornography, recreational drug use, or any other currently contested moral issue.

But what if Alex and Bertha are both "reasonable people"? If reasonable people disagree about whether an act is immoral, does that mean that no objective truth exists about the matter, that there is only subjective opinion? Not necessarily. Their disagreement may simply mean that either Alex or Bertha is mistaken or that both are. Even reasonable people are fallible and are sometimes less than fully informed.[1] Alex or Bertha might be partially or wholly ignorant of, or insufficiently attentive to, some relevant fact or value. One or the other (or both) might be making a logical mistake or some other error in reasoning. Prejudice of one sort or another might be impeding a crucial inference or other insight.

Of course, people who believe (as I do) in objective moral truths do not suppose that those truths are always obvious and that moral questions are never difficult. On the contrary, certain moral questions are exceedingly difficult.

Some moral questions are intrinsically difficult; others are difficult for people in cultural circumstances in which ignorance, prejudice, self-interest, or other factors tend to obscure relevant facts or values and impede critical insights, even for reasonable people. To say that a moral question is difficult, however, is in no way to suggest that it admits of no right answer. Even reasonable disagreement does not indicate an absence of objective truth.[2]

Thus far, I have been concerned with showing that, contrary to what one hears at cocktail parties and in undergraduate classrooms, the absence of objective moral truth does not follow from the existence of disagreement—even "reasonable disagreement," that is, disagreement about moral issues of sufficient difficulty that reasonable people, in a prevailing set of circumstances, can find themselves disagreeing about them. There is, however, a less direct but considerably more sophisticated way of arguing from the fact of moral disagreement among reasonable people to liberal conclusions about certain morally charged issues of law and public policy. John Rawls's most recent work appeals to what he calls "the fact of reasonable pluralism" as a premise for a form of liberal constitutionalism[3] that includes, among other things, a "duly qualified" right to abortion.[4] In constructing his argument, Rawls eschews any appeal to moral subjectivism or relativism, even of a limited type.[5] At the same time, he offers no refutation of the arguments advanced by opponents of abortion in support of their belief in the fundamental equal dignity of unborn human beings. His strategy is not to identify false premises or errors of reasoning in the case that opponents of abortion publicly advance. Rather, he suggests that their claims, *even if true,* cannot be defended except by appeal to principles drawn from what he calls "comprehensive doctrines."[6] He maintains that principles drawn from such doctrines—whether secular, such as Marx's communism or the "comprehensive" liberalism of Kant or Mill (as opposed to Rawls's noncomprehensive or "political" liberalism),[7] or religious, such as Judaism or Catholicism—cannot serve as legitimate grounds for making public policy on issues, such as abortion, that touch on what he calls "constitutional essentials" and "matters of basic justice."[8]

Rawls's argument applies what he calls the "criterion of reciprocity": namely, the idea that "our exercise of political power is proper only when we sincerely believe that the reasons we offer for our political action may reasonably be accepted by other citizens as a justification of those actions."[9] He maintains that when it comes to the issue of abortion, for example, reasonable people who subscribe to certain comprehensive forms of liberalism, or other comprehensive doctrines that also support a woman's right to abortion (in the first trimester of pregnancy, at least, and possibly beyond), cannot be expected to accept the reasons for prohibiting abortion advanced by those who subscribe to competing comprehensive doctrines, which include the belief that the unborn have a right not to be deliberately killed. The arguments advanced by opponents of abortion—even if those arguments appeal to reason alone and not to revelation or other forms of religious authority, and, indeed, even if the position they are advanced to support is true—therefore fail to qualify as "public reasons," as Rawls conceives them:[10] that is, reasons that provide legitimate grounds for making public policy when it comes to fundamental political questions. Public policies based on such arguments and reasons violate what Rawls calls "the liberal principle of legitimacy."[11]

Therefore, to analyze the problem of abortion in Rawlsian terms, people who believe that abortion is wrongful killing (and as such a violation of human rights) and who are prepared to defend this belief, not (or not exclusively) by appeal to authority or revelation but by appeal to scientific facts and to moral principles accessible to rational persons as such, should nevertheless desist from the exercise of political power to secure legal protection for abortion's unborn potential victims. As a violation of the liberal principle of legitimacy, advocacy and action to restrict abortion are contrary to political justice and, in that way, unreasonable.

But we must ask, How can it be unreasonable for people to seek legal protection for the unborn if they are prepared to provide rational arguments (which may well be sound) for believing that the unborn are human beings with human rights? Precisely because the issue is fundamental—going to the question of who is to count as a member of the human community, one whose rights must therefore be respected and protected—it would seem important for any nation to settle its law and public policy on the subject of abortion in accordance with the best moral judgment of its policymakers and citizens.

It is true that arguments in favor of a fetal right to life cannot avoid appealing to certain metaphysical and moral propositions that are currently in dispute among reasonable people. But the same is true of arguments for a right to terminate pregnancy and deliberately bring about fetal death. Rawls's treatment of abortion provides an apt example. He declares that "any reasonable balance" of the values at stake in the debate about abortion "will give a woman a duly qualified right to decide whether or not to end her pregnancy during the first trimester. . . . [Moreover, it] may allow her such a right beyond this, at least in certain circumstances."[12] Yet a great many thoughtful people, including most opponents of abortion, reject Rawls's idea that the right to life is properly subject to "balancing" against competing values in the making of public policy. Is the rejection of this idea somehow unreasonable? Certainly on its face it is not, and Rawls provides no argument for believing it to be so. Indeed, any argument that Rawls, or someone sharing his view, might make in support of the idea that the question of abortion is properly resolved by balancing, let alone the particular conclusions that he claims follow from a proper balancing, will unavoidably appeal to principles drawn from comprehensive liberalism or for some other comprehensive view that many reasonable people reasonably reject.[13] Consequently, in the end Rawls's argument offers reasonable citizens who happen not to share his belief in a right to abortion no reason that they can reasonably accept to refrain from acting in the political sphere to vindicate the basic human rights of unborn human beings whom they reasonably believe to be potential victims of unjust killing in abortion.

Should we conclude, then, that the fact of moral disagreement has no relevance whatsoever to the deliberations of citizens, legislators, and judges who must make decisions about abortion and other morally charged issues of law and public policy? Gutmann and Thompson argue powerfully for a more limited, although far from trivial, relevance of the fact of moral disagreement to democratic deliberation and legal reasoning. Although their work fits comfortably into the liberal tradition of thought about morality, politics, and law that has been so powerfully shaped in our time by Rawls's writings, they are centrally concerned with the implications of the fact of moral disagreement for the manner in which morally charged issues about which reasonable people disagree should be debated and resolved in democratic politics instead of with the substantive outcomes that ought to be reached.

Deliberative Democracy in the Face of Reasonable Disagreement

Gutmann and Thompson develop and defend the ideal of "deliberative democracy," which they describe as "a conception of democracy that secures a central place for moral discussion in political life" (1). Its "core idea" is that "when citizens or their representatives disagree morally, they should continue to reason together to reach mutually acceptable decisions" (1). Thus, the deliberative conception of democracy differs from nondeliberative conceptions. For example, a nondeliberative conception of democracy is understood to constitute nothing more lofty than a desirable means of resolving conflicts among citizens who are motivated, for example, purely by self-interest or ideological commitments. The deliberative conception of democracy, on the other hand, has the more elevated goal of also attempting to promote reasonable discussion and mutual respect, even when consensus is unlikely to be achieved.

The "constitution" of deliberative democracy, as Gutmann and Thompson conceive it, includes as its central principles "publicity," which requires that citizens and public officials justify their actions publicly (95), the "accountability" of members of the democratic polity to their fellow citizens and others who live under their rule (128), and the need for law and public policy to respect "basic liberty" and to afford to all "basic opportunity" and "fair opportunity" (12). The "first principle" of deliberative democracy, however, is "reciprocity," which Gutmann and Thompson define as citizens "seeking fair terms of social cooperation for their own sake" (2). They add to this requirement the need to try "to find mutually acceptable ways of resolving moral disagreements" (2). In sum, citizens who are faithful to the ideal of deliberative democracy and who find themselves in fundamental, albeit reasonable, disagreement with their fellow citizens over important moral issues must, in attempting to resolve the conflict, make their arguments in ways that respect their opponents as fellow citizens and reasonable people.

This mutual respect among citizens has intrinsic as well as instrumental value. Reciprocity is more than merely a requirement of prudence for the sake of social peace or even sound public policy, though it will certainly advance the former goal and may even conduce to the latter. Reciprocity is above all a constitutive moral value of deliberative democracy, something that democratic citizens owe to one another as a matter of justice. It is what might be called a "common good" of the political community, a mutual moral benefit to all concerned, even (or perhaps especially) when people find themselves in irresolvable disagreement over fundamental moral issues. As such, the mutual respect citizens owe to one another provides a kind of moral bond between them, their substantive moral disagreements notwithstanding, and it requires them to search for political accommodation whenever possible.

The politics of moral disagreement in a deliberative democracy is not, then, simply a matter of putting together a majority for one's position, and it is certainly not a matter of gaining a majority by whatever rhetorical or other means necessary. The ideal of reciprocity is realized in practice when, or to the extent that, citizens understand and accept the obligation to justify their positions to those fellow citizens who reasonably disagree. If democracy is, as Supreme Court Justice Antonin Scalia says, the idea that "the majority rules,"[14] deliberative democracy, as Gutmann and Thompson conceive it, adds the demand that the winners do their best to justify their position to the losers, thus giving them the respect to which they are justly entitled. In the less-than-ideal circumstances of real-life politics, Gutmann and Thompson maintain, "citizens who reason reciprocally can recognize that a position is worthy of moral respect even when they think it morally wrong" (2–3).

To flesh out their conception of deliberative democracy and to illustrate some of its implications, Gutmann and Thompson explore a wide range of political questions that are morally charged, including surrogate motherhood (chap. 7), welfare reform (chap. 8), and affirmative action (chap. 9). Their leading and most frequently invoked example, unsurprisingly, is abortion. They distinguish abortion and other moral questions that give rise to true "deliberative disagreements" from moral questions about which people may happen to disagree but that do not qualify as matters of deliberative disagreement (73–74).[15] They cite, as an example of a possible disagreement that is not deliberative, a dispute "about a policy to legalize discrimination against blacks and women" (3). The difference, they say, is that the claims on both sides of the debate about abortion "fall within the range of what reciprocity respects" (74).

Although their sympathies seem to fall on the pro-choice side of the debate over abortion, Gutmann and Thompson forthrightly observe that the pro-life position cannot be dismissed, as it often is by their fellow liberals, on the ground that it represents an attempt to impose a religious view on citizens who do not accept it.[16] "Although pro-life advocates sometimes invoke a religious conception of human life, the belief that the fetus is a human being with constitutional rights does not depend on a distinctively religious conception of personhood" (75). The pro-life view, they say, "may also derive its plausibility from secular considerations such as the similarity of successive stages in the natural development from fetus to infant," whereas the pro-choice position "gains some credibility from the striking differences among a zygote, a five-month-old fetus, and an infant" (75). Gutmann and Thompson conclude that "in these respects both [the] pro-life and pro-choice positions seem reasonable" (75).

Indeed, Gutmann and Thompson seem to maintain that the pro-life and pro-choice positions are more or less equally reasonable, which means that "the disagreement is fundamental and irresolvable, at least within the limits of our present moral understanding" (75). The debate over the humanity and moral status of the unborn is, they conclude, a "deadlock"—for now, at least (76–77). In defending this obviously highly controversial claim, they say that when it comes to the debate about abortion, "the effect of reading and listening to the arguments on both sides, at least for citizens who are open to opposing views, has been to conclude that neither side has yet refuted its rival" (75). Here, surely, the authors are illicitly generalizing their own conclusion. The fact is that thoughtful people "open to opposing views" who have examined the issue have reached various conclusions. Some, to be sure, have drawn Gutmann and Thompson's conclusion that the matter is rationally deadlocked. A great many others, however, have concluded that one side or the other has the stronger (even much stronger) rational case.

Obviously, the sheer fact that reasonable people disagree about the issue of abortion is no warrant for believing that the pro-life and pro-choice positions are roughly equal in rational strength. After all, the fact that reasonable people on both sides of the debate disagree with Gutmann and Thompson's conclusion that the issue is rationally deadlocked does not mean that their conclusion is incorrect. The proposition that the issue of abortion is rationally deadlocked is just one controversial view among a range of controversial views about abortion. In trying to decide which view is correct, the fact of disagreement settles nothing. Anyone who wishes to form a sound judgment has no choice but to examine critically the arguments and counterarguments put forward by champions of the various positions.

To their credit, Gutmann and Thompson present and carefully criticize arguments advanced by several leading proponents of the pro-choice position, including Ronald Dworkin[17] (75–77) and Cass Sunstein[18] (375, n. 21). Unfortunately, however, they do not present and criticize arguments advanced by pro-life thinkers.[19] In fact, their presentation of the pro-life case suffers from inadequacies that obscure its rational strength. What Gutmann and Thompson describe entirely abstractly as "the natural development of fetus to infant" (75) is concretely something's (or, more precisely, some being's) natural development from the fetal stage of *its* life into *its* infancy. It is the natural development of a distinct, unitary substance—a human being—who begins as a zygote and develops without substantial change through the embryonic and fetal stages of its life, then through its infancy, childhood, adolescence, and finally into adulthood. The "similarity" of the "successive stages" in a human being's development consists of nothing less than the fact that these stages are stages in the life of a particular human being, with its unity, distinctness, and identity remaining intact through the successive stages of its development.[20] Each of us who is now an adult is the same human being who was at an earlier time an adolescent, a child, an infant, a fetus, an embryo, and a zygote. Thus, however striking one finds the differences between zygote, fetus, and infant, these differences cannot bear the moral weight necessary to warrant the conclusion that killing X at an early enough stage of X's development is not killing a human being, or, indeed, is not killing X.

In view of these considerations, John Finnis has concluded that people who "[attend] strictly to the arguments and [are] not distracted by the numbers and respectability of those who propose them . . . will find that (apart from the question whether killing is intended in cases where the pregnancy itself threatens the mother's life) the issue is not even a close call."[21] If Finnis is right (or, for that matter, if he is very badly wrong and the pro-choice argument is the clear winner), does this mean that abortion does not qualify for treatment as a matter of deliberative disagreement as Gutmann and Thompson conceive it?

In my view, people ought to respect the principle of reciprocity whenever they find themselves in disagreement with reasonable people of goodwill, regardless of whether they find the position (or even the arguments) advanced by such people to be worthy of respect. It is not the worthiness of a position (or argument) that makes this principle applicable. Rather, it is a matter of respecting people's reasonableness (even when they are defending a view that one can only judge to be fundamentally unreasonable) and their goodwill (even when they are defending practices or policies that one can only judge to be gravely unjust or in some other way immoral). By observing the principle of reciprocity in moral and political debate, one is indicating respect not necessarily for a position (which one perhaps reasonably judges to be so deeply immoral as to be unworthy of respect) but for the reasonableness and goodwill of the person who, however misguidedly, happens to hold that position. The point of observing the requirements of reciprocity is to fulfill one's obligations in justice to one's fellow citizens who are, like oneself, attempting to think through a moral question as best they can.

However, reciprocity does not necessarily require compromising with one's opponents in circumstances in which political compromise is not a matter of practical necessity; for when it comes to issues such as abortion, no moral compromise is possible without doing injury to someone's rights (that is, the rights of the fetus if, in truth, abortion violates the rights of the unborn, or the rights of the woman if, in truth, women have a right to abortion). Reciprocity does entail, however, that supporters of a right to abortion are entitled to a respectful hearing for their arguments, that opponents of abortion have an obligation to consider these arguments and meet them with counter-arguments, and vice versa. It follows, then, that the obligations of the principle of reciprocity will, under certain circumstances, apply even in disagreements in which one side cannot but view the other as denying the equal dignity of a class of their fellow human beings.

Here the test case is surely the issue of slavery. Prior to its abolition, clearheaded people whose understanding was not impeded by prejudice, self-interest, pseudoscience, or other prevalent cultural conditions (of which slavery was itself partially a cause and partially an effect) saw slavery for the intolerable moral evil that it was (and is). Almost everybody today thinks of these "abolitionists" as moral heroes. Many of us imagine that had we been around in those days, we would have stood with them. We should allow, however, that some defenders of slavery, although tragically mistaken and objectively guilty of grave injustice toward the enslaved, were not people of bad will. Opponents of slavery, however much they (rightly) held in contempt the proslavery position and proslavery arguments, had reason to respect the principle of reciprocity in dealing with those persons who, misguidedly but in good faith, held that position and made those arguments,[22] even as they forcefully rebutted those claims and struggled in the political sphere for slavery's abolition. Today, however, in a society in which the institution of slavery has long been abolished, and which fortunately is largely free of the fundamental misconceptions and prejudices that made it possible for reasonable people—even people of goodwill—to rationalize so monstrous an evil, it would be wrong to say that those who would enslave others or rationalize their enslavement deserve treatment in accordance with the principle of reciprocity. Thus, there is no reason to give a respectful hearing to those who would revive those prejudices or stir up the residue of racial prejudice that, alas, remains.

Gutmann and Thompson are therefore right to treat arguments for the reinstitution of slavery or policies of racial discrimination as unworthy of reciprocity. However, I think the reasons they are right go beyond their belief that citizens have greater reasons for certainty on the subjects of slavery and discrimination than on abortion (77). In my view, the key distinction between slavery and racial discrimination, on the one hand, and abortion, on the other, to the extent that the requirements of reciprocity are concerned, is that whereas ours is (thank God) no longer a society in which it is difficult sometimes even for honorable people to see the wickedness of slavery, it is a society that tends to obscure even for many reasonable people of goodwill the injustice of abortion. Therefore, even those who share my view that abortion is an evil parallel to that of slavery in its denial of the equal dignity of a particular category of human beings can reasonably judge the disagreement about abortion to require them to respect the principle of reciprocity in debating the issue with their opponents, under current circumstances, even as they hope and pray that the day is not far off when people will look back on the era of abortion on demand the way we now look back on the era of chattel slavery.

To be clear, I am not suggesting that the people who perceived the enormity of the evil of slavery prior to its abolition should not have opposed it with resolution and determination, or that they should have refrained from protest and civil disobedience in the cause of ending it. The opposite is true. I also do not suggest that slavery was somehow less evil when it had respectable advocates than it would be today, when no respectable person would defend it. What I propose is that a certain sensitivity to the ways in which cultural factors in some cases facilitate, and in others hinder, sound moral understanding can legitimately enter into assessing whether those who perceive and oppose a grave moral evil are obliged to adopt a stance of civility toward their opponents and even a certain (if limited) attitude of respect toward their arguments (namely, a willingness to give their arguments an honest hearing, and a felt obligation to meet them with counterarguments, rather than dismissing them as mere rationalizations for positions adopted in bad faith).

I am not suggesting, however, that the evil of slavery (or abortion) is culturally relative. Slavery was no less unjust in the United States in 1857 than it would be here (and is in the Sudan, where it still exists)[23] in 1999. What can be culturally relative, however, is whether advocates of what one judges to be a grave injustice deserve to be treated in accordance with the principle of reciprocity. My suggestion is that the principle of reciprocity should govern moral debate whenever cultural circumstances or other factors make it possible for reasonable people of goodwill to be mistaken about a putative moral evil; and reasonable people of goodwill can be mistaken about even serious moral evils when ignorance, prejudice, self-interest, and other factors that impair sound moral judgment are prevalent in a culture or subculture.[24]

Conclusion

Democracy, in practice, often seems incapable of being morally deliberative; the achievement of Gutmann and Thompson has been to show how genuine deliberation is possible in a democracy even in the face of serious and protracted moral disagreement. In commenting on their book, I have not so much dissented from their view of the importance of reciprocity to proper democratic deliberation as I have attempted to reinforce and extend it, by suggesting that the applicability of the principle of reciprocity can be affected by the bearing of cultural circumstances upon people's abilities to recognize serious evils for what they are.

More than a few people today wonder how the institutions of American constitutional democracy can meet the challenges presented by profound and seemingly intractable moral disagreement. *Democracy and Disagreement* goes far toward providing an answer. At the same time, it makes it clear that much depends on the willingness of participants in public debates, at every level, to renew their dedication to honesty, self-criticism, civility, good faith, and respect for their opponents, however misguided they may believe them to be.

Notes

The author is grateful to William C. Porth for much good advice.

1. Cf. John Rawls, *Political Liberalism* (New York: Columbia University Press, 1993), 54–58 (discussing the "burdens of judgment" that may generate disagreement between "reasonable persons").

2. Of course, to show that the mere fact of moral disagreement does not logically entail the absence of moral truth is by no means to disprove the moral subjectivist's claim that there are no objective moral truths. The question whether morality is objective or merely subjective is itself a difficult one. The argument from disagreement is perhaps the weakest in the arsenal of moral subjectivists. I shall not address their stronger arguments here, however, because the topic of this review is not subjectivism as such but rather the question of what, if anything, follows from the fact of moral disagreement. For strong, capably defended arguments for moral subjectivism, see Jeffrey Goldsworthy, "Fact and Value in the New Natural Law Theory," *American Journal of Jurisprudence* 41 (1996): 21, 38–45. For my criticisms of these arguments, see Robert P. George, "A Defense of the New Natural Law Theory," *American Journal of Jurisprudence* 41 (1996): 47, 56–61.

3. Rawls, *Political Liberalism*, 36, above n. 5.

4. Ibid., 243, n. 32. I should point out that Rawls's formal treatment of abortion is brief and is proposed as a mere illustration of his general argument. However, in his introduction to the paperback edition of *Political Liberalism*, Rawls appears to endorse, subject to several (unspecified) addenda, an argument for a right to abortion advanced in Judith Jarvis Thomson, "Abortion," *Boston Review*

(Summer 1995): 11–15, at 11. See Rawls, *Political Liberalism* (1993; New York: Columbia UP, 1996), lvi, n. 31. For my criticism of Thomson's argument and a more detailed critique of Rawls's treatment of abortion, see Robert P. George, "Public Reason and Political Conflict: Abortion and Homosexuality," *Yale Law Journal* 106 (June 1997): 2475–2504.

5. Heidi Hurd, in an illuminating review of *Political Liberalism*, explains that "Rawls is not premising his liberalism on skepticism; on the contrary, he is seeking to premise his liberalism on [religious, philosophical, and moral] agnosticism and is therefore as loathe to embrace skeptical claims as to embrace realist ones." Heidi M. Hurd, "The Levitation of Liberalism," *Yale Law Journal* 105 (1995): 795, 796, n. 6.

6. Rawls, *Political Liberalism*, 59, above n. 5.

7. Ibid., 145.

8. Ibid., 137–38. Rawls qualifies this prohibition somewhat by allowing that principles drawn from comprehensive doctrines may legitimately be invoked in political debate, even if that debate concerns constitutional essentials and matters of basic justice, when they are introduced in support of policies that could be successfully defended by appeal to a purely "political" conception of justice: that is, a conception that is not derived from a comprehensive doctrine. See ibid., 249–52; see also ibid., li–lii, above n. 8 (detailing his further qualifications of the prohibition on the invocation of principles drawn from comprehensive views).

9. Ibid., xlvi, above n. 8. For a detailed critique of Rawls's "criterion of reciprocity" and his inferences about abortion, see George, "Public Reason and Political Conflict."

10. Rawls, *Political Liberalism*, 213–16, above n. 5.

11. Ibid., 137.

12. Ibid., 243, n. 32.

13. See Jean Hampton, "The Common Faith of Liberalism," *Pacific Philosophical Quarterly* 75 (1994): 186, 208–9; Peter de Marneffe, "Rawls's Idea of Public Reason," *Pacific Philosophical Quarterly* 75 (1994): 232, 235; Philip L. Quinn, "Political Liberalisms and Their Exclusions of the Religious," in *Religion and Contemporary Liberalism*, ed. Paul Weithman (Notre Dame, IN: University of Notre Dame Press, 1997).

14. Antonin Scalia, "Of Democracy, Morality, and the Majority," address at Gregorian University, May 2, 1996, reprinted in *Origins* 26 (1996): 82, 88.

15. Gutmann and Thompson describe a "deliberative disagreement" as "one in which citizens continue to differ about basic moral principles even though they seek a resolution that is mutually justifiable. The disagreement persists within the deliberative perspective itself. It is fundamental because citizens differ not only about the right resolution but also about the reasons on which the conflict should be resolved" (73).

16. The most sophisticated version of the claim that laws prohibiting abortion constitute an imposition of a religious position is the one advanced in Ronald Dworkin, *Life's Dominion: An Argument about Abortion, Euthanasia, and Individ-*

ual Freedom (New York: Alfred A. Knopf, 1993). Gutmann and Thompson's rebuttal of Dworkin's argument (75–77) is, to my mind, entirely successful.

17. See ibid., 30–147, above n. 20.

18. See Cass R. Sunstein, *The Partial Constitution* (Cambridge: Harvard University Press, 1993), 270–85.

19. It would be interesting to know what Gutmann and Thompson would say in response to the pro-life arguments advanced, for example, in Patrick Lee, *Abortion and Unborn Human Life* (Washington, DC: Catholic University Press of America Press, 1996); John Finnis, "Abortion and Health Care Ethics II," in *Principles of Health Care Ethics*, ed. Raanan Gillon and Ann Lloyd (Chicester, NY: John Wiley and Sons, 1994), 547–57; and Germain Grisez, "When Do People Begin?," *Proceedings of the American Catholic Philosophical Association* 63 (1990): 27. Gutmann and Thompson also do not directly address arguments for the existence of moral personhood from the moment of conception, such as those presented in Dianne Nutwell Irving, "Scientific and Philosophical Expertise: An Evaluation of the Arguments of 'Personhood,' " *Linacre Quarterly* 60 (1993): 18, 21; and Helen Watt, "Potential and the Early Human," *Journal of Medical Ethics* 22 (1996): 222, 223, 225.

20. In criticizing Ronald Dworkin's defense of the pro-choice position, Gutmann and Thompson correctly observe that the fetus "is already a human being (as Dworkin acknowledges) and will naturally develop the sentience and consciousness of an infant if it is not killed" (76). They suggest, however, that although pro-life advocates can reasonably believe that the right to life does not depend on the actual attainment of sentience and consciousness, such advocates are not able to provide an argument strong enough to dislodge the (also reasonable) belief of their pro-choice opponents that human beings who have not yet attained sentience and consciousness do not have a right to life—at least not of the sort that would entitle them to the status of "constitutional [persons who] deserve the same protection that infants and women should enjoy" (76). I think that such an argument has, in fact, been provided, for example, in Lee, *Abortion and Unborn Human Life*, 50–54, and by the other authors cited in the preceding note.

21. John Finnis, "Is Natural Law Theory Compatible with Limited Government?," in *Natural Law, Liberalism, and Morality*, ed. Robert P. George (Oxford: Clarendon Press, 1996), 1, 18. Gutmann and Thompson contend that certain hypothetical examples of justified killing that Judith Jarvis Thompson previously advanced should, by analogy, "convince even people who perceive the fetus to be a full-fledged person that to permit abortion is not obviously wrong in the case of a woman who becomes pregnant through no fault of her own (for example, by rape)" (85). These examples do show, I think, that abortion prior to fetal viability in the case of forcible rape need not be what traditional moralists condemn as "direct killing," that is, the deliberate bringing about of (fetal) death as an end in itself or as a means to some other end, as opposed to "indirect killing," where death is foreseen and accepted as a side effect but is not, strictly speaking, intended. On this distinction and its significance for moral analysis, see John Finnis, "Intention and Side-Effects," in *Liability and Responsibility: Essays in Law and Morals*,

ed. R. G. Frey and Christopher W. Morris (Cambridge: Cambridge University Press, 1991), 32, 44–64. In cases of "indirect killing" (for example, the foreseen but unintended killing of noncombatants in otherwise justified strikes against military targets in war), the moral norm, the sound application of which distinguishes justified from wrongful killing, is the requirement to treat others fairly. As to whether the indirect killing of an unborn human being conceived in an act of rape is unfair, I agree with Gutmann and Thompson that the answer is not obvious. Even people who recognize the humanity and equal dignity of the unborn might consider the question of abortion in this case a "close call." For an argument that abortion is unfair to its unborn victim even in the case of rape, see Lee, *Abortion and Unborn Human Life*, 120–24. For an argument that administration of a postcoital birth control pill for the purpose of preventing conception after rape can be legitimate (that is, involve no injustice to the unborn), despite the risk that it will cause abortion (as a side effect) if it happens that conception has already occurred, see Finnis, "Abortion and Health Care Ethics II," 553–54.

22. Of course, not all of slavery's defenders were in good faith. Many saw perfectly clearly slavery's cruelty and wickedness and defended it out of malice, greed, or some other ignoble motive.

23. See Nina Shea, *In the Lion's Den* (Nashville, Tenn.: Broadman and Holman Publishers, 1997), 33–34, 121, nn. 5–9; see also Joseph R. Gregory, "African Slavery 1996," *First Things* 63 (1996): 37, 38–39 (describing slavery in Mauritania and the Sudan).

24. It should sober anyone who thinks about the issue of abortion to remember that among the defenders of slavery were a far from insignificant number of otherwise generally decent people, including, let us not forget, some who strenuously objected to separating slave families and to other egregious forms of inhumane treatment. See Eugene D. Genovese, *A Consuming Fire: The Fall of the Confederacy in the Mind of the White Christian South* (Athens, Ga.: University of Georgia Press, 1998).

14

Enabling Democratic Deliberation

How Managed Care Organizations Ought to Make Decisions about Coverage for New Technologies

NORMAN DANIELS

An Addition to "Middle Democracy"

I will sketch a sympathetic addition to the house that Amy Gutmann and Dennis Thompson build in *Democratic Disagreement*. Because they are fearful that democratic deliberation theory has put all of its effort into thinking about foundations, or constitutional issues, they design a structure to occupy "middle democracy," a space where much more of the action in our political lives takes place. My addition expands that living space to include certain nonpublic, nondemocratic organizations and the role they can play in enabling a broader, if not formal, democratic deliberation. In designing the addition, I pay more attention to functional detail than the original. That is, I focus more specifically on how constraints on deliberation in these institutions might actually affect the process of deliberation. In contrast, Gutmann and Thompson pay less attention to institutional function and design and instead provide us with an instructor's manual showing how we might reconstruct, deconstruct, and sometimes resolve controversies of the sort originally raised in their case book *Ethics and Politics* in light of their principles.

Some Complaints about the Architecture of the Original

Designing an addition to a house does not imply agreement with all of the architectural decisions in the original, and before revealing the addition, I want to register, quite briefly, a few complaints about the construction—especially the foundations—of the original.

Gutmann and Thompson offer a constitutional form of deliberative democracy, specifying principles that constrain democratic deliberation. At the same time, they strain to distinguish themselves from constitutionalism of the sort developed by Rawls. In reading their discussions of welfare reform, affirmative action, and other issues, however, I am left wondering just how such vaguely "agreed on" principles as "basic liberty," "basic opportunity," and "fair opportunity" are supposed to constrain deliberation about specific issues. Where these principles seem to have some specific substance, they obtain it—I believe—from the fact that these notions have, for twenty-five years, largely been fleshed out and examined in debate about the adequacy of Rawls's theory and its extensions. By eschewing appeal to any such underlying theory, Gutmann and Thompson leave it unclear just how their version of these constitutional ties that bind actually work to constrain outcomes.

I am more sympathetic to an approach that is clearer about the foundations for its constitutional principles. Such foundations provide insight into how we should use constitutional constraints in the democratic deliberation needed to carry out institutional design and policy development. I shall illustrate the point with an example that provides a bridge to the issues raised later in this chapter.

For ten years, starting in the late 1970s, I argued that we could use an extended version of Rawls's fair equality of opportunity principle to give us guidance in allocating health care resources under reasonable resource constraints. Specifically, I suggested that we think about the impact on an individual's fair share of the normal opportunity range as a guide to the relative importance of a health care need and the services that should be allocated for it.[1] Early in the last decade, I became convinced that general principles of justice, such as the fair equality of opportunity principle, provided less guidance in designing institutions than I had hoped. They do guide our thinking about fundamental features of design, such as the provision of universal insurance coverage or the need to design a benefit package in which coverage turns on the functional importance of different health care services rather than on the category of service into which they fall.[2] For example, the theory argues for parity between mental and physical health care and between preventive, curative, and long-term care.

Nevertheless, these general principles of justice are too indeterminate to resolve key rationing issues.[3] The fair equality of opportunity principle tells us, for example, to give some priority to helping the sickest patients, but it does not tell us how much. Nor does it tell us how much weight to give to uses of scarce resources that produce "best outcomes"—measured by net health benefit—as opposed to giving all eligible patients fair chances at receiving some benefit. Nor does it tell us when it is morally permissible or required to aggregate modest benefits to larger numbers of patients so that this aggregation outweighs giving more significant benefits to fewer people. Serious moral controversy surrounds these "priorities," "best outcomes/fair chances," and "aggregation" problems.

Rationing problems like these are not peripheral issues in the theory of distributive justice. Exactly similar sorts of problems arise throughout "middle democracy" in thinking about the design of educational institutions or the distribution of legal aid or income support, or fundamental decisions in economic growth policy in developing countries. What, then, does it mean to say, as Rawls does, that a general principle of justice should "guide" the thinking of legislators responsible for institutional design? How does a very general principle give guidance if it is so indeterminate?

One strategy would be to find a middle level of moral principles to bridge the gap between general principles of justice and these questions about institutional design. For example, Kamm's brilliant exploration of trolley and other hypothetical cases is intended to uncover the underlying moral structure of "our" commitments to saving lives under resource constraints.[4] I believe this approach should be explored and mined for its insights in the ways Kamm so cleverly employs. Doing so might reveal some principles on which there is more consensus than there might seem to be at first. But I fear this strategy ignores the significant moral disagreement that surrounds solutions to these hypothetical problems, at least the disagreement I find among students and in audiences of health professionals when such hypotheticals are discussed.[5] If it is unlikely that we can find consensus on such intermediary principles, or if we cannot do so in the real time of policy formation, we must resort to fair procedures for resolving these disputes.

But what should count as a fair procedure for resolving *moral* disputes of this sort? Simply voting on these matters, tallying preferences (whether in committees of experts or in public agencies), is inadequate for all the reasons that early democratic deliberation theorists like Joshua Cohen and others,[6] and more recently Gutmann and Thompson, offer against "pure" proceduralism. The middle ground, I became persuaded, requires a deliberative model of fair procedures.

Nevertheless, I construe this account of fair procedures as a necessary extension of a constitutionalist approach in which there is some foundational account of what the principles of justice involved in constitutional constraints require. For me, developing the deliberative middle ground does not involve rejecting the theory of justice (or Rawls's politicized version of it), for example, as a way of grounding the constitutional constraints.[7] Without that theory, I find that Gutmann and Thompson's invocation of basic liberty, basic opportunity, and fair opportunity as constitutional constraints lacks adequate support and clarity. Even if Rawls's theory leaves much to democratic deliberation in the interpretation and refinement of basic principles of justice, there is some guidance given in the arguments for those principles about the way in which the principle constrains democratic deliberation. I fear that Gutmann and Thompson eclectically appeal to elements of such a theory while distancing themselves from it.

Gutmann and Thompson's description of the deliberative approach embodies an ambiguity or vagueness about the concept of "shared" reasons that closely resembles the problem they ascribe to the (Rawlsian) constitutionalism they reject. Their principle of reciprocity says that we must restrict our reason-giving to considerations that all can agree on, that are shared or can come to be shared by all appropriately motivated citizens, despite their not sharing other values. But if democratic deliberators can "share" a commitment to "basic opportunity" even if they still disagree about what that includes, then why reject Rawlsian constitutionalism because we still must use deliberation to settle disagreements about how to interpret and apply its principles? Perhaps their approach leaves more to deliberation, as they suggest, but this may be more "spin" than real difference.

A troubling ambiguity runs through much of the democratic deliberation literature, including Gutmann and Thompson's reciprocity principle. As a democratic deliberator, I am at least constrained to give reasons or to cite principles that others can "accept" in the *attenuated* sense that they recognize their relevance, even if they attribute a different weight or importance to them. But am I also constrained to restrict my reasons or principles to those to which others ascribe exactly the same weight or importance, to ones that they see not only as relevant but that they actually accept in just the same way?

Such *full acceptance* seems much too strong. It would probably stop deliberation before it starts. Nevertheless, it captures more than attenuated acceptance the core idea that we should not be bound by principles we cannot accept. The full acceptance view also misdescribes the outcome of a vote after appropriate deliberation. After a vote to break a deliberative disagreement, the majority *fully accepts* a principle governing the decision and its weighting, but the minority gives it only *attenuated* acceptance.

The weaker constraint, which I invoke in what follows, may appear to fail to provide the full legitimacy that full acceptance claims, but it better describes the typical outcome of practical deliberation. Gutmann and Thompson should modify or clarify their view so that their reciprocity principle appeals only to this more attenuated or weaker version of "agreement" or "acceptance" of principles. In any case, only this attenuated version captures the sense in which parties to the debates they reconstruct could be said to agree on principles.

Limits to Coverage: Legitimacy and Deliberation in MCOs

The work on "middle democracy" I describe here grows out of, three-year project in which my collaborators and I studied how collaborating managed care organizations (MCOs) make decisions about coverage for new technologies.[8] Our goal was to identify "best practices" and make recommendations about improving these decisions. These decisions effectively limit access to care that may fundamentally affect the well-being of patients. MCOs obviously face a problem of trust: Many people assume that all decisions are driven by costs or "the bottom line." Beyond the issue of trust, however, there are the philosophically more basic problems of legitimacy and fairness.

The *legitimacy problem* asks under what conditions authority over fundamental matters of well-being should be placed in the hands of private organizations. The *fairness problem* asks when a patient or clinician who thinks that an uncovered service is appropriate or even medically necessary has sufficient reason to accept as fair the morally controversial limit-setting decisions of MCOs. These problems are distinct, since legitimate authorities can make unfair decisions and nonlegitimate decision-makers can make fair ones, but related, since legitimacy is undermined by repeated unfairness.

Some people argue that because these organizations are private and because people can "choose" their insurers, no problem about legitimacy arises. People "consent" to the limits just as they do when consumers "consent," through their purchases to quality decisions made by an auto manufacturer. People who do not like choices made by the manufacturer can respond with their own choices.

Buying cars, however, is not like buying health care coverage. Not only does greater uncertainty keep us from being informed choosers of health insurance, but most Americans cannot choose their coverage at all—their employers choose for them. In addition, we often discover a limit-setting decision only when it is too late to change insurers; moreover, no better choices may be available to us in the market. More important, there are social obligations to distribute health care justly;[9] no similar obligations apply to meeting people's "car needs." Finally, our use of a mixed public private system does not suspend the accountability the private system must have to the public to conform to requirements of justice. Given that it is a social obligation to assure the just provision of needed services, private organizations in a mixed system must be publicly accountable for the reasonableness of the decisions they make. Otherwise there is no way to assure that society meets its own obligations.[10]

Some people may mistakenly believe that coverage decisions about new technologies involve little moral controversy because they are primarily technical assessments of evidence about efficacy and safety. This view is false. Certainly, if MCOs engaged in comparative decisions in which they had to assess the "opportunity cost" of one new technology against alternative new or old ones for other conditions, then all the unsolved moral problems about rationing I noted earlier would arise. But even where MCOs compare new treatments to older ones for the same conditions one at a time and without explicit budget constraints, moral controversy arises, for example, about how to weigh the stewardship of resources and protection of the public good of gathering knowledge in clinical trials against the urgency of patient demands for "last-chance" treatments.[11]

We would take a giant step toward solving the problems of distrust, legitimacy, and fairness that face MCOs if the following four conditions were satisfied:

1. Decisions regarding coverage for new technologies (and other limit-setting decisions) and their rationales must be publicly accessible.
2. The rationales for coverage decisions should aim to provide a *reasonable* construal of how the organization (or society) should provide "value for money" in meeting the varied health needs of a defined population under reasonable resource constraints. Specifically, a construal will be "reasonable" if it appeals to reasons and principles that are accepted as relevant by people who are disposed to finding terms of cooperation that are mutually justifiable.
3. There is a mechanism for challenge and dispute resolution regarding limit-setting decisions, including the opportunity for revising decisions in light of further evidence or arguments.
4. There is either voluntary or public regulation of the process to ensure that conditions 1–3 are met.

These four conditions capture at least the central necessary elements of a solution to the legitimacy and fairness problems for coverage decisions about new treatments.[12] Condition 1 requires publicity or transparency with regard to reasons for decisions. Condition 2 involves some constraints on the kinds of reasons that can play a role in the rationale: It recognizes the fundamental interest all parties have in finding a justification all can accept as reasonable. Conditions 3 and 4 provide mechanisms for making deliberative decisions within MCOs accountable to a broader deliberative process. These conditions were developed independently but fit reasonably well with Gutmann and Thompson's framework of principles for democratic deliberation. Condition 1 corresponds to their principle of publicity, condition 2 approximates their principle of reciprocity, and conditions 3 and 4 capture elements of their principle of accountability, though there are differences in accountability between public and private institutions.

The guiding idea behind the four conditions is to convert private MCO solutions to problems of limit-setting into part of a larger public deliberation about a major, unsolved public policy problem, namely, how to use limited resources to protect fairly the health of a population with varied needs. This problem is made progressively more difficult by the successes of medical science and technology. In the end, keeping the focus of problem solving within delivery systems may yield more coherent and defensible practices than proclamations by public commissions (as in Europe), provided that these delivery systems are properly connected to a broader public deliberation and provided that the results of that broader public deliberation can modify or constrain the decisions made within particular elements of the delivery system.

If met, these conditions help these private institutions to enable or empower a more focused public deliberation that involves broader democratic institutions. They may indeed be a model for how solutions to this problem should be approached in public systems as well, since there is a tendency for these systems to establish highly visible, publicly accountable commissions, while remaining secretive and nonaccountable at the level where decisions are really made.[13] The broader public deliberation envisioned here is not necessarily an organized democratic procedure, though it could include the deliberation underlying public regulation of the health care system. Rather, it may take place in various forms in an array of institutions, spilling over into legislative politics only under some circumstances.[14]

The first condition requires that rationales for decisions be publicly accessible to clinicians, patients, and would-be subscribers. One MCO, for example, decided (like others) to cover growth hormone treatment, but only for children who are growth hormone deficient or who have Turner's syndrome. It deliberated clearly about the reasons for its decision, which included the lack of evidence of efficacy or good risk/benefit ratios for other groups of patients and a commitment to restrict coverage to the treatment of disease and disability (as opposed to enhancements); but, like other MCOs, it did not state these reasons in its medical director's letter to clinicians or in support materials about the procedure that were used in "shared decision-making" with patients and families. These were defensible reasons aimed at a public good all can understand and see as relevant—the provision of effective and safe treatment to a defined population under resource constraints—although the restriction to treatment rather than enhancement requires a moral argument.[15]

One important effect of making public the reasons for coverage decisions is that, over time, the pattern of such decisions will resemble a type of "case law." The virtues of a case law model will help us see that the benefits of the publicity requirements of condition 1 are both internal and external to MCOs committed to it. Internally, the requirement leads to more efficient, coherent, and fairer decisions over time. Externally, the emerging case law will strengthen broader public deliberation and contribute to the perceived legitimacy of the decision-makers. A body of case law establishes the presumption that if some individuals have been treated one way because they fall under a reasonable interpretation of the relevant principles, then similar individuals should be treated the same way in subsequent cases. In effect, the institution generating the case law is saying, "We deliberate carefully about hard cases and have good reasons for doing what we have done, and we continue to stand by our reasons in our commitment to act consistently with past practices."

To rebut this presumption that a subsequent case should be treated similarly to an earlier one requires showing either that the new case differs in relevant and important ways from the earlier one, justifying different treatment, or that there are good grounds for rejecting the reasons or principles embodied in the earlier case. Case law does not imply past infallibility, but it does imply giving careful consideration to why earlier decision-makers made the choices they did. It involves a form of institutional reflective equilibrium, a commitment to both transparency and coherence in the giving of reasons. The quality of decision-making improves if reasons must be articulated. Fairness improves over time, both formally, since like cases are treated similarly, and substantively, since there is systematic evaluation of reasons. To the extent that we are then better able to discover flaws in our moral reasoning, we are more likely to arrive at fair decisions. Over time, people will understand better the moral commitments of the institutions making these decisions.

The second condition imposes two important constraints on the rationales that are made publicly accessible. Specifically, the rationales for coverage decisions should aim to provide (a) a *reasonable* construal of (b) how the organization (or society) should provide "value for money" in meeting the varied health needs of a defined population under reasonable resource constraints. Both constraints need explanation.

We may think of the goal of meeting the varied needs of the population of patients under reasonable resource constraints as a characterization of the *common or public good* pursued by all engaged in the enterprise of delivering and receiving this care. It is a goal that is avowed in their mission statements and marketing by many MCOs, whether they are for-profit or not. It is avowed by the clinicians engaged in treatment, who have professional obligations to pursue their patients' best interests. Finally, it is avowed by patients seeking care, who want their needs met but also want a cooperative scheme that provides affordable, nonwasteful care.

It is not enough simply to specify the goal of the cooperative enterprise. Reasoning about that goal must also meet certain conditions. Specifically, a construal of the goal will be "reasonable" only if it appeals to reasons, including values and principles, that are accepted as relevant by people who are affected by them and who are disposed to finding mutually justifiable terms of cooperation. For example, these criteria are commonly used in the (noncomparative) decisions about new technology made by the national Blue Cross/Blue Shield Technology Evaluation Center (MAP) and by many other organizations:

1. The technology must have final approval from the appropriate government regulatory body.
2. The scientific evidence must permit conclusions concerning the effect of the technology on health outcomes.
3. The technology must improve the net health outcome.
4. The technology must be as beneficial as any established alternative.
5. The improvement must be attainable outside the investigational setting.

Although there might be controversy about acceptable levels of risks and benefits, all these criteria are applicable with publicly accessible methods of reasoning and meet both constraints in condition 2.

To see their appropriateness more clearly, contrast these criteria with a reason that a religious patient (or clinician) might offer. Such a patient might insist that her religion requires her to pursue every avenue for survival and that some technology that fails to meet the MAP criteria nevertheless might turn out to be the occasion for a miraculous cure. Compelling though this reasoning might be to the patient, it has no relevance at all for those who lack the appropriate faith. This patient, in contrast with a Christian Scientist, would still recognize the relevance of the five criteria.

Recall the restriction of the use of growth hormone treatment to those with growth hormone deficiency. Some object that a theory that emphasizes protecting equal opportunity, as mine does, should also use medical interventions to eliminate extreme but normal shortness if it is disadvantaging. Still, proponents on both sides of this dispute can recognize that reasonable people might disagree about the specific requirements of a principle protecting opportunity. Both sides of the dispute about the scope of the goals of medicine nevertheless must recognize the relevance and appropriateness of the kind of reason offered by the other, even if they disagree with the interpretation of the principle or the applications to which it is put.[16]

"Including this treatment benefits me (and other patients like me)," just like "excluding this treatment disadvantages me (and other patients like me)," is not the kind of reason that meets the constraints on reasons. Because comparative coverage decisions always advantage some and disadvantage others, mere advantage or disadvantage is not a relevant reason in debates about coverage. If, however, a coverage decision disadvantages me compared to other patients similar to me in all relevant ways, then this is a reason based on disadvantage that all must think is relevant. Also, if a coverage decision disadvantages someone (and others like him) more than anyone need be disadvantaged under alternatives available, then this too is a reason that all must consider relevant.

How should we view the claim that a treatment "costs too much"? First, suppose this is a claim about relative cost-effectiveness or-worthiness. People who share in the goal of meeting the varied medical needs of a population covered by limited resources would consider relevant the claim that a particular technology falls below some defensible threshold of cost-effectiveness or relative cost-worthiness.

Suppose, however, the claim that something "costs too much" refers to its effects on profits or competitiveness. Supporting this claim often requires providing information that MCOs will not reveal (for good business reasons), often turns on economic and strategic judgments requiring special experience and training, and ultimately depends on a much more fundamental claim about the design of the system—namely, that a system involving competition in this sort of market will produce efficiencies that work to the advantage of all who have medical needs. My point is not that these reasons necessarily fail to meet condition 2—they do not—but that providing support for them requires information that is often not available, that is hard to understand when it is available, and that ultimately depends on fundamental moral and political judgments about the feasibility of quite different alternative systems for delivering health care. These reasons are likely to fuel further disagreement, not resolve it.

Conditions 3 and 4 require organizations to have institutional mechanisms in place for dispute resolution and the appeal of decisions. These mechanisms assure accountability that goes beyond the publicity requirements of the first two conditions. When patients or clinicians use these procedures to challenge a decision, and the results of the challenge lead effectively to reconsideration of the decision on its merits, the decision-making process is made iterative in a way that broadens the input of information and argument. Parties who were excluded from the decision-making process and whose views may not have been clearly heard or understood find a voice, even if after the original fact.

The dispute resolution mechanisms—like the rest of the four conditions—do not empower enrollees or clinicians to play a direct, participatory role in the actual decision-making bodies. Direct participation does not happen in many public democratic processes either. Moreover, while such participation may be feasible in some "cooperative" private organizations, it would not be in many others. Because of the frequent "capture" of community representatives, for example, participation is neither necessary nor sufficient to establish legitimacy by assuring that the appropriate deliberation takes place. Nevertheless, the dispute resolution requirements, supplemented by the other conditions, do empower enrollees to play a more effective role in the larger social deliberation about the issues, including in those public institutions that can play a role in regulating MCOs or otherwise constraining their acts. The mechanisms we describe thus play a role in assuring broader accountability of private organizations, such as MCOs, to those who are affected by limit-setting decisions.

The four conditions hold MCOs accountable for acting reasonably in deciding how to meet diverse patient needs under resource constraints. This *accountability for reasonableness* goes beyond the *market accountability* that is often advocated by consumer groups.[17] Market accountability is intended to facilitate informed choices about a product. Thinking that market accountability is sufficient to establish legitimacy through "choice" presupposes what I argued earlier was absent for many: an opportunity to exercise market choice in a well-functioning market. In contrast, accountability for reasonableness aims more directly at the issue of legitimacy and the facilitation of a broader societal deliberation about the unsolved problems with which each MCO must grapple. The arrangements required by the four conditions provide connective tissue to, not a replacement for, broader democratic processes that ultimately have authority and responsibility for guaranteeing the fairness of limit-setting decisions.

It is possible to specify features of institutional design in MCOs that embody the four conditions and thus assure more accountability for reasonableness. For example, the National Committee for Quality Assurance (NCQA) establishes standards that must be met if managed care organizations are to receive accreditation. Among those standards are some that call for organizations to have a process for assessing new technologies. Those standards should be modified to require that coverage decisions for new technologies be accompanied by publicly available rationales and to require that those rationales specify the evidence, reasons, and principles used in deliberating about how patient needs will be met under resource constraints.[18] Similarly, the standards requiring that there be grievance procedures can be strengthened to ask for similar accountability for reasonableness and to provide a way for grievances to influence reconsideration of policy decisions.

Space prohibits my giving more detail about how features of institutional design in this area of "middle democracy" can assure more effective democratic deliberation. Still, these suggestions underlie my earlier remark that more attention to function and institutional design is needed than Gutmann and Thompson provide. Despite this and earlier reservations, I offer this analysis of deliberation in private organizations as an addition that I hope blends in well with the many laudable features of their original structure.

Notes

A version of this chapter was presented at the Pacific Division of the American Philosophical Association in March 1997 at an "Authors Meet Critics" symposium on *Democratic Disagreement.* I have benefited from discussions with Joshua Cohen and Larry Sager. The discussion of managed care organizations is drawn from collaborative work with James Sabin. A fuller discussion of the issues raised here can be found in Norman Daniels and James Sabin, "Limits to Health Care: Fair Procedures, Democratic Deliberation, and the Legitimacy Problem for Insurers," *Philosophy and Public Affairs* 26:4(Fall 1997): 303–50. I wish to acknowledge support for that research provided by the National Science Foundation, the Retirement Research Foundation, the Greenwall Foundation, the Robert Wood Johnson Foundation, and the Harvard Pilgrim Health Care Foundation.

1. Norman Daniels, "Health Care Needs and Distributive Justice," *Philosophy and Public Affairs* 10, no. 2 (1981): 146–79, and reprinted in Norman Daniels, *Justice and Justification: Reflective Equilibrium in Theory and Practice* (New York: Cambridge University Press, 1996), chap. 9; Norman Daniels, *Just Health Care* (New York: Cambridge University Press, 1985).

2. For a detailed discussion of implications of the theory for the design of a system, see Norman Daniels, *Seeking Fair Treatment: From the AIDS Epidemic to National Health Care Reform* (New York: Oxford University Press, 1995), chap. 8, and Norman Daniels, Donald Light, and Ronald Caplan, *Benchmarks of Fairness for Health Care Reform* (New York: Oxford University Press, 1986); for an overview of the implications of the theory for rationing, see "Rationing Medical Care: A Philosopher's Perspective," *Economics and Philosophy* 14 (April 1998): 569–85.

3. In my "Rationing Fairly: Programmatic Considerations," *Bioethics* 7, nos. 2–3 (1993): 224–33, and in prepublication versions discussed while I was a Fellow in the Harvard Ethics and Professions Program in 1992–93, I argued that this indeterminacy of principles forced us to seek an account of a fair procedure for resolving disputes. Nevertheless, my view is characterized in *Democratic Deliberation* (see 215) as one that might not recognize the inability of general principles to specify appropriate rationing strategies.

4. Frances Kamm, *Morality and Mortality,* vol. 1: *Death and Whom to Save from It* (Oxford: Oxford University Press, 1993).

5. Norman Daniels, "Kamm's Moral Methods," *Philosophy and Phenomenological Research* 58, No. 4 (December 1998): 947–54.

6. See Joshua Cohen, "Deliberation and Democratic Legitimacy," in *The Good Polity: Normative Analysis of the State,* ed. Alan Hamlin and Philip Pettit (Oxford: Basil Blackwell, 1989), 17–34; also "Procedure and Substance in Deliberative Democracy," in *Democracy and Difference: Changing Boundaries of the Political,* ed. Seyla Benhabib (Princeton: Princeton University Press, 1996), 95–119.

7. It would take me beyond the scope of this chapter to explain why I think Gutmann and Thompson exaggerate the degree to which in *Political Liberalism* Rawls modifies or moves away from the basic principles he argues for justice as fairness. See Rawls's rejection of such a claim in the introduction to the paperback edition: John Rawls, *Political Liberalism* (New York: Columbia University Press, 1996), xlviii.

8. Collaborating sites in this project included Harvard Pilgrim Health Care, Kaiser Permanente of Northern California, Oregon Blue Cross/Blue Shield, Group Health of Puget Sound, Health Partners, Aetna, and the Oregon Health Resources Commission.

9. Norman Daniels, *Just Health Care* (New York: Cambridge University Press, 1985).

10. My point is that society must impose these obligations of public accountability on private organizations, not that they have already been imposed and that organizations are blameworthy for violating them.

11. See James Sabin and Norman Daniels, "Last Chance Therapies and Managed Care: Pluralism, Fair Procedures and Legitimacy" (under review).

12. These conditions are not sufficient for the broader problem of limit-setting. For example, the list does not include being open about incentive arrangements with clinicians. It does not exclude some clinician incentive arrangements that pose unacceptable conflicts of interest. Both of these omissions bear on broader limit-setting concerns, even if they do not bear directly on decisions about coverage for new treatments. These omissions and others would have to be corrected by any comprehensive solution to the fairness and legitimacy problems.

13. See, for example, Chris Ham and Susan Pickard, *Tragic Choices in Health Care: The Story of Child B* (London: Kings Fund, in press).

14. See Joshua Cohen and Charles Sobel, "Directly Deliberative Polyarchy," *European Law Journal* (forthcoming), for a discussion of the value of democratic deliberation in decentralized institutions that converges with points sketched here.

15. Norman Daniels, "Growth Hormone Therapy for Short Stature: Can We Support the Treatment/Enhancement Distinction?" *Growth, Genetics, and Hormones* 8 (1992, supplement 1): 46–48; James E. Sabin and Norman Daniels, "Determining 'Medical Necessity' in Mental Health Practice," *Hasting Center Report* 24, no. 6 (1994): 5–13.

16. See my *Justice and Justification*, chaps. 10, 11.

17. See Norman Daniels and James Sabin, "The Ethics of Accountability and Managed Care Reform," *Health Affairs* 17, No. 5 (1998): 50–64.

18. We are working with our collaborators to seek just such NCQA changes in standards.

15

Everyday Talk in the Deliberative System

JANE MANSBRIDGE

What I will call "everyday talk" does not meet all of the criteria implicit in the ordinary use of the word "deliberation." It is not always self-conscious, reflective, or considered. But everyday talk, if not always deliberative, is nevertheless a crucial part of the full deliberative system that democracies need if citizens are, in any sense, to rule themselves. Through talk among formal and informal representatives in designated public forums, talk back and forth between constituents and elected representatives or other representatives in politically oriented organizations, talk in the media, talk among political activists, and everyday talk in formally private spaces about things the public ought to discuss—all adding up to what I call the deliberative system—people come to understand better what they want and need, individually as well as collectively. The full deliberative system encompasses all these strands.[1]

If a deliberative system works well, it filters out and discards the worst ideas available on public matters while it picks up, adopts, and applies the best ideas. If the deliberative system works badly, it distorts facts, portrays ideas in forms that their originators would disown, and encourages citizens to adopt ways of thinking and acting that are good neither for them nor for the larger polity. A deliberative system at its best, like all systems of democratic participation, helps its participants understand themselves and their environment better. It also helps them change themselves and others in ways that are better for them and better for the whole society—though sometimes these goals conflict. How one judges a deliberative system thus depends heavily on what one believes to be a "good" or "bad" way of thinking or acting and what one judges to be a better or worse understanding of self and environment. Such judgments will always be heavily contested.

This chapter has two aims. First, it argues that theorists of deliberation ought to pay as much attention to citizens' everyday talk as to formal deliberation in public arenas. Although talk intended to conclude with a binding decision differs from talk that has no such intention, that difference is not significant for judging the quality of the deliberation for democratic purposes. Second, it argues that existing criteria for judging democratic talk are inadequate and need revision. The analysis calls throughout for a democratic theory that puts the citizen at the center.

One of the major aims of Amy Gutmann and Dennis Thompson's *Democracy and Disagreement* is to widen the scope of public reason to include not only its judicial exemplifications but also the democratic deliberations characteristic of legislatures at their best. Indeed, they extend the concept of public forum to include meetings of grassroots organizations, hospital committees, and sports and professional associations (113, 359). I see no reason not to widen the scope still further, to include in the arena of democratic deliberation what I call everyday talk, as well as the media, interest groups, and other venues of discussion.

Everyday talk anchors one end of a spectrum at whose other end lies the public decision-making assembly. Everyday talk produces results collectively, but not in concert. Often everyday talk produces collective results the way a market produces collective results, through the combined and interactive effects of relatively isolated individual actions. A decision-making assembly, by contrast, produces results in concert, usually through the give-and-take of face-to-face interaction. Everyday talk is not necessarily aimed at any action other than talk itself; deliberation in assembly is, at least in theory, aimed at action. Everyday talk may be almost purely expressive; deliberation in the assembly, being aimed at action, is usually intentional. Deliberation in a public assembly is often aimed at creating a collectively binding decision.

It may seem, then, that everyday talk and decision-making in an assembly differ in kind rather than in degree, because only a governmental assembly aims at and creates a collectively binding decision. Yet everyday talk among citizens on matters the public ought to discuss prepares the way for formal governmental decisions and for collective decisions not to "decide." One can trust formal governmental decisions to reflect the considered will of the citizenry only insofar as that will has gone through a process of effective citizen deliberation—in the everyday talk of homes, workplaces, and places where a few friends meet, as well as more formal talk in designated public assemblies.[2]

Few of the standards that various theorists have offered for judging deliberation map onto the one great difference between governmental assemblies and other forms of deliberation: that such assemblies (including the governing bodies of grassroots organizations, hospital committees, and sports and professional associations) aim at producing a decision binding on the participants and other venues for talk do not. I conclude, both from this lack of fit and from analyzing the features of everyday talk directly, that the larger deliberative system (including everyday talk) should be judged by much the same standards as classic deliberation in assemblies. Those standards must be loosened to accommodate the more informal character of the nongovernmental parts of the deliberative system, but in this loosening they do not lose their character. In both legislative bodies and the rest of the deliberative system, the concept of "public reason" should be enlarged to encompass a "considered" mixture of emotion and reason rather than pure rationality. The standards of publicity and accountability, which in Gutmann and Thompson's presentation are designed primarily for representative assemblies, have counterparts elsewhere in the deliberative system, including everyday talk. Reciprocity applies well to everyday talk. So do the standards of freedom, equality, consideredness, accuracy in revealing interests, and transformative capacity that arguably apply to the deliberations in assembly whose procedures democratically legitimate their conclusions.

In the full process of citizen deliberation, the different parts of the deliberative system mutually influence one another in ways that are not easy to parse out. Television, radio, newspapers, movies, and other media both influence their intended audiences and are influenced by them. So too in social movements, which work as much by changing the way people think as by pressuring governments to enact legislation, the intentionally political talk of political activists both influences and is influenced by the everyday talk of nonactivists.[3]

The interaction between activists and nonactivists in a social movement, for example, combines the dynamics of a market and a conversation. In a market, entrepreneurs put forth a product, which consumers then buy or do not buy. By making this binary choice, to buy or not to buy, consumers shape what the entrepreneurs produce. In an ideal market, entrepreneurs try to understand the present and potential desires of the consumers in order to produce a product the consumers will buy; entrepreneurs who offer an undesired product will go out of business. Conversations, by contrast, do not depend on binary signals. An ideal conversation, like Jürgen Habermas's ideal speech situation, aims at understanding. But even a conversation has a component that works a little like a market: Each partner advances words, which the other does or does not understand, does or does not find interesting. Even a partner who does not speak can shape what the other says by nonverbally indicating understanding or confusion, interest or boredom. Nonactivists affect what activists say and think in part by being speaking partners in conversation with the activists or intermediate actors and in part by responding to those offerings with understanding or confusion, interest or boredom, appropriation or rejection.

The interaction of activists and nonactivists only begins the real work of nonactivists. In everyday talk and action the nonactivists test new and old ideas against their daily realities, make small moves—micronegotiations—that try to put some version of an idea into effect, and talk the ideas over with friends, sifting the usable from the unusable, what appears sensible from what appears crazy, what seems just from what seems tendentious. In their micronegotiations and private conversations, nonactivists influence the ideas and symbols available to the political process not only aggregatively, by favoring one side or another in a vote or in a public opinion survey, but also substantively, through their practice. They shape the deliberative system with their own exercise of power and reasoning on issues that the public ought to discuss. The activism of nonactivists, which has its greatest effect through everyday talk, includes even the snort of derision one might give at a sexist television character while watching with friends. That snort of derision is, in my analysis, a political act.

Once More into "The Personal Is Political"

Outside the discipline of political science, the subfield of political theory, and the subculture of certain activist groups, the label "political" may have little relevance or laudatory power. Inside that discipline, subfield, and subculture, however, the label has a legitimating function for objects of study, a normative function in bringing into play criteria of judgment specific to political things, and a valorizing function in marking a particular activity as "serious." The reader who balks at giving the label "political" to the kind of everyday actions and talk that this chapter describes may, for almost all of the purposes of this chapter, simply think of them as "prepolitical." But because I am interested in the normative criteria appropriate to political things, I will argue that these everyday, informal forms of action and deliberation are best understood as political.

I propose that we define as political "that which the public ought to discuss," when that discussion forms part of some, perhaps highly informal, version of a collective "decision."[4] As a collective, we the people (bounded by some large or small perimeter that we or our forebears have set) make many more "decisions" than appear in our formal state apparatus. Large numbers of mutually interacting individual choices, weighted unequally through patterns of domination and subordination, chance, and other justifiable and un-justifiable inequalities, together create a host of collective choices. Those collective choices, or "decisions," then affect, often substantially, the individual choices of each member of the collective. To "politicize" one of these collective choices—to make it "political"—is to draw it to the attention of the public, as something the public should discuss as a collectivity, with a view to possible change. What the public ought to discuss is explicitly a matter for contest.[5]

This process of bringing a collective "decision" to public attention, as something the public ought to discuss, need not involve the state. We may bring to public attention not a decision made in concert but rather one that has emerged from highly informal, unconscious, and aggregative processes. Nor need we involve the state in the discussion or resolution of the issue. A medieval maxim concludes that "What touches all should be decided by all."[6] If that maxim means, as it seems to have been intended to, "decided by all" through formal government with its legitimate monopoly of force, I propose that it is simply wrong. A public might rightly decide, collectively but informally through the evolution of norms, that certain questions that affect all in a particular area should not be decided by all through formal government. My action as CEO of General Motors, or cardinal of the Catholic Church, or anchorwoman for NBC, or simply as a private individual might subtly affect literally everyone in the polity, but collectively though informally the public might decide not to allow formal governmental decision to touch the areas in which the CEO, cardinal, anchorwoman, or individual acts.

Too much has been written on the subject of "the political" to cover in any detail here.[7] For the moment, however, let me explain how I came to the definition I suggest, give some examples of what I want to cover and why, and explain why previous definitions do not seem to me fully satisfactory.

Carol Hainisch first used the phrase "The personal is political" in print, expressing an idea developed in the group to which she belonged, New York Radical Women. In the article with that title, Hainisch (1970) explained to critics within the women's movement why consciousness-raising groups, which often discussed issues such as individual women's experiences with menstruation or sexual orgasm, were as "political" as more action-oriented groups. Hainisch argued that such issues as feeling ashamed of menstruation or believing incorrectly that vaginal orgasms were different from and better than clitoral orgasms were, in my terms, matters that the public should discuss. These feelings and beliefs require public discussion because they support a structure of male dominance that for reasons of justice ought to be changed. Although that change had to be collective in the broadest sense, it did not necessarily require action in concert or by a formal government. Indeed, many of these issues were almost certainly best left outside the realm of formal government. The personal became political once individual struggles were linked conceptually with a larger normative struggle for equal status in the polity as a whole.

By coining the phrase "The personal is political," feminists meant that a host of concerns, previously trivialized as "personal" and experienced as individual or idiosyncratic, we now saw as "political," experienced by women as a group or by subgroups of certain women, and deserving of collective discussion with a view to deciding whether or not it was appropriate to take collective (though perhaps informal and piecemeal) action. An issue becomes "political" when it deserves public discussion and possibly action.

Defining the political as whatever involves "power," by contrast, includes too much and too little. It includes too much: All else equal, I exercise power but it is not "political" if I hold a gun to your head and demand your money, if I threaten anger when you want the last cookie, or if I constrain your ability to use the car because I took it to Wisconsin. More important, the definition includes too little: It excludes all that involves persuasion rather than power. It excludes all that creates and fosters commonality. In this vein, Jean Elshtain convincingly took to task several early feminist writers for concluding, as Kate Millet did, that power "is the essence of politics" (cited in Elshtain 1981, 218), or, as Nancy Henley put it, that "the personal is political" means "there is nothing we do—no matter how individual and personal it seems—that does not reflect our participation in a power system" (cited in ibid.).

The opposite mistake is to say, with Hannah Arendt and Sheldon Wolin, that "the political" is only the ground of "commonality," when commonality excludes procedural arrangements, such as majority rule, for deciding matters of fundamentally conflicting interest through relatively legitimate forms of power, or as Arendt called it, "violence."[8] The political should neither exclude the grounds of commonality, the way a definition based solely on power is likely to do, nor be confined to commonality.

Finally, what the public ought to discuss is a matter of collective concern and in a sense a matter of collective "decision," but it is not always a matter for positive action. Whether or not to take action is one of the issues that the public ought to discuss. We might discuss an issue collectively (formally or informally) and decide collectively (formally or informally) that we ought not to take action on that issue, either through formal government or through the most informal, individual processes. In this I disagree with Benjamin Barber, who defines the realm of "politics" as "circumscribed by conditions that impose a necessity for public action" (1984, 121, 137, 161, 174, and passim). I adapt the formulation of Ronald Beiner, who depicts "politics" as the medium in which human beings try to "make sense of their common situation in discourse with one another" (1983, 148), adding that "making sense" almost inevitably has decisional implications for action, when "decision" and "action" are defined in the highly informal, weakly collective sense that I define them here.[9]

Does defining the political this broadly "[erode] the terms of the private sphere" (Elshtain 1981: 333)? I believe it does—in small part. To suggest that the public should discuss many intimate and familial matters, at least in general terms, destroys one strong defense against the invasion of the private world by the public. That strong defense is simply to say that what goes on in the family, or in the sphere of intimacy, is not for public discussion. Appropriate norms should put sexual orgasm or child-rearing practices, for example, simply off-limits. Informal prohibitions on public speech about these issues constitute one of the strongest defenses I can imagine against the invasion of the public into the private. I would argue, however, that the private sphere can be protected sufficiently against serious incursions from formal government without so limiting public discussion.

What the public ought to discuss is contested and essentially contestable. The question "Is this political?" demands an argument aimed at convincing the interlocutor that an issue ought to, or ought not to, be discussed by the public. This kind of argument has to produce reasons why the matter in question should be of larger collective concern, why it should go beyond the two of us (or the four or ten of us).

An argument of this sort would not collapse the distinction between the public and private realms. It would not eliminate either or subordinate either to alternative concepts. It would not demand that the private be integrated fully within or subsumed by the public. It would not insist that the public realm be privatized. It would not devalue the private sphere or suggest that the relationships that characterize that sphere had little significance or value.[10] But it would say that some matters, hitherto thought too intimate for the public to discuss, or of so little importance that they did not need to be discussed by the public, were matters on which the collective, the public, ought to deliberate.

Everyday Activism and Everyday Talk

Everyday activism occurs when a nonactivist takes an action in order to change others' actions or beliefs on an issue that the public ought to discuss. Much everyday activism takes place through talk. Here is an African American woman reporting an instance of everyday activism to other participants in a focus group:

> I was born and raised in Chicago, and I've never been south in all of my life. But all my in-laws are from the South. So I go to this big family dinner and I'm just waiting, you know, sitting at the table, waiting. And

all of a sudden all the men shift [speaker makes a funny shifting noise; laughter from others] to one side of the room. And all of a sudden all of the women shift [makes another shifting noise] into the kitchen. And I'm sitting there at the table by myself scratching my head. And the women come out with the plates, handing out the plates, and my husband says: "You gonna fix my plate?" "I don't fix your plate at home. Why would I do it here?" Well, it ties in. It's a generation thing. It's a cycle, a never-ending cycle. His father did it, and his father's father did it. They just sit there and wait while the women go [shifting sound] around.

[Others in the group chime in, ask questions.]

Well, what I did was I ended up like liberating the other women in the family and then all of a sudden they stopped serving them all of a sudden—[Others interrupt with their stories].[11]

With this small act—a combination of speech and, in this case, nonperformance of an expected action—the nonactivist intervened in her own and others' lives to promote a relatively new ideal of gender justice, exemplified by her verb "liberating." She intended to affect the others by her actions and words. She undoubtedly also believed that the issues on which she acted were issues that the public ought to discuss.

On the issue I am currently studying—changing conceptions of gender justice—the everyday activism of the nonactivists I have met has relied less on power, that is, the threat of sanction or the use of force, than on influence, that is, persuading another of a course of action on its merits.[12] In one or two incidents that my informants described, a form of power did most of the work of social change—as when a woman phoned the company of a sexist window salesman to get him fired. In several other incidents, power in the form of a threat of personal anger and withdrawal played an important role. Yet even in those incidents in which power played the greatest role, persuasive appeals to justice underlay my informants' approach to the conflict.

Consider the act of calling someone a "male chauvinist." The hurling of an epithet, often in anger, surely ranks near the bottom of a scale of articulated, nonmanipulative, and humane forms of deliberation. It falls far short of the ideal that deliberation should be conducted in a context of mutual respect, empathy, and listening. It serves itself as a sanction, and it implicitly threatens further sanctions, thus fitting solidly within the particular constellation of causal effects that I call "power." Yet the summary indictment captured in the term "male chauvinist" also works as a crude and shorthand form of influence. It inherently makes two claims—one structural, the other normative. Descriptively, it claims that the behavior in question results in part from a structure of gender relations that extends beyond the particular individuals engaged in this interaction. Normatively, it claims that the man's behavior is not merely disagreeable but also unjust. Persuading others to act or refrain from acting on the basis of shared and contested ideals of human interaction often takes just such a shorthand form.

Here is a professional-class woman, self-identified as "conservative" on a liberal-conservative spectrum, reporting that she had called her husband a male chauvinist.

> JM: What was your husband's reaction to you saying something like that to him?
>
> R: I remember him being surprised and then saying that he didn't think he was, but as he thought about he guessed he was a little. It never occurred to him that he was male chauvinist before I said it.
>
> JM: Do you think he took it as a criticism?
>
> R: Yes. I don't think he wanted to be that way—especially since he values my intelligence and that is why he married me. I think he has improved; I am looking back a couple of years, and he is better now.[13]

In some of the reported instances of women calling a man a "male chauvinist," the phrase sparked an interchange that led to changed behavior, primarily through persuasion based on an implicit appeal to justice. In many instances, men simply laughed the criticism off or got angry, and the women in the interaction thought there was no chance the men would change. In several instances the women did not challenge the men directly at all. Instead, they talked with one another "backstage," using the phrase and the analysis it embodies to reinforce one another in an emerging sense of injustice that they did not yet dare to bring into the open.[14]

In social movements, new ideas—and new terms, such as "male chauvinist" or "homophobia"—enter everyday talk through an interaction between political activists and nonactivists. Activists craft, from ideals or ideas solidly based in the existing culture, ideals or ideas that begin to stretch that base. Social enclaves in which activists talk intensely with one another foster this kind of innovation. The activists, along with others who for various reasons find themselves in these enclaves, discuss and try to put into practice these extensions and revisions of received ideas. In the protected space of the enclave, and also on the borders between that enclave and mainstream society, activists experiment with persuading others. They discover through empathy, intuition, logic, and trial and error which ideas move others to change their own ideas and behavior and which do not. The enclave nourishes the development of extreme ideas—such as that gun control advocates consciously intend to destroy citizens' capacities to resist government, or that babies should be produced in test tubes by cybernetricians. The enclave confirms some of its participants in the reality of their perceptions, both accurate and inaccurate. It stokes collective anger. It encourages creative, sometimes harebrained, solutions to collective problems. It helps remove the deadening conviction that nothing can be done. It stirs the intellectual and emotional pot.

From the enclave crucible and the surrounding ferment emerge ideas that may or may not get anywhere in the larger society. To change the thinking and behavior of large numbers of people, an idea must be sufficiently congruent with existing ideas to find a niche in the schemas people already employ to interpret the world. It must explain hitherto unexplained phenomena or apply old lessons to something relatively new. A new idea will often emerge from a new material base. But the powerful role of interpretative schemas, both in the particular cultures of competing enclaves and in the often conflicting strands of mainstream thought, ensures that no new idea can be predicted simply from material change.

As the activists, with their many tendencies and factions, take their ideas out into the larger society, they become willy-nilly entrepreneurs, or carriers of infection, or participants in a somewhat one-sided conversation. Whether in the market many consumers buy the ideas, whether in the epidemic many become infected, or whether in the conversation many eyes light up or glaze over, depends on the activists, on translators with one foot in the enclave and one in the larger society, and on the needs and ideas of members of the society at large.

As new ideas enter the larger society, different kinds of people pick them up and try them on, for different reasons. Some find in these ideas a new club with which to beat old enemies, others an enticement with which to seduce would-be friends. Some find in them the answer to intellectual and emotional puzzles. Some see them as healthy extensions of ideals they already hold. Pundits weigh in. Newsmagazines run side articles, then possibly lead articles or even cover stories. Television programs lightly air the new ideas, then drop or focus on them. If the ideas have relevance to the lives of ordinary citizens, those citizens begin to take positions and talk the ideas over with their friends. Women may talk with their husbands and the other women in the family. They may stop fixing plates and may call the men they know "male chauvinists."

If parts of the new ideals begin to win more general acceptance, many people, including nonactivists, begin changing their lives in order to live up to those ideals in a better way. Those whose material lives are improved by putting the new ideals into practice have incentives to promulgate those ideas. Those whose material lives will be harmed have incentives to denigrate them. But material loss and gain do not fully explain adherence to or rejection of an idea. People are governed in part by their ideals, and they often want to act consistently. Showing that a new ideal is consistent with an old ideal, or that previous arguments for why the new ideal did not apply are wrong, can make at least some contemporary human beings change their ideas of right relationships, their ideas of right action, and their lives.

The ideas and ideals that generate and are generated by this process can be either good or bad. The process that generates, over time, a growing conviction that schools should be racially integrated is the same process, in its outlines, as the process that generates, over time, a conviction that Jews should be sent to concentration camps. But although the outlines may be the same, the process in its details may not be the same. The ideals of good deliberative process have been derived, in part, from long human observation of what procedures produce good decisions over time, as well as, in part, from understanding what procedures have elements that are good in themselves. The democrat's faith is that good deliberative systems will, over time, produce just outcomes. Yet what the criteria for good deliberation are is at the moment an open question. It is also unclear whether the criteria for good deliberation in a public assembly are the same as the criteria for a good deliberative system.

Criteria for Judging Deliberation and Everyday Talk

Gutmann and Thompson suggest the standards of reciprocity, publicity, and accountability as criteria for judging deliberation in a public assembly. These criteria apply in a modified manner to the larger deliberative system, including everyday talk. The criteria also need revision to capture adequately what distinguishes good democratic talk from bad in an assembly or in everyday talk.

Publicity, as Gutmann and Thompson present it, is primarily a virtue of representative assemblies, which typically produce a binding decision. Jürgen Habermas and Immanuel Kant suggest that the deliberative system as a whole should also foster publicity in ideas.[15] Yet neither formal nor everyday talk should make a fetish of publicity. Secrecy often produces better deliberation than "sunshine." In a formal decision-making assembly, proceedings are often more productive if the doors are closed and members do not have to watch their words. Similarly, in the everyday talk of the larger deliberative system, creative thought often thrives in protected space. A better criterion than publicity pure and simple would be some mixture of protection and publicity in the early stages of a deliberative process, but maximum feasible publicity in the final stages (see Elster 1998, 117).

Accountability might seem, even more than publicity, the virtue of a representative body. Yet in a larger sense, all the citizens of a polity are accountable to one another. Because neither journalists nor ordinary citizens are formally accountable to their readers or fellow citizens, the standard of accountability must be interpreted broadly in the deliberative system as a whole. In most instances of everyday talk it makes sense to mandate only an informal sense of responsibility to others, and it is worth discussing what that undoubtedly contested responsibility might be.[16] "Hate speech," for example, could usefully be analyzed in the larger frame of parsing out the forms of mutual accountability appropriate to good democratic talk. Beginning to do so raises the point, applicable as well to deliberative assemblies, that constant accountability to others does not always produce the most creative and authentic deliberation, or even a deliberation that is ultimately the most helpful to the polity as a whole. Human beings may sometimes need spaces protected from accountability as well as from publicity in order to think most freely about the problems that face them. Again, a good criterion for deliberation would not mandate full accountability in the creative stages of the process but only in the later most public stages.

The standard of reciprocity applies fairly unproblematically to everyday talk. Gutmann and Thompson group under the heading of "reciprocity" the values of mutual respect, the goals of consistency in speech and consistency between speech and action, the need to acknowledge the strongly held feelings and beliefs of others, and the values of openmindedness and "economy of moral disagreement" (seeking rationales that minimize the rejection of an opposing position). Gutmann and Thompson incorporate in reciprocity, by making it an early step in the deliberative process, Lynn Sanders's (1997) proposed alternative to deliberation of "testimony," or stating one's own perspective in one's own words, an action that both has expressive value and helps change others' interpretive schemas. All of these values can apply straightforwardly to everyday talk.

Along the same lines, Benjamin Barber (1984) discussion of "strong democratic talk" stresses the mandate to listen. Amitai Etzioni (1996, 102–6) proposes for informal moral dialogues among citizens rules of engagement that include appealing to an overarching or external value that might reconcile participants in a given conflict, not affronting the deepest moral commitments of others (including leaving some issues out of the debate[17]), and when possible substituting for the language of rights the language of needs, wants, and interests. Daniel Yankelovitch (1991) spells out some of the ways in which, ideally, public judgment should differ from a mere aggregation of preferences—including "working through" controversial public matters as one would work through grief after death. Iris Young (1996) opens up the process of deliberation to participants disadvantaged by traditional elite understandings of "reason-giving" by adding the elements of "greeting" (explicit mutual recognition and conciliatory caring), "rhetoric" (forms of speaking, such as humor, that reflexively attend to the audience), and "storytelling" (which can show outsiders what values mean to those who hold them). Young's suggestions apply easily to everyday talk; all of these other writers explicitly apply their expanded understandings of "reciprocity" to everyday talk.

Yet even interpreted so expansively, reciprocity cannot stand unchallenged as a criterion for judging either formal deliberation or everyday talk. Gutmann and Thompson insightfully conclude their section on reciprocity by commenting that "the politics of mutual respect is not always pretty." In order to attract attention to a legitimate position that would otherwise be ignored, they point out, citizens may need "to take extreme and even offensive stands . . . refuse to cooperate with opponents, and even threaten retaliation" (90). The same is true in everyday talk, and more so. Because public statements go on record, because being made to look a fool in public is more wounding than a comparable insult in private, and because the sequencing of interaction in an assembly of several speakers makes it harder to correct misinterpretation or soften a harsh remark with a subsequent compliment, speakers in a public forum must be particularly careful to weigh their words and give others at least formal respect. The looser and less accountable settings of everyday talk foster greater incivility.

Both in a public forum and in everyday talk, there are justifiable places for offensiveness, noncooperation, and the threat of retaliation—even for raucous, angry, self-centered, bitter talk, aiming at nothing but hurt. These forms of talk are sometimes necessary not only to "promote mutual respect in the long term" (Gutmann and Thompson 90), but also to achieve authenticity, to reveal (as in "testimony") the pain and anger, hate, or delight in another's pain, that someone actually feels, when expression or knowledge of those feelings furthers the understanding that is the goal of deliberation. These uncivil forms of talk are also often necessary as means to the end of approaching both liberty and equality in deliberation. Sometimes only intensity in opposition can break down the barriers of the status quo. No one always listens attentively to everyone else, and members of dominant groups are particularly likely to find they do not need to listen to members of subordinate groups. So subordinates sometimes need the battering ram of rage.[18]

Everyday talk sometimes provides spaces, such as the arms of a best friend, in which the most corrosive and externally harmful words can be uttered, understood, assimilated, and reworked for more public consumption. The corridors of public forums provide the same function. Everyone who has deliberated frequently in a public forum, even if that forum is no bigger than the twenty-five or so members of an academic department, knows that good deliberation has to include what goes on before and after, as individuals talk over their positions with likeminded and opposing others, as anger is worked up against the enemy in order to provide the impetus to speak, and as tempers are cooled, misunderstandings explained, compromises brokered—or positions sharpened, obfuscations skewered, and shoddy attempts at consensus revealed as internally contradictory. These processes work best in groups of only two or three, where the flow of communication, both verbal and nonverbal, is relatively unfettered.[19] Everyday talk, the New England town meeting, the state legislature, and the U.S. Congress are alike in these respects. They all require their spaces of unmediated authenticity, which sometimes require nonreciprocity toward the outside world. Both in public forums and in the deliberative system as a whole, therefore, the criterion for good deliberation should be not that every interaction in the system exhibit mutual respect, consistency, acknowledgment, openmindedness, and moral economy, but that the larger system reflect those goals.

Joshua Cohen (1989) was the first theorist to specify criteria by which one might judge the democratic legitimacy of deliberation, that is, the degree to which suitably structured deliberation generates the legitimate authority to exercise power. His criteria for legitimate deliberation apply equally well to deliberation in public assemblies and to everyday talk, for the quality of everyday talk affects the normative legitimacy of our many informal collective "decisions." Yet his criteria too require revision.

Cohen's first criterion is that a deliberation be free. This criterion is best reinterpreted as the Habermasian ideal of "freedom from power," that is, freedom from the threat of sanction or use of force.[20] Although Foucault is right that no situation can be "free" from power, and each of us both is constituted by power and exercises power in every interaction, nevertheless, some spaces for talking and acting are, although never fully free, more free than others.[21] We seek out such spaces both in democratic constitution-making and in our everyday search for self-understanding and the creation of commonality. Democratic constitutions often try to insulate public deliberative forums from the worst effects of external power: The United States Constitution, for example, exempts congressional representatives from liability for their official acts. Negotiations are often arranged so that with two parties (such as labor and management) each side has an equal number of representatives and votes, allowing the formal power of each to cancel out the formal power of the other. To guarantee sufficient freedom for everyday talk, a polity must not only provide the specific liberties of speech, press, and association needed for good deliberation (Dahl 1989, Knight and Johnson 1994) but also generate for all groups some spaces that are relatively free from power.[22]

Equality, another of Cohen's criteria, applies to judging both everyday talk and formal deliberation. Deliberation is never fully free of power. Therefore, Cohen points out rightly that the criterion of equality requires making participants "substantively equal in that the existing distribution of power and resources does not shape their chances to contribute to the deliberation" (Cohen 1989, 23). Insofar as threats of sanction and force do enter the deliberative arena, each participant should have equal resources to use as the basis for the threat of sanction and the use of force. Asymmetries should not give unfair advantage to any participant (Knight and Johnson 1998, 293;

Mansbridge 1988). When systemic power, derived from a history of domination and subordination, produces a set of naturalized expectations and norms that disadvantage subordinates, both classic deliberation and everyday talk must, in order to approach the condition of equality, draw from a stream of alternatives to those expectations. The need to solicit and encourage previously excluded constituents in order to come closer to equality (Knight and Johnson 1994, 1998; Young, this volume) does not mean that every forum need include all those affected, but rather that in the deliberative system as a whole no participants should have an unfair advantage.[23]

Yet the equality appropriate to either everyday talk or formal deliberation does not require equal influence. Although Cohen writes that each participant should have "an equal voice" in the decision, deliberative equality should not mean that each participant ought to have an equal effect on the outcome. Rather, the force of the better argument (including, as we shall see, the force of good arguments based on emotion) should prevail, no matter from whom that argument originates or how frequently it originates from one or more participants.[24] In practice, influence is not easy to separate from power, but both a smoothly functioning public assembly and a group of friends in everyday talk will try to perform that separation as best they can. They will take a good idea from any source but will reject attempts to exercise power, particularly unequal power, in the sense of the threat of sanction and the use of force.[25]

The criterion of equality also mandates some form of mutual respect among participants. Mutual respect, a major component of Gutmann and Thompson's reciprocity, requires listening (Barber 1984). It requires your trying, through imagination and empathy, to put yourself in another's place (Williams 1962, Minow 1987, Benhabib 1991). It also requires recognizing the differences between you and others that make it impossible for you fully to put yourself in their place (Young 1997). Until the recent work of Black feminist and post-colonial writers (e.g., Harris 1990), theories of mutual respect did not emphasize, or even recognize, the need to honor those differences.

The criterion of equality in deliberation should therefore be modified to mandate equal opportunity to affect the outcome; mutual respect; and equal power only when threats of sanction and the use of force come into play.

Cohen's next criterion is that deliberative outcomes should be settled only by reference to the "reasons" participants offer. Yet requiring of legitimate deliberation that it be "reasoned" implicitly or explicitly excludes the positive role of the emotions in deliberation. Amelie Rorty (1985) and Martha Nussbaum (1995) point out the flaws in dichotomizing "reason" and "emotion." The emotions always include some form of appraisal and evaluation, and reason can proceed only rarely without emotional commitment, if only an emotional commitment to the process of reasoning. Nussbaum's positive account of the role of emotions in deliberation further singles out the emotion of compassion as an essential element of good reasoning in matters of public concern. Other emotions, such as solidarity, play equally important roles. Because making the best sense of what we collectively ought to do requires a finely tuned attention to both cognitions and emotions, the third criterion for normative legitimacy should be that a deliberation be "considered" rather than "reasoned."[26]

Cohen's fourth criterion is the degree to which deliberation "aims to arrive at a rationally motivated *consensus*" (Cohen 1989, 23, emphasis in original). This is not, in my view, an appropriate criterion for legitimate deliberation. Even at the formal assembly level, normatively legitimate deliberation should aim not only at consensus but also at clarifying conflict, sharpening that conflict if necessary. Similarly, Cohen's criteria for an "ideal deliberative procedure" include that it should be "focused on the common good" (1989, 19), but such a singular focus on the common good makes it harder to recognize that deliberation may legitimately conclude correctly that the interests of the participants are fundamentally in conflict (Mansbridge [1980] 1983, 1992; Knight and Johnson 1994, 1998; Young 1996; Sanders 1997). The conscious or unconscious pressure to frame one's argument in terms of the common good can seriously distort participants' understandings of the issue, making it far harder to resolve it through legitimate bargaining (e.g., taking turns or equalizing outcomes with sidepayments).

For the same reasons, deliberation should not ideally shape the "identity and interests of citizens" only "in ways that contribute to the formation of a public conception of the common good" (Cohen 1989, 19). Formal deliberation, everyday talk, and other forms of democratic participation should enable citizens to see conflict more clearly when that conflict has previously been masked (e.g., by elite "nondecisions" and by hegemonic definitions of the common good; see Bachrach and Baratz 1963, Bachrach 1974; see also the criterion of "enlightened understanding" in Dahl 1979, 104–5). Women, for example, have often been socialized to put the interests of others ahead of their own in ways that interfere with understanding their own interests. The articulation of self-interest has a legitimate role in democratic deliberation, particularly in discussions of fair distribution (Mansbridge 1992a, Stoker 1992, Knight and Johnson 1998). A legitimate deliberation should therefore meet the criterion of helping citizens understand their interests better, whether or not these interests can be forged into a larger common good.

Revised in these ways, both Gutmann and Thompson's criteria for justifiable decisions in a public assembly and Cohen's criteria for legitimate decisions in a binding forum turn out also to be reasonable criteria for judging everyday talk. In settings of relative liberty and equality, considering both reason and emotion, both everyday talk and more formal deliberation should help participants understand their conflicts and their commonalities. I will not try to resolve here how we may judge formal deliberation and everyday talk on the basis of their capacity for transforming a participant from a "private person" to a "citizen."[27] In both venues, we should judge these transformations by the *kinds* of solidarity and commitment to principle they involve.[28]

A Range of Forums, a Range within Standards

The venues for deliberation fall along a spectrum from the representative assembly (Bessette 1994), to the public assembly producing a binding decision (Cohen 1989, Gutmann and Thompson), to the "public sphere" (Habermas [1962] 1989), to the most informal venues of everyday talk. Moving along this range entails moving along a similar range, from formal to informal, within the same standards for good deliberation.

Jürgen Habermas has drawn a bright line between the binding assembly, as the locus of "will-formation," and the rest of the deliberative system, as the realm of "opinion-formation."[29] But this line does not, I believe, imply any great difference in the standards for deliberation. Habermas's public sphere is not restricted to a binding forum. Nor do his two constitutive elements of the public sphere—that in it "the private people . . . come together to form a public" and that it evince critical reasoning—define or map onto the binding/nonbinding distinction.[30]

The criteria for judging deliberation thus fall along a continuum that may not break at the binding/nonbinding distinction. At the most stringent end should be the standards that help create political obligation (Applbaum 1992). Possibly less stringent, but possibly no different, are the standards that generate the legitimate authority to exercise power (Manin 1987, Cohen 1989). Less stringent still are standards that allow us to judge which arguments are "justifiable" to other citizens (Gutmann and Thompson), adequate for continued cooperation (Bohman 1996), or simply productive of higher-quality decisions (Estlund 1993). The line between the forums that produce binding decisions and all other venues does not correspond, Gutmann and Thompson contend, to the line between legitimacy and mere justifiability. Gutmann and Thompson avail themselves explicitly of the line between binding and nonbinding decisions, making their analysis apply only to binding decisions. Yet they also make it clear throughout that they are working not within the framework of legitimacy but within the far broader frame of justifiability.[31] If we do not draw from the distinction between binding and nonbinding forums qualitatively different standards for judging deliberation on either side of that line, we are left with one set of standards that simply apply more and more loosely as the participants in talk are less and less formally accountable to one another.

Everyday talk in this respect differs from classic deliberation in an assembly not in kind but only in degree.

I do not deny that formal representation differs in important ways from informal accountability. Assemblies with the authority to produce binding decisions also differ from the informal conversations that comprise everyday talk. The outstanding question is whether any of the criteria for judging the quality of deliberation, with which Gutmann and Thompson and others concern themselves, change at the binding/nonbinding boundary or at the boundary between formal and informal representation. With the possible exception of accountability, which obviously becomes formal with the institution of formal representation, this analysis claims that these criteria do not change; they simply become looser in application. Public deliberation stretches across a spectrum in which the various divisional points—state/non-state, representative, binding/nonbinding—have as yet no coherent relation to the criteria for deliberation. As we ask what can motivate good deliberation within our formal and binding assemblies we should also ask what can motivate good deliberation in our interest groups, our media, and or everyday talk. All of these constitute important parts of the larger deliberative system.

Everyday talk was once revered as the prime locus of the formation of public judgment. Today it appears too rarely in the theoretical literature on deliberation,[32] as theorists direct their attention primarily toward deliberation in formal and binding assemblies. It is time to broaden our descriptive and analytic horizons again and give adequate credit, as a critical component of democracy, to the entire deliberative system, including its centerpiece, the citizen's everyday talk.

Notes

I would like to thank Michael Bratman, Kimberly Curtis, Jean Elshtain, Stephen Macedo, and Andrew Sabel for comments on all or parts of this chapter, and Kimberly Curtis, Marshall Ganz, and Amy Gutmann for conversations that persuaded me to change my earlier phrase "everyday deliberation" to "everyday talk." This chapter was prepared while I was a Fellow at the Center for Advanced Study in the Behavioral Sciences. I am grateful for financial support provided by National Science Foundation Grant #SBR-9601236.

1. By using the word "system" I do not want to imply that the parts of the whole have a mechanical or perfectly predictable relation to one another, although both of these attributes are connotations of the words "system" and "systematic" in ordinary speech. Rather, I want to imply an interrelation among the parts, such that a change in one tends to affect another. (See Christiano 1996b for interest groups and political parties as part of what I call the deliberative system.)

2. Although Habermas includes in his deliberative "public sphere" privately

owned settings with restricted access, such as the coffeehouses in England in the late seventeenth century ([1962] 1989), he does not include the kitchens and bedrooms that often host everyday talk.

3. In a 1989 representative survey, about a third of the U.S. public reported not engaging in any political act beyond voting (Verba, Schlozman, and Brady 1996, 83). By "nonactivists" I mean people like these. By "activists" I mean people who identify with a social movement, who feel an obligation toward that social movement, that is, a commitment to pay some price to promote the ends of the movement), and who actively discuss, craft, and propagate the ideas of the movement as a major part of their identities and lives. The majority of citizens in the United States today fall somewhere between these groups. They may have moments of activism, but in most of their identities and actions they are nonactivists. My term "nonactivists" also applies to the nonactivist sectors of the lives of this great majority of partially active citizens. The analysis in this paper chapter does not, I believe, depend on the exact definition of either group. It also focuses on only one aspect of the deliberative system—the everyday talk of nonactivists—and not on other aspects of the deliberative system or on other ways nonactivists influence the political process.

4. This formulation is intended to be more specific than Habermas's ([1974] 1979, 49) "matters of general interest" or Benhabib's (1994, 26) "matters of common concern." It is not intended to be much more specific, as all of these formulations leave open to contest the meaning of "general," "common," and "what the public ought to discuss." This formulation, however tries to underline that openness to contest by making the "ought" explicit. Note that Habermas used the phrase "matters of general interest" to describe the "public," not the "political;" he wrote that citizens "behave as a public body when they confer in an unrestricted fashion . . . about matters of general interest" ([1974] 1979, 49). By contrast he used the adjective "political," modifying "the public sphere," to designate discussion that "deals with objects connected to the activity of the state" (ibid.). The formulation I suggest does not restrict the meaning of the political to issues connected with the activity of the state. Other words, such as "state" and "governmental," allow us to retain the important distinction between matters of state decision and matters of collective decision outside the state. Young (1990, 9) quotes Hannah Pitkin (1981, 343) and Roberto Unger (1987, 145) as defining politics, respectively, as "the activity through which relatively large and permanent groups of people determine what they will collectively do, settle how they will live together, and decide their future, to whatever extent this is within their power," and the "struggle over the resources and arrrangements that set the basic terms of our practical and passionate relations. Preeminent among these arrangements is the formative institutional and imaginative context of social life." These definitions are highly compatible with mine.

5. Simply allowing certain issues, such as pedophilia, into public debate gives them a legitimacy grounded in the possibility that such debate might usher in approval. Jean Elshtain (personal communication) argues on these grounds for excluding such issues from public debate and therefore from the realm of the

political. For different but parallel reasons, John Stuart Mill (1840, 272–73) suggested keeping certain fundamental values "*above* discussion" (his emphasis).

6. Cited in, e.g., Walzer 1983, 292. This is a relatively common understanding in modern theory as well. Dewey, for example, defined "public" matters as those whose consequences "affect the welfare of many others" and are "so important as to need control." He defined "the public" as "all those who are affected by the indirect consequences of transactions to such an extent that it is deemed necessary to have those consequences systematically cared for" ([1927] 1994, 12, 16). Leaving aside the problematic indefinite subject in "is deemed," this definition leaves unexplored the meaning of "control" and "systematically," in which much of the meaning must lie if the definition does not simply extend the boundaries of the public to anyone even indirectly (though "seriously") affected ([1926] 1994, 35). See below, n. 23 on the boundaries of the polity and n. 27 on the normative dimensions of Dewey's "public."

7. On the private/public distinction, see, e.g., Elshtain 1981, 217–18, 331–53; Dietz 1985; Young 1987, 74; Benhabib [1987], 1988, 177, n. 12; Okin 1990, 124–33; MacKinnon 1989, 120; Mansbridge and Okin 1993.

8. For a critique of the position on this subject of Wolin (1960, 1996), Arendt (1965), and Habermas ([1976] 1985), and an argument for the democratic legitimacy of "power" defined as the threat of sanction or use of force, see Mansbridge 1995a.

9. My definition is compatible with Barber's if one defines "action" to include the decision not to take action and "public" to include the informal collective processes with which I am primarily concerned as well as the formal processes of state action.

10. These comments respond to arguments in Elshtain 1981.

11. Focus group, 1994, drawn from a representative Chicago sample, of African American women who had said in an earlier survey that they had less than a college education and considered themselves "feminist."

12. For an elaboration of this distinction between power and influence, see Mansbridge 1995a. I would like to avoid the purely rationalist implication of "persuasion on the merits" but cannot find in English a phrase that includes a legitimate appeal to the relevant emotions along with a legitimate appeal to the relevant reasons. For the legitimate appeal to relevant emotions, see below pp. 225–26.

13. From a 1994 in-depth follow-up to a survey earlier in 1994, in which 63 percent of women in a representative sample of the Chicago area reported having used the phrase "male chauvinist."

14. See Scott 1990 for parallels.

15. Much of the late eighteenth- and early nineteenth-century literature extolling the virtues of "public opinion" (Habermas [1962] 1989, 90–102) applies specifically to what I call "everyday talk." Habermas (100–01) also supports the application of the criterion of publicity to everyday talk. Following Bentham on "the regime of publicity," he applies the criterion both "inside and outside the parliament, and quotes Kant on the importance to the development of public

reason of "the course of conversation in mixed companies [including] . . . businesspeople or women" (106).

16. See Mansbridge [1980] 1983, 248–51, for active citizens as informal representatives of the inactive, and Mansbridge 1995b, 1997b, for informal accountability in the representative sector.

17. Gutmann and Thompson are rightly leery of this sometimes necessary solution, because it forestalls attempts to generate deliberation within disagreement.

18. Linguists point out that human cultures differ dramatically in the degree to which various forms of expression are permitted and how these forms are interpreted (see, e.g., Kochman 1981 on black/white differences in the United States). As theorists explore further the role of the emotions and uncivil acts in the democratic process, it will be important to distinguish those speech forms and actions that are likely to promote mutual understanding across cultures from those that simply reflect the cultural habits of the writer.

19. The backstage does not, however, solve the problems of deliberative inequality. In backstage action and in everyday talk as well as in the deliberative forum, members of the professional classes are more likely than working-class or lower-middle class participants to have the skills that generate greater influence (Mansbridge [1980] 1983, 201). How unfettered such talk should be is, again, a matter of contest. See Christiano 1996a on the "inherent contestability of deliberative equality," Knight and Johnson 1998 for a critique of Rawls's "precepts of reasonable discussion," and Rawls himself (1971) on the conditions for legitimate civil disobedience.

20. Cohen categorizes Habermas's concept not under the criterion of freedom but under the criterion of a reasoned decision. Cohen's own criterion of "freedom" includes not being "constrained by the authority of prior norms or requirements" (1989, 22). This condition seems problematic unless it means, as I assume Cohen intended it to mean, *absolutely* constrained by the *traditional* authority of prior norms or requirements. Our lives and selves have no meaning apart from prior norms and requirements. One might almost say that our lives and selves are made up of prior norms and requirements. Many of those norms and requirements are right and just. Some (like language) are in many ways merely convenient but also contain elements of the use of force against the interests of some, often subordinate, groups. Some of the norms and requirements are highly unjust. Deliberation, even in the ideal sense, should be constrained by these priors when they are neutral or just. It should not be absolutely constrained; nor should it be constrained merely by tradition or by other requirements that cannot stand up under scrutiny. These considerations are included in my definition of freedom from power.

Conceptually, what I call "freedom" has strong links to Bentham's and Kant's understanding of publicity. Habermas describes how Kant's principle, that political actions are "in agreement with law and morality only as far as their maxims were capable of, or indeed in need of, publicity," derived from his thinking about the role of giving reasons everyday talk (Habermas [1962] 1989, 108). Kant's conclusion that "the public use of one's reason must always be free" (quoted 106), which animates his distinction between "private" and "public" reason, is fully appropriate as a regulative ideal in everyday talk.

All these criteria, including freedom, should be understood as regulative ideals, that is, as ideals that can never be fully achieved but serve instead as standards at which to aim. As such, the regulative ideals of deliberative democracy parallel the regulative ideals of aggregative (or "adversary") democracy, e.g., that in the aggregation each should count for one and none for more than one. In practice, neither deliberative democracy nor aggregative democracy can ever fully live up to its regulative ideals. This fact does not mean we should reject these ideals as goals, or fail to use them to judge the degree of legitimacy (which will never, therefore, be full) of existing democratic practice. It is therefore not an appropriate criticism of a regulative ideal (such as "love thy neighbor as thyself") to say (with, e.g., Sanders 1997) that it cannot fully be reached in practice. It is an appropriate criticism of such an ideal to say that aiming at it produces ill effects in utility, justice, or other values, or that aiming at an ideal that cannot fully be achieved in practice itself produces ill effects. (See Christiano 1996b for a good critique of making only deliberation the basis for legitimacy.)

21. See Allen 1970 and Evans and Boyte 1986 on "free space"; Mansbridge 1990, 1995a, on deliberative enclaves; Fraser [1992] 1997 on subaltern counterpublics; Scott 1990 on sequestered spaces; and Johnson 1997 for an interpretation of Foucault as searching for spaces of concrete freedom.

22. Freedom in deliberation might also include what John Rawls (1971) called "the worth of liberty," but I categorize those considerations under equality.

23. Young (1990), Fraser [1992] 1997), and Mansbridge (1990, 1995a), among others, address the institutional requirements that usually increase equality in deliberation. See Maier 1953 and Hastie 1993 on encouraging minority voices in deliberation. The question of inclusion involves norms regarding the boundaries of the polity (Dahl 1956, 64–67). Without putting bounds on the polity, the maxim "What affects all should be decided by all" could entail weighting the power of individuals in a decision (including their capacity to block consensus and therefore retain the status quo) by the degree to which the decision would affect them.

24. For the effect of equality in opening an arena for the authority of the better argument, see Habermas [1962] 1989, 36; for deliberation not requiring equal influence, see Mansbridge [1980] 1983, esp. 235–44, and more recently Warren 1996 and Brighouse 1996, 125. When Cohen (1989, 22) uses the term "equal voice" as a requirement for participants in legitimate deliberation, he presumably does not mean to imply equal numbers of words from each participant or an equal effect on the outcome. The term "equal voice" does not as yet have an exact or even a frequently stipulated meaning in democratic theory. A new generation of theorists has recently begun to tackle the formidable problems involved in formulating a concept of equality congruent with deliberative ideals. In their excellent essay on the subject, Knight and Johnson's most challengeable argument is that "deliberation requires equal capacity to advance persuasive claims," including "the ability to reason, articulate ideas, etc." (1998, 281). One could, it

is true, argue for such an ideal, stressing its regulative and unachievable side, on the grounds of full agency, self-development, and the precisely faithful representation of one's interests in deliberation. But it is not clear that equality in these capacities is required for deliberation or even deliberative equality. Many participants in deliberation might prefer Christiano's formulation, in which although "I have a great interest in having my views expressed . . . it is not essential that I do the expressing" (1996a, 259). Christiano's further formulation, that for equality to prevail in deliberation "equal time should be given" to different opinions, is, however, overly mechanical, unsuited to how thinking and deliberation actually work (when one point may be made well in five words and another may require 500). Bohman's (1996) institutional suggestions for furthering equality in deliberation are more persuasive than his analysis of the normative ideal (see 107, 113, 122, 124, 126, 131, for differing formulations of that ideal).

25. Legitimate influence does not encompass manipulation (getting others to agree to positions against their deepest interests through persuasion that has the external form of "the better argument"). Manipulation is illegitimate in any democratic deliberation, including everyday talk.

26. See Mansbridge 1992b, 1997; Lindblom 1990, 32; Barber 1984, 174; Knight and Johnson 1998, 284.

27. Habermas [1962] 1989. Dewey ([1926] 1994) also wanted "The Public" to "form itself" (31), "define and express its interests" (146), and become "organized" (28), in contrast to the "mass," which he saw as "scattered, mobile and manifold" (146), forming "too many publics" (126). See also Barber 1984.

28. For an invigorating skepticism on transformation, see Rosenblum 1998; also Knight and Johnson 1994.

29. By 1992, Habermas had borrowed from Nancy Fraser ([1992] 1997) the idea that the "general" public sphere consists of both a "strong" public sphere that engages in making binding decisions and a "weak" public sphere that engages exclusively in opinion-formation and consists of "overlapping, subcultural publics" that can form "collective identities" ([1992] 1996, 307–8, esp. n. 26). I argue here that the weak public sphere should include the full range of everyday talk on matters that the public should discuss. This weak public sphere is responsible for the "informal opinion-formation that prepares and influences political decision making" (171). As the realm of "opinion-formation," it differs from the realm of "will-formation," that is, the formal arena making binding decisions (314).

30. Habermas [1962] 1989, 25. Although these two criteria of coming together to form a public and critical reasoning do not exclude nonbinding forums such as the coffeehouse, they might seem to exclude everyday talk. On the first criterion, informal everyday talk itself can "pull [] together the scattered critical potentials" of the public (Habermas [1962] 1989, 382). Ideas, loosed upon a population by individuals linked with social movements, governments, a differentiated media and other sources of intellectual ferment, do some of the required "pulling together." Whether the group then forms a "public" raises a contested question. My portrayal of the public sphere intentionally blunts the critical edge of both Dewey's conception of the "Public" (see note 27 above) and Habermas's

ideal public sphere (which should produce a transformation from "private person" to "citizen") on the grounds that if these concepts require the citizenry to aim at a common good (even while disagreeing, sometimes violently, on that good), they do not define the only appropriate ends and if they do not require such an aim their meaning is ambiguous. On the second criterion, "critical consideration" of appropriate reasons and emotions seems a better requirement for a public sphere (see above, pp. 225–26), particularly if that consideration encompasses forms of deliberative shorthand, such as entire arguments summed up in a word, rules of thumb, and other time-and cognition-saving heuristics (Popkin 1991).

31. Gutmann and Thompson do link the binding quality of decisions to their justifiability. The decisions they analyze "are collectively binding, and they should therefore be justifiable, as far as possible, to everyone bound by them" (13). However, how one comes to be "bound" is not fully clear. Gutmann and Thompson may, like Rawls, base a citizen's duty to obey the law solely on the near-justice of the overall constitutional system, provided that the law in question does not exceed certain limits of injustice. This stance would be congruent with their explicitly rejecting the idea that deliberative democracy will necessarily produce a just outcome (18), and also explicitly rejecting the idea that an outcome is legitimate if the process that produced it was legitimate (200). Most importantly, they reject the dichotomy that asks "whether democratic procedures have priority over just outcomes or just outcomes over democratic procedures" (27). Rather, "neither the principles that define the process of deliberation [the "conditions of deliberation," i.e. the principles of reciprocity, publicity and accountability] nor the principles that constitute its content [the "content of deliberation," i.e. the principles of basic liberty, basic opportunity, and fair opportunity] have priority in a deliberative democracy. Both interact dynamically in ways that overcome the dichotomy between procedure and outcome" (27).

It is not easy to parse out the relation of these six dynamically interacting principles to whether or not a law that results from a given deliberation is justified. In most of the argument in the book, justifiability lies along a spectrum, so that the "more nearly the conditions [that is, the principles of reciprocity, publicity and accountability] are satisfied, the more nearly justifiable are the results likely to be" (17). But some sections of the book suggest a more either/or structure, in which if one or more of any of the principles is violated, the results of the deliberation are not justified. For example, "liberty and opportunity join reciprocity, publicity and accountability as the constitutional principles of a deliberative democracy" (199; also 201), while constitutional principles are "standards that public officials and citizens *must not* violate in the making of public policy in order that those policies can be provisionally justified to the citizens who are bound by them" (199, emphasis added). This sounds as if justifiability falls upon violation of any one of the six principles. This interpretation is strengthened by their statement that "public policies that violate [a constitutional principle] are *not justifiable*, even if they are enacted in a process that otherwise satisfies the conditions of deliberation" (199–200, emphasis added). On the other hand, these strong either/or sentences all appear in the section on liberty and opportunity. They may well therefore apply not to all six principles but only to the three principles that constitute the "content" of deliberation, namely liberty, opportunity and fair opportunity. This counter-interpretation is strengthened not only by the context but also by recognizing that part of the role of these "content" principles is to act in analogy with rights or other forms of priority, constraining (199, 229, 354, 355), restraining (209) and ruling out (225) certain actions within and resulting from deliberation. Yet if the second three principles (liberty, opportunity and fair opportunity) have a stronger either/or role, making policies that violate them "not justifiable," this difference from the first three principles is not spelled out. Guttman and Thompson state far more weakly that each of the six principles constrains and restrains all the others (355), although the content principles are "more constraining" than the conditions principles (199).

32. For past concern for everyday talk, see n. 15 above. For the current literature on deliberation see citations in Gutmann and Thompson, and more recently, Weithman 1995; Bohman 1996; Bohman and Rehg eds. 1998; Elster ed. 1998; and Herzog 1998, chap. 4.

References

Allen, Pamela. 1970. *Free Space: A Perspective on the Small Group in Women's Liberation.* New York: Times Change Press; shorter version reprinted in Anne Koedt, Ellen Levine and Anita Rapone, eds., *Radical Feminism* (New York: Quadrangle Press, 1973, pp. 271–9).

Applbaum, Arthur Isak. 1992. "Democratic Legitimacy and Official Discretion." *Philosophy and Public Affairs* 21:240–74.

Arendt, Hannah. 1965. *On Revolution.* New York: Viking.

Bachrach, Peter. 1974. "Interest, Participation, and Democratic Theory." In *Participation in Politics: NOMOS XVI,* ed. J. Roland Pennock and John W. Chapman. New York: Lieber-Atherton.

Bachrach, Peter, and Morton Baratz. 1963. "Decisions and Non-Decisions: An Analytical Framework." *American Political Science Review* 57: 632–42.

Barber, Benjamin R. 1984. *Strong Democracy: Participatory Politics for a New Age.* Berkeley: University of California Press.

Beiner, Ronald. 1983. *Political Judgement.* London: Methuen.

Benhabib, Seyla. [1987] 1988. "The Generalized and Concrete Other." In *Feminism as Critique,* ed. Seyla Benhabib and Ducilla Cornell. Minneapolis: University of Minnesota Press.

———. 1991. *Situating the Self.* New York: Routledge.

———. 1994. "Deliberative Rationality and Models of Democratic Legitimacy." *Constellations* 1:26–52.

Bessette, Joseph M. 1994. *The Mild Voice of Reason: Deliberative Democracy and American National Government.* Chicago: University of Chicago Press.

Bohman, James. 1996. *Public Deliberation.* Cambridge: MIT Press.

Bohman, James, and William Rehg, eds. 1998. *Deliberative Democracy.* Cambridge: MIT Press.

Brighouse, Harry. 1996. "Egalitarianism and the Equal Availability of Political Influence." *Journal of Political Philosophy* 4:118–41.

Bury, J. P. [1920] 1932. *The Idea of Progress.* New York: Macmillan.

Christiano, Thomas. 1996a. "Deliberative Equality and the Democratic Order." In *Political Order: NOMOS XXXVIII*, ed. Ian Shapiro and Russell Hardin. New York: New York University Press.

———. 1996b. *The Rule of the Many: Fundamental Issues in Democratic Theory.* Boulder, Colorado: Westview Press.

Cohen, Joshua. 1989. "Deliberation and Democratic Legitimacy." In *The Good Polity: Normative Analysis of the State*, ed. Alan Hamlin and Philip Pettit. Oxford: Basil Blackwell.

Dahl, Robert A. 1956. *After the Revolution?* New Haven: Yale University Press.

———. 1979. "Procedural Democracy." In *Philosophy, Politics and Society*, ed. Peter Laslett and James Fishkin New Haven: Yale University Press.

———. 1989. *Democracy and Its Critics.* New Haven: Yale University Press.

Dewey, John. [1926] 1994. *The Public and Its Problems.* Athens: Swallow Press/ Ohio University Press.

Dietz, Mary G. 1985. "Citizenship with a Feminist Face: The Problem with Maternal Thinking." *Political Theory* 13:19–37.

Elshtain, Jean Bethke. 1981. *Public Man, Private Woman: Women in Social and Political Thought.* Princeton: Princeton University Press.

Elster, Jon. 1998. "Deliberation and Constitution Making." In *Deliberative Democracy*, ed. Jon Elster. Cambridge: Cambridge University Press.

Elster, Jon, ed., 1998. *Deliberative Democracy.* Cambridge: Cambridge University Press.

Estlund, David M. 1993. "Who's Afraid of Deliberative Democracy? On the Strategic/Deliberative Dichotomy in Recent Constitutional Jurisprudence." *Texas Law Review* 71:1437–77.

Etzioni, Amitai. 1996. *The New Golden Rule.* New York: Basic Books.

Evans, Sara M., and Harry C. Boyte. 1986. *Free Spaces.* New York: Harper & Row.

Foucault, Michel. 1982. "The Subject and Power." Afterword in Hubert Dreyfus and Paul Rabinow, *Michel Foucault: Beyond Structuralism and Hermeneutics.* Chicago: University of Chicago Press.

Fraser, Nancy. [1992] 1997. "Rethinking the Public Sphere." In *Justice Interruptus.* New York: Routledge.

Gutmann, Amy, and Dennis Thompson. 1996. *Democracy and Disagreement.* Cambridge: Harvard University Press.

Habermas, Jürgen. [1962] 1989. *The Structural Transformation of the Public Sphere.* Trans. Thomas Burger and Frederick Lattimore. Cambridge: MIT Press.

———. [1973] 1975. *Legitimation Crisis.* Trans. Thomas McCarthy. Boston: Beacon Press.

———. [1974] 1979. *Communication and the Evolution of Society.* Trans. Thomas McCarthy. Boston: Beacon Press.

————. [1976] 1985. "Hannah Arendt's Communications Concept of Power." In *Philosophical-Political Profiles*, trans. Frederick G. Lawrence. Cambridge, Mass.: MIT Press.

————. [1992] 1996. *Between Facts and Norms.* Trans. William Rehg. Cambridge: MIT Press.

Hainisch, Carol. 1970. "The Personal is Political." In *Notes from the Second Year: Women's Liberation, Major Writings of the Radical Feminists*, ed., Shulamith Firestone and Anne Koedt. New York: Radical Feminists.

Harris, Angela. 1990. "Race and Essentialism in Legal Theory." *Stanford Law Review* 42:581–616.

Hastie, Reid, ed. 1993. *Inside the Juror.* Cambridge: Cambridge University Press.

Herzog, Don. 1998. *Poisoning the Minds of the Lower Orders.* Princeton: Princeton University Press.

Johnson, James. 1997. "Communication, Criticism, and the Postmodern Consensus." *Political Theory* 25:559–83.

Knight, Jack, and James Johnson. 1994. "Aggregation and Deliberation: On the Possibility of Democratic Legitimacy." *Political Theory* 22:277–96.

————. 1998. "What Sort of Political Equality Does Democratic Deliberation Require?" In *Deliberative Democracy*, ed. James Bohman and William Rehg. Cambridge: MIT Press.

Kochman, Thomas. 1981. *Black and White Styles in Conflict.* Chicago: University of Chicago Press.

Lindblom, Charles E. 1990. *Inquiry and Change: The Troubled Attempt to Understand and Shape Society.* New Haven: Yale University Press.

MacKinnon, Catharine A. 1989. *Toward a Feminist Theory of the State.* Cambridge: Harvard University Press.

Maier, Norman. 1953. "An Experimental Test of the Effects of Training on Discussion Leadership." *Human Relations* 6:161–73.

Manin, Bernard. 1987. "On Legitimacy and Political Deliberation." *Political Theory* 15:338–68.

Mansbridge, Jane. [1980] 1983. *Beyond Adversary Democracy.* Chicago: University of Chicago Press.

————. 1988. "The Equal Opportunity to Exercise Power." In *Equality of Opportunity*, ed. Norman E. Bowie. Boulder, Colo.: Westview Press.

————. 1990. "Feminism and Democracy." *American Prospect* 1: 127–36.

————. 1992a. "A Deliberative Theory of Interest Representation." In *The Politics of Interests*, ed. Mark P. Petracca. Boulder, Colo.: Westview Press.

————. 1992b. "Self-Transformation within the Envelope of Power." Paper delivered at the annual meeting of the American Political Science Association, Chicago, Ill., Sept. 2.

————. 1995a. "Using Power/Fighting Power: The Polity." In *Democracy and Difference*, ed. Seyla Benhabib. Princeton: Princeton University Press.

————. 1995b. "What Is the Feminist Movement?" In *Feminist Organizations: Harvest of the New Women's Movement*, ed. Myra Marx Ferree and Patricia Yancey Martin. Philadelphia: Temple University Press, 1995.

————. 1997a. "Activism Writ Small; Deliberation Writ Large." Paper delivered at the annual meeting of the American Political Science Association, Washington, D.C., August 28.

————. 1997b. "The Many Faces of Representation," Working Paper, Politics Research Group, John F. Kennedy School of Government, Harvard University.

————. 1999. "You're Too Independent!" In *Race, Class and Culture*, ed. Michele Lamont. New York: Russell Sage.

Mansbridge, Jane and Susan Moller Okin. 1993. "Feminism." In *A Companion to Contemporary Political Philosophy* ed. Robert E. Goodin and Philip Petit. Oxford: Blackwell.

Mill, John Stuart. 1840. "Coleridge." *London and Westminster Review*, March.

Minow, Martha. 1987. "Foreword to the Supreme Court 1986 Term." *Harvard Law Review* 101: 10–95.

Nussbaum, Martha Craven. 1995. "Emotions and Women's Capabilities." In *Women, Culture, and Development*, ed. Martha Craven Nussbaum and Johnathan Glover. Oxford: Oxford University Press.

Okin, Susan Moller. 1990. *Justice, Gender and the Family*. New York: Basic Books.

Pitkin, Hannah. 1981. "Justice: On Relating Public and Private." *Political Theory* 9: 327–52.

Popkin, Samuel. 1991. *The Reasoning Voter*. Chicago: University of Chicago Press.

Rawls, John. 1971. *A Theory of Justice*. Cambridge: Harvard University Press.

Rorty, Amélie Oksenberg. 1985. "Varieties of Rationality, Varieties of Emotion." *Social Science Information* 2: 343–53.

Rosenblum, Nancy L. 1998. *Membership and Morals: The Personal Uses of Pluralism in America*. Princeton: Princeton University Press.

Sanders, Lynn M. 1997. "Against Deliberation." *Political Theory* 25: 347–76.

Scott, James C. 1990. *Domination and the Arts of Resistance: Hidden Transcripts*. New Haven: Yale University Press.

Stoker, Laura. 1992. "Interests and Ethics in Politics." *American Political Science Review* 86: 369–80.

Unger, Roberto. 1987. *Social Theory: Its Situation and Its Task*. Cambridge: Cambridge University Press.

Verba, Sidney, Kay Lehman Schlozman, and Henry G. Brady. 1996. *Voice and Equality*. Cambridge: Harvard University Press.

Walzer, Michael. 1983. *Spheres of Justice*. New York: Basic Books.

Warren, Mark. 1996. "Deliberative Democracy and Authority." *American Political Science Review* 90: 46–60.

Weithman, Paul H. 1995. "Contractualist Liberalism and Deliberative Democracy." *Philosophy and Public Affairs* 24: 320–40.

Williams, Bernard. 1962. "The Idea of Equality." In *Philosophy, Politics and Society*, ed. Peter Laslett and W. G. Runciman. Oxford: Blackwell.

Wolin, Sheldon S. 1960. *Politics and Vision*. Boston: Little, Brown.

————. 1996. "Fugitive Democracy." In *Democracy and Difference*, ed. Seyla Benhabib. Princeton, N.J.: Princeton University Press.

Yankelovich, Daniel. 1991. *Coming to Public Judgment.* Syracuse, N.Y.: Syracuse University Press.

Young, Iris Marion. 1987. "Impartiality and the Civic Public." In *Feminism as Critique: On the Politics of Gender,* ed. Seyla Benhabib and Drucilla Cornell. Minneapolis: University of Minnesota Press.

———. 1990. *Justice and the Politics of Difference.* Princeton: Princeton University Press.

———. 1996. "Communication and the Other: Beyond Deliberative Democracy." In *Democracy and Difference,* ed. Seyla Benhabib. Princeton, N.J.: Princeton University Press.

———. 1997. "Assymetrical Reciprocity: On Moral Respect, Wonder, and Enlarged Thought." *Constellations* 3: 340–63.

PART III

Reply to the Critics

16

Democratic Disagreement

AMY GUTMANN AND DENNIS THOMPSON

What is the value of deliberative democracy? What are its limits? The thoughtful commentaries in this volume help us answer these questions more fully than we did in *Democracy and Disagreement*. The first group of commentators calls into question the desirability of deliberation. In reply, we develop our views about the value of deliberation. The second group agrees that deliberation is desirable, and some of these commentators even call for a greater role for deliberation than we defend. In reply, we examine the limits of deliberation. Although we cannot address every point made by every commentator, we try to address the most challenging issues and to proceed throughout in the spirit of deliberative democracy, seeking agreement where it is possible and maintaining mutual respect where it is not.

The Role of Deliberation

Before turning to the individual responses, we need to clarify a fundamental distinction between the principles and the practice of deliberative democracy. In doing so, we show that the practice of deliberation is not sufficient and not always necessary to constitute the principles of deliberative democracy.

Insufficient Practice

Our theory of deliberative democracy expresses a set of principles that prescribe fair terms of cooperation. The most important principle is reciprocity, which says that citizens owe one another justifications for the laws they collectively enact. Other principles specify terms of cooperation that satisfy reciprocity. The theory is "deliberative" because the terms of cooperation take the form of reasons that citizens or their accountable representatives give to one another in an ongoing process of mutual justification.

The practice of deliberation also seeks to realize the root value of reciprocity that should prevail among democratic citizens. Citizens who have effective opportunities to deliberate treat one another not merely as objects who are to be judged by theoretical principles but also as subjects who can accept or reject the reasons given for the laws and policies that mutually bind them. The reasons are not to be regarded as binding unless they are presented to citizens who have the chance to consider and reject them either directly or through their accountable representatives in a public forum. But passing the test of deliberation is no guarantee of justifiability; the policy may still not be right, because deliberative democracy expresses a set of principles, not only a practice.

The principles of deliberation are a powerful critical tool for challenging the actual practice of deliberation—both the substance of policies and the process by which they are made. Consider Oregon's experience in setting priorities for its publicly funded health care under Medicaid in the early 1990s. The priorities list of the Oregon Health Services Commission, based mainly on utilitarian cost-benefit calculations, provoked much justifiable criticism (capping a tooth ranked much higher than an appendectomy). The commission then began consulting with people who were previously excluded from the priority-setting process. Community meetings were organized at which participants were "asked to think and express themselves in the first person plural . . . as members of a statewide community for whom health care has a shared value." Eventually, after still more deliberation, the commission presented a revised list, which was an improvement over the original plan. However, the commission could not correct the most serious flaw in the scheme: because only the poor were eligible, only the poor had to sacrifice to improve the list. When the deliberation continued in the legislature, the legislators saw what treatments on the list would have to be eliminated under the projected budget, and they managed to find more resources by increasing the total budget for health care for the poor.

Judged by deliberative principles, the deliberative practice in Oregon improved the situation of some poor citizens compared to that of the earlier process and policy. The process forced officials and citizens to confront a serious problem that they had previously evaded and to confront it in a more reciprocal ("first-person plural") spirit. As a result, even the basic unfairness in the policy—its failure to secure for poor citizens the basic opportunity of adequate health care—was somewhat lessened. But the deliberative practice did not produce a policy that fully provided the basic opportunity of health care for Oregon's poor citizens (or, alternatively, a decision that they were not entitled to this basic opportunity).

Neither did the deliberative practice in Oregon live up to reciprocity's requirement that citizens be effectively represented, especially those citizens whose lives are most affected by the decisions reached in the deliberations. To the extent that the deliberation conducted by the Oregon Commission excluded the poor, who would be most affected by its policy, it failed to be fully reciprocal and was therefore less legitimate. The practice of deliberation was in this case, as it is in general, insufficient to constitute deliberative democracy. The most defensible response to this serious problem is the more inclusive deliberation that reciprocity requires, not more unaccountable expert decision-making, as is implied by Ian Shapiro's call for "firm action from above." Reciprocity is a response to the incomplete moral and empirical understanding possessed by a single citizen or group of citizens. Exclusive deliberation by unaccountable experts will generally fail to produce a mutually justifiable policy.

Deliberative principles also serve as guides for making political practice not only more inclusive but also more deliberative. Because the principles can be satisfied to greater or lesser degree, they can help identify and assess changes designed to improve the practice of deliberation. An accurate assessment of a deliberative practice requires an evaluation of not just one phase of a process in isolation (such as the commission's deliberations) but of all related phases (including, for example, the legislature's later appropriation of new funds). That the commission's process exposed a serious injustice that the legislature later acted to correct is therefore not a "fortunate externality," as Shapiro suggests, but an integral and desirable part of the practice of deliberative democracy. The reiterative character of the deliberative process in Oregon enabled citizens and officials to criticize the defects in both the process and results and to propose changes to improve both at each stage, including the last.

Unnecessary Practice

Deliberative democrats do not consider the hypothetical justification proposed by some social contract theorists to be sufficient: justifications must be actually given at some stage in a political process. But there is no reason that every single law and public policy must be publicly deliberated, and there are good reasons of economy and competence that argue against universal deliberation. Taking such reasons into account, citizens and officials may abridge or omit deliberation in making some decisions. Deliberative democracy requires only that the decision not to deliberate be made publicly and by agents who are accountable. Citizens or their accountable representatives decide deliberatively the circumstances and nature of the policies that are not to be deliberatively decided. Experts on health care, for example, might conduct a (nondeliberative) empirical inquiry in Oregon and present their conclusions to citizens (or their accountable representatives). Citizens or their representatives could then decide deliberatively how to proceed, whether to engage in deliberation themselves or adopt some other procedure.

Deliberative democrats therefore do not have to claim, as Shapiro seems to assume they do, that the only legitimate way to set health care priorities in Oregon was through a deliberative process. We think the actual process came closer to satisfying not only the deliberative principles presented in *Democracy and Disagreement* but also the principles defended by most of our commentators than did the top-down approach that he evidently favors, which in this case produced the first set of objectionable priorities.

But it is partly an empirical question, as Frederick Schauer suggests, as to what extent deliberative practices produce deliberative results. Deliberative standards such as accountability can guide such empirical work. Schauer himself relies on these standards in describing the potential pitfalls of various imperfect decision-making methods: decision-making by experts, for example, may undermine accountability. But the findings of an empirical investigation, even if they were to show that a deliberative process is less likely to produce the correct result in certain cases, would not settle the matter. Other values such as reciprocity and accountability may legitimately influence citizens' choice of a decision-making process. One could of course call for still more empirical investigation to see if deliberation is the best way to decide whether to deliberate. But at some point in a democracy, citizens and their accountable representatives have to decide how to decide.

The Value of Deliberation

Although virtually all of our commentators see some value in deliberation, the first group has serious doubts about whether it should have the central role in democracy that we propose. Some also argue that it may undermine other important democratic values.

Deliberation for Its Own Sake (Schauer)

Schauer questions whether, even on its own terms, deliberation is as desirable as we suggest. He presents his argument in the form of a dilemma that he thinks our theory cannot resolve. Insofar as our theory of deliberative democracy is to be applied under ideal conditions, deliberation, he thinks, is unnecessary. But insofar as the theory is applied under nonideal conditions, deliberation is often undesirable. Under ideal conditions, Schauer believes, all disagreement would be reasonable—"untainted by prejudice, selfishness, and related pathologies"—and deliberation would therefore not be needed to produce reasonable results. Almost any decision procedure would do as well.

But deliberation serves purposes other than merely eliminating unreasonable disagreement. As we discuss in *Democracy and Disagreement* (41–43), laws that are adopted after mutual consideration of conflicting moral claims are more likely to be legitimate than those enacted after only strategic calculation of the relative strength of competing political interests. Such enhanced legitimacy would be valuable even under ideal conditions. Schauer may assume that under ideal conditions, citizens would be so public-spirited that they would readily accept as legitimate any decision within the range of reasonable disagreement, even if they never engaged in deliberation over the merits of decisions with which they disagreed. But limited generosity is not the only source of moral disagreement. Scarce resources, conflicts among moral values themselves, and incomplete moral understanding, as we show in *Democracy and Disagreement* (18–26), give rise to deep and persistent disagreement. Schauer surely would not define ideal conditions so as to exclude all of these circumstances, and so long as they exist, deliberation would still have plenty of work to do.

But there is the other horn of the dilemma: is deliberation undesirable under nonideal conditions that prevail in actual democracies now? "A decision to prefer a talk-based decision procedure," Schauer warns, "runs the risk . . . of producing less rather than more . . . idealized deliberation." (Shapiro makes a similar point when he argues that "as deliberation operates on the ground that Americans increasingly inhabit, it is often an obstacle to providing . . . [basic opportunity] goods.")

Some kinds of talk, including some of the dominant forms in today's political discourse, do not advance justice or democracy and may be worse than other procedures. But the principles of deliberative democracy provide ways of *criticizing* these kinds of talk and of proposing political practices that are alternatives to deliberation. By contrast, procedural theories concentrate mainly on voting and other similar practices and thereby neglect the problem of political discourse.

Even if deliberative talk is not all there is to deliberative democracy, do we expect too much from its use in politics? Schauer acknowledges that we do not expect talk alone to resolve moral problems in politics. The form of deliberation that we defend is constrained by both the content and the condition principles, which are each independently valuable. If it could be shown that among available procedures, judicial review best protects certain rights required by the principle of basic liberty, then our conception of deliberative democracy could recommend judicial review in those cases. It would of course take an extensive empirical investigation to determine in what kinds of cases judicial review (or any other procedure) does in fact best protect basic liberty today. But because not only facts but also values (such as accountability) are centrally at stake, no empirical investigation would be sufficient. Furthermore, any conclusion that courts rather than legislatures should decide certain kinds of cases would still have to be justified to the citizens who would be bound by the judicial decisions.

Deliberation versus Power (Shapiro)

Shapiro argues that deliberative democracy attends "too little to the degree to which moral disagreements in politics are shaped by differences of interest and power." As a consequence, "what is often needed is not widespread deliberation but firm action from above to protect the vulnerable." But who should take this action from above, and on what principles should they act? If the actors from above are unaccountable philosophers or politicians who use their power to impose their own conceptions of justice, Shapiro's alternative begins to look less like a critique of deliberative democracy than like a rejection of democracy itself. In the politics of power, "firm action from above" is especially likely to favor those who already have power. If Shapiro assumes that the actors from above are accountable and act on principles they try to justify to their fellow citizens, then his alternative is hardly an alternative at all. It is consistent with deliberative democracy. When action from above is the only means of securing basic liberty and opportunity for the most vulnerable citizens, then deliberative democrats should favor it; but they and those who practice it must still justify this action, if not prospectively then at least retrospectively, to those who are bound by it.

Shapiro sometimes writes as if democratic theorists must take as given the pattern of underlying interests. That would be the most natural consequence of making power and interest the sovereign principle of a theory. But Shapiro is also prepared to make his own moral judgments, some quite critical of the actual distributions of power that exist in modern democracies. As long as he offers his moral judgments merely for consideration by his fellow theorists, he can continue to regard politics as only a realm of power. But if (as he seems to assume) his judgments are worthy of having some influence on political practice, he should be prepared (as deliberative democrats urge) to justify those judgments to his fellow citizens, who would be bound by them.

Shapiro acknowledges that deliberation does not always ignore differences of power and interests and may even help to bring them to public attention. But he sees little value in the capacity of deliberation to expose differences in interest because he neglects the possibility that it can alter what he calls the "underlying interests." We do not claim that it does so alone, only that it is often a necessary step in any effort to change the prevailing patterns of power. Deliberating about campaign finance reform, for example, brings to light the power of money in American politics. It also exposes the underlying interests of incumbents and the powerful people and groups who oppose any reform. Debate about campaign finance reform in the United States falls short of the deliberative ideal partly because political incumbents, powerful lobbying groups, and commercial media all find it in their interest to prevent more and better deliberation on the subject. Without the exposure of these interests that deliberation encourages, the chances of reform would be even less than they are now.

In *Democracy and Disagreement*, we describe several cases in which deliberation exposed differences in interests and led to a better outcome, but one is especially worth recounting. It also shows that the content of deliberation need not exclude emotional appeals or forceful rhetoric. The deliberation provoked by Senator Carol Moseley-Braun, when she threatened a filibuster on the floor of the Senate over what was previously thought to be a routine matter of renewing a patent on the Confederate flag insignia, brought profound differences to light that had previously been ignored by many members and citizens alike. "On this issue," Moseley-Braun argued, "there can be no consensus. It is an outrage. It is an insult. It is absolutely unacceptable to me and to millions of Americans, black and white, that we would put the imprimatur of the United States Senate on a symbol of this kind of idea." Her speech stimulated a debate that changed senators' minds, or at least their public positions. Over a three-hour period of deliberation, twenty-seven senators reversed their earlier vote, defeating the amendment seventy-five to twenty-five. Senator Howell Heflin said that his ancestors "might be spinning in their graves" but that he would reverse himself and join Moseley-Braun in voting against the Confederate flag because "we must get racism behind us."

It might be said in reply that Heflin's underlying interests must have been on the side of voting with Moseley-Braun. But such a reply would turn Shapiro's claim into a tautology. If deliberation leads to changed positions, they are assumed to be in line with underlying interests. If it does not change positions, then the underlying interests are assumed to have triumphed over deliberation. In either case, deliberation virtually by definition cannot get any credit, whether or not it had an effect. It is both empirically and normatively more fruitful to keep open the possibility that underlying interests can change and that the deliberation that reveals them may contribute to such change. Deliberation has an important role even if its main effect is to make it too embarrassing for, and therefore less in the interest of, powerful people to take racist positions in public.

But on some issues, Shapiro believes, deliberation is not merely powerless but also dangerous. "Intense—particularly religious—differences" are best "kept out of organized politics as much as possible" because of their "explosive potential." The strongest constitutional case for removing these differences from politics, Shapiro suggests, is in this sense pragmatic. It is not that courts are better able to resolve such differences but that no democratic political body is capable of doing so on a principled basis, as deliberative democracy requires. That the Constitution prohibits the establishment of religion shows, Shapiro thinks, that American democracy recognizes that religious differences cannot be settled on a principled basis, as deliberative democrats seem to suggest. Shapiro allows that there may be a deliberatively democratic reply to this pragmatic case, but he notes that we do not offer one in our book. We can suggest here the form that a deliberative case for these constitutional protections would take.

The constitutional provisions protecting religion are better understood as deliberative agreements than as pragmatic bargains. Their deliberative character is reflected in the most common way of describing religious toleration in this country. Citizens are said to agree to disagree about their religious differences, not simply to ignore them. Furthermore, equal freedom for all religions is not the most likely result of a political bargain negotiated on the basis of relative power. The mutual assurance that Americans enjoy to agree to disagree about religious differences developed out of the extensive discussion that led up to the First Amendment and continued to shape laws and policies throughout history. Such deliberations helped create a political context in which American citizens today can reasonably believe that these constitutional protections are publicly justifiable to those who are bound by them.

Deliberative democrats are committed to "promoting attempts to resolve religious disagreements in the public sphere" only in the sense that the question of which disagreements should be so resolved is to be decided deliberatively. Where to draw the line between religious differences that should and those that should not be part of ongoing political debate is still a very live issue in American politics. It is, moreover, a live issue for moral reasons, which are neglected by any view that, like Shapiro's, would remove issues only because of their "explosive potential." As we show in the book in the case of abortion, the decision to take major issues such as those involving religion off the agenda is not neutral. It has effects on the moral positions of all parties to the dispute, and it requires a moral justification just as much as the decision to try to resolve the dispute in a public forum. The public debate about the place of religion continues today, and the outcome is not likely to be anything as simple as Shapiro's rule that intense religious differences should be kept out of politics "as much as possible." In light of this history of quite complex and intensely contested decisions, this rule is practically elusive at best, morally mistaken at worst.

Deliberation and Toleration (Galston)

The complexity of this continuing debate about the place of religion in politics is brought out well in William Galston's commentary. Galston thinks that toleration is the best way to deal with religious differences and also, by extension, with many other intense moral conflicts. But unlike Shapiro, who wants to keep religion out of politics for the sake of protecting politics, Galston wants politics to give religion more scope in private life for the sake of protecting religion. Also unlike Shapiro, he directly challenges on moral grounds our view that democracies should decide deliberatively what issues should be on the political agenda.

We agree with Galston that toleration is "a morally significant achievement." It is valuable in its own right and also provides the foundation on which democracies can develop other virtues of deliberative democracy, such as mutual respect (which is a more demanding form of agreeing to disagree). We would therefore no longer refer as we did in the book to "*mere* toleration," though we would still stand by the argument about abortion in which we used that phrase. Toleration alone cannot resolve the abortion controversy, as some liberals claim it can. Indeed, the abortion controversy offers strong evidence in support of the deliberative democratic idea that toleration is not sufficient. Mutual respect, which does not require agreement on the substance of an issue either, goes significantly beyond toleration in supporting the kind of constructive interaction with people that is necessary for the other virtues of democracy (which Galston himself favors) to flourish in the face of fundamental moral disagreement.

Our disagreement with Galston is not about whether toleration and mutual respect are important values but about precisely when citizens should agree to disagree rather than decide a controversial matter collectively on its merits, and how *this* disagreement can most justifiably be settled in politics. Galston argues, first, that citizens should agree to disagree more than deliberative democracy recommends, and second, that deliberation is therefore less important than deliberative democracy presumes. Even if Galston is right on the first point (which we do not think he is), the second does not follow. It presumes that deliberation is not necessary to determine when citizens should agree to disagree.

Our dispute with Galston on the "controversial curriculum" case (*Mozert v. Hawkins County Board of Education*) is itself an instance of what we call a deliberative disagreement. Galston disagrees with our conclusion, which supports the school board against fundamentalist parents who sought to exempt their children from basic reading classes. The parents, he suggests, could have presented an argument based on the reciprocity principle, which would have justified overturning the school board's decision. The argument that Galston offers on their behalf is better than the ones the parents or their advocates presented in the actual case. But the "fact" of the parents' belief is not itself sufficient, as Galston suggests it is, to conclude that a court must override the deliberative judgment of a democratically elected school board. Such a judicial decision would thereby set a precedent for requiring school boards to exempt all children from all parts of a public school curriculum that offend their parents' religious beliefs.

Galston's proposal represents not an alternative to deliberation but rather another argument that (like ours) deserves a hearing in a deliberative forum. He evidently would prefer a judicial resolution, but the validity of his argument for the parents does not depend on that preference. The argument he puts in the mouths of the fundamentalist parents may even be more effective in a meeting of a local school board than in a court of law. But even if his claim on behalf of the parents is right on the merits, he would need a further argument to overcome the objection that courts should not overturn the decisions of public school boards on matters of reasonable curricular requirements. Both his argument for the parents and his further claim that the courts should decide such questions—precisely because they are reasonable—give greater support to our appeal for more deliberation than to his plea for less.

If our defense of the school board's decision in the *Mozert* case implied that children were the mere creatures of the state, then our disagreement with Galston would be unreasonable. But our position, as Galston recognizes, affirms a sphere of parental authority that is not subject to state control. Galston's position, as we recognize, affirms a sphere of public authority that is not subject to parental control. Children are not the mere creatures of their parents, either. In the face of a deliberative disagreement of this kind, all of us (the parents, the school board, and theorists like Galston and us) have no morally justified alternative but to try to make our arguments in an actual deliberative process.

We should have made clearer in *Democracy and Disagreement* that there is a prior question to be answered before political decision-making on some issues begins: "Does the state possess the legitimate power to make collectively binding decisions on this issue?" If the answer is negative, "the question of how such decisions should be made is never reached." The value of personal integrity, for example, places limits on what government and society should demand of citizens, and what citizens should demand of one another. Because the deliberative democratic state is committed to protecting basic liberty as a constitutional right, as we argue, (230–72), it should not determine how or whether citizens worship, what ideas they profess or publish, whom they marry or with whom they live, whether they conceive children, and many other matters for which individual liberty is essential to respecting the integrity of persons.

Nevertheless, there is a question that is prior to Galston's question, and that is who should answer his question. In a successful deliberative democracy, this prior question will not be asked about many of the issues just mentioned. Citizens and officials will take for granted that basic liberty prevents government action. Prior understandings, cultural taboos, and institutional devices will check most tendencies to legislate in these areas. But democrats must assume that this question has been answered at some point, at least implicitly, by citizens or their accountable representatives, and deliberative democrats must assume further that it would be answered deliberatively if it became a genuine disagreement again. Galston himself appeals to constitutional values to defend religious freedom and other liberties that no government should violate. Those values must be interpreted—whether by the courts, the legislature, or citizens—and the interpretation ultimately becomes part of the political process, at least potentially subject to democratic deliberation.

The Bias of Deliberation (Simon)

What if some citizens object to the very idea of making decisions according to the principles of deliberation? William Simon argues that while we may make deliberation seem attractive for most theorists and most citizens, we neglect the people who find its demands biased against their moral and political commitments. He is particularly concerned about politically engaged religious fundamentalists and defenders of identity politics. Many members of these groups accept most of the principles of deliberation and try to offer arguments that are accessible to their fellow citizens who do not share their religious views. But Simon plausibly assumes that some religious citizens would reject deliberation, and then he appropriately asks how deliberative democrats should respond to them.

What can deliberative democrats say to those religious fundamentalists who believe that the revealed truth, to which only they and members of their church have access, requires them not to deliberate? They are of course free to take part or not in the deliberative process, but the critical question is whether the reasons they give can be justifications for legislation that would deny some basic liberties and opportunities to others who do not share their religious faith. Deliberative democrats can only engage with the fundamentalists' arguments and consider the strongest claims that can be made on their side. But ultimately we, like they (and Simon), must take a side in a political argument. Although there are many sides and none should be regarded as fixed forever, the one that is enacted into law should be justified in terms accessible to citizens who do not share the fundamentalists' faith.

What about citizens who reject deliberation not out of conviction but out of strategic motives? Simon warns against deliberating with people who are "simply not open to reflection," because "at best it could be a waste of time, and at worst you could help the person present himself to others as more reasonable than he is." But deliberative democrats following their own principles and practices are quite capable of exposing bad faith in politics, in just the way that Simon himself exposes the bad faith of some of the contributors to the debate over welfare reform. Simon's concerns about the bad faith in the welfare debate implies a need for not less but more deliberation about the issue. If his critique is to have some influence in actual democratic politics beyond the academic debates about welfare reform, it must find a place in the rough-and-tumble of actual political discourse, bad faith and all. Even if engaging in deliberation enables some people to present their motives in a more favorable light than they really merit, that result may be desirable. It is better than what typically happens in contemporary political discourse, in which participants and commentators far too readily assume bad faith on the part of their political opponents.

Proponents of identity politics, Simon argues, have especially good reasons to distrust deliberation. Identity groups "define and constitute themselves through the assertion of their claims" rather than by deliberating with their political opponents. We agree that creating solidarity and encouraging mobilization among the ranks of the politically disadvantaged are often first steps to bringing about more justice. But solidarity and successful mobilization of an identity group should not be confused with political success. If the followers of Malcolm X sought to change only their own minds and not "the white man's mind," then they let too many of their fellow citizens off the moral and political hook and gave up on securing respect for themselves and justice for their cause. It is generally a sign of hopelessness when a disadvantaged minority abandons the effort to seek support from people who do not share their group identity.

In contrast, Martin Luther King Jr.'s leadership of the civil rights movement exemplifies a politics of deliberative engagement. He mobilized African Americans around a moral cause that he publicly justified in reciprocal terms, appealing to principles that could move his country closer to a society with liberty and justice for all citizens. He practiced an economy of moral disagreement by publicly invoking values that all Americans could acknowledge as important—"citizenship rights" based on the "self-evident truth" that "all men are created equal." The rhetoric was certainly not parochial. He furthered the cause of civic integrity by calling on American citizens to live up to their professed principles, and he appealed to American leaders to live up to their constitutional commitments. A model of civic magnanimity, King did not find engaging in deliberation with those who were not African American threatening to African American identity.

Deliberative democracy therefore does not disrespect the "separateness of groups," but it does distrust the kind of separatist identity politics that Simon sympathetically describes (without firmly committing himself to defending it). More often than not, such politics is a woefully inadequate means of bringing about more justice for disadvantaged groups. Simon writes that he himself likes deliberative politics: "It's my kind of politics." Since he declines to take his own side in this particular argument, we take it for him.

Spheres of Deliberation (Walzer)

A deliberative democracy, as Michael Walzer points out, must include many activities besides deliberating—educating, organizing, mobilizing, demonstrating, bargaining, lobbying, campaigning, fund-raising, voting, and ruling. We also agree with Walzer that deliberation is not just another activity on the list—but for a reason that gives deliberation more prominence than he suggests. Deliberative democrats are not committed to making all political activities in all places at all times more deliberative, but they are committed to assessing all political activities by deliberative principles. Through deliberation, citizens can modify these other activities, and by doing so they can improve them—for example, by making bargaining, campaigning, voting, and ruling more public-spirited in both process and outcome. From this perspective, American democracy today suffers from a deliberative deficit (which Walzer himself has recognized in other writings), and its politics could be improved if citizens and their representatives were more often prepared to deliberatively assess the activities on Walzer's list.

Two general characteristics of politics cause Walzer to doubt that deliberation should have any place at all on his list of political activities: the "prevalence of inequality" and the "permanence of conflict." The first, he thinks, supports his objection that deliberation favors the interests of the powers-that-be. We addressed this kind of objection briefly in responding to Shapiro and Simon, and at greater length in *Democracy and Disagreement* (132–37, 301–6). But it is worth emphasizing that the principles of deliberative democracy do not prevent adopting any of the means that Walzer suggests for advancing the claims of the disadvantaged, and they provide positive reasons for advancing those claims. Furthermore, the principles imply that to the extent that the practice of deliberative democracy is characterized by unjust inequalities, its procedures and policies are less justified.

The other general characteristic Walzer mentions—the permanence of conflict—is in our view not an objection to deliberative democracy but a consideration in its favor. As we show in the book, the "persistence of moral disagreement" forms the basis for much of the argument for the need for deliberative democracy (18–26, 39–49), which in our view is as much concerned with living with continual conflict as with trying to resolve it. In face of this "endless return to . . . disagreements and conflicts," Walzer rejects deliberative democracy in favor of winning "whatever temporary victories are available." Winning "more people than the other side has" is "what makes the victory legitimate."

But this is not really an alternative to deliberative democracy. Walzer must be assuming that the victory takes place in a process that is otherwise just, as judged by standards other than the rule of the many. Walzer himself does not think majority rule justifies laws and policies when they deny basic liberties and opportunities to citizens for no reason other than that they happen to be in the minority. "It is not only . . . inclusiveness that makes for democratic government. Equally important is what we might call the rule of reasons." This cogent statement from Walzer's own *Spheres of Justice* (304) supports our conception of deliberative democracy.

The rule of reasons is too important to be left to hypothetical rulers. Good reasons are more likely to yield good laws when they inform not merely the arguments of academics but also the decisions of citizens. (Academic argument, which is not directed toward practical decision-making, should not be confused with political deliberation, which is.) Deliberative democracy denies that either the better argument or the greater number alone suffices to justify the exercise of coercive political power. Minority usurpation of democratic authority and majority tyranny are both unjust. Our defense of deliberative democracy is intended to show that democratic politics should be both inclusive and reasonable.

Deliberation by the Elite (Bell)

Is our deliberative democracy *too* inclusive? Daniel Bell prefers a version of democracy that would give a more prominent role in government to intellectual elites, who would be minimally accountable and could therefore better resist the pressures of populist democracy. Bell defends what he takes to be the true meaning of deliberative democracy by advocating an institution that he claims is both feasible and desirable: a Chinese-style "House of Scholars," whose members are selected on the basis of competitive examinations rather than competitive elections.

From Bell's perspective, our mistake is that we do not appreciate how difficult it would be to realize this kind of democracy in the United States, rather than in a country like China, where the traditional social understandings are more compatible with rule by an intellectual elite. Although Bell thinks we do not pay enough attention to questions of feasibility, our proposals in *Democracy and Disagreement* for making American democracy more deliberative (discussed below) are surely more feasible than creating a House of Scholars even in China, let alone any analogous institution in the United States.

Democracy and Disagreement concentrates on questions of desirability, and Bell's argument for the House of Scholars reinforces our view that these questions should be prior to those of feasibility. Bell makes the claim—which is partly empirical, partly normative—that "the examination process [for members of the House of Scholars] would help to ensure the selection of talented decision-makers," of more "talent and integrity" than those likely to be selected by democratic elections. But he fails to explain how the examination could test the kind of abilities that are central to defensible democratic decision-making. These abilities surely include moral as well as empirical judgment and, in a deliberative democracy, the reciprocal willingness to justify one's decisions to those affected by them.

Bell's conception of the House of Scholars implicitly rejects reciprocity as a basic principle of deliberative democracy. His scholars do not seem especially interested in justifying their decisions to anyone but their colleagues. Yet Bell never tries to show why reciprocity should not be a requirement of a deliberative democracy. That would in any case be a difficult task. He would have to demonstrate that coercive laws, policies, and institutions need not be justified to the people who are bound by them, either as a general proposition or as one that holds for the particular context of contemporary China.

Bell's defense of a House of Scholars serves an important although perhaps unintended purpose. It helps to distinguish our conception of deliberative democracy from those that emphasize deliberation at the expense of democracy. It makes clear that our deliberative democracy does not favor a politics of "elegant, nonadversarial, and informative" conversation, which advances the class interests of intellectuals. If that were a main aim of our deliberative democracy, the House of Scholars should be a desirable, if not a feasible, institutional addition to it. But such an institution is in principle incompatible with deliberative democracy as we understand and defend it. Our understanding aims at a society of free and equal citizens and requires principles of reciprocity, publicity, and accountability. It also welcomes inelegant, impassioned, and adversarial arguments (such as the one made by Moseley-Braun on the floor of the Senate) that are addressed to both the merits of the issue and the moral constituents of the deliberator. On our view, deliberative democracy should be no less democratic than deliberative.

Deliberation as Exclusion (Fish)

Stanley Fish denies that deliberation plays any positive role in politics and argues that it excludes positions with which its proponents disagree. Referring to our example of Senator Carol Moseley-Braun's speech against congressional endorsement of the Confederate flag, Fish writes that "the response of Senator Heflin and others on this occasion had nothing to do with argument, and everything to do with Mosley-Braun's success in painting her colleagues into an unhappy political corner." Fish insists that actions like Moseley-Braun's are strategic, not deliberative.

Fish's insistence depends entirely on the false dichotomy he has created between strategy and deliberation. They are not mutually exclusive. One of the brushes that Moseley-Braun used to paint some of her colleagues into a political corner was a deliberative argument: To put the Senate's imprimatur on a symbol of racism is morally wrong. The argument caused Heflin to change his vote and to publicly affirm that "we must get racism behind us." The argument would probably not have had this positive effect in a different political context, one in which electoral success depended generally on taking racist positions. But neither would the argument have succeeded if it had been purely strategic, asserting only a claim of interest and making no appeal to moral principle. Deliberative democrats judge political practices according to deliberative principles, but they do not condemn and indeed may recommend strategic action as long as it is consistent with these principles.

Fish thinks our conception of deliberative democracy excludes not only strategic politics but also moral arguments if they run against our substantive views. Deliberative democracy denies that some claims are a legitimate basis for coercive legislation, but it does not exclude those claims from public forums (as Fish seems to suggest). We argue that public policies based on a doctrine of racial inferiority, for example, are not mutually justifiable. We never suggest that "anyone who favors racial discrimination is just sick." We offer *reasons* for not counting such claims as a legitimate basis for legislation: racial discrimination violates reciprocity because it denies basic liberties and opportunities to people merely on the basis of their race.

We doubt that Fish would want to maintain that the reasons for extending equal rights to all human beings regardless of skin color are no better than the reasons offered for slavery and racial discrimination. Surely he does not think it is reasonable to deny some people the right to vote because of their race. If he were to hold that racial inferiority and civic equality are equally defensible, then his critique of deliberative democracy would undermine virtually all forms of democracy. But if he acknowledges that racial inferiority is not as mutually defensible as civic equality, then his critique undermines itself.

Fish tries to evade this dilemma by making a metalevel move: His views are simply his views, no more or less reasonable than ours. The move does not save his critique. The metalevel claim itself presupposes a shared perspective by which to judge whether reasonableness is an appropriate standard. Any such judgment, moreover, will include some moral considerations. Fish's critique trades on the presumption that the metalevel claim itself is reasonable, more reasonable than those he is rejecting. (So does his underlying assumption, which motivates much of the critique, that exclusion is an undesirable feature of democratic theory and practice.)

Fish's effort to debunk his opponents' claims to reasonableness is ultimately as self-defeating as his attempt to deny the substantive claims about racial discrimination. Fish's readers will be convinced only to the extent that they misunderstand him to be presenting reasonable arguments, which he must (as an honest and intelligent writer) deny he is doing. Once readers recognize that his rules of argument authorize him to say anything that helps him win, and winning is merely a matter of causing people to accept his view (whatever it happens to be), his arguments dissolve into self-assertion.

This kind of self-assertion is common enough in contemporary politics, but it is not a kind of politics that democrats, deliberative or otherwise, should wish to encourage. Or if they do, they would need to provide some arguments that could be accepted by their fellow citizens, and they would have entered again into the forums of deliberative democracy that invite the reasonable arguments that Fish resists.

Fish asserts that what deliberative democrats really mean by "reasonable" is "what [their] friends and [they] take to be so." Yet in *Democracy and Disagreement* we defend the pro-life position as reasonable, although it is not the position that we take to be the right one. We argue—against the views of many liberal philosophers and some of our friends—that the strongest available pro-life position begins with plausible premises, builds a logical argument on the basis of those premises, and arrives at a reasonable conclusion in favor of restricting the right to abortion.

Fish says our conception of deliberative democracy leaves people out of the conversation "not because they exhibit a character, logical, or cognitive flaw but because they don't believe what Gutmann and Thompson believe." Pro-life advocates do not believe what we believe about the rightness of legalizing abortion, yet we do not exclude them from the conversation or claim that they exhibit character, logical, or cognitive flaws. We advocate not only tolerating but also respecting them. We claim that our fundamental beliefs about the fetus's moral and constitutional status differ from theirs in a way that is for now irreconcilable.

If we are right about the abortion controversy, then Fish is wrong to characterize our conception of deliberative democracy as not respecting people whose political positions differ from our own. If we are wrong about the abortion controversy, then Fish is wrong to claim that reason cannot resolve any moral controversies in politics. Either way, Fish's critique—which should on its own terms be self-serving—turns out to be self-effacing.

Deliberation versus the Sovereign (Hardin)

Russell Hardin finds it "hard to imagine a theory of democracy . . . that would not require publicity and accountability on the part of officals." We welcome Hardin's agreement on these principles. Part of our defense of these principles in the book was to show that any adequate democratic theory should accept such principles. But the theorists whom we criticize in chapters 3 and 4 for implicitly or explicitly rejecting the implications of these principles are real enough. These principles are also more demanding than Hardin seems to recognize. They would, for example, constrain some forms of utilitarianism—

perhaps even Hardin's own. Citizens have not only preferences about, but also ideals of, what the political process should be. Many of these ideals cannot be easily accommodated within a utilitarian calculus, since they implicitly assume a process that does not treat all claims as preferences and in this respect is anti-utilitarian. The accountability principle is to this extent incompatible with this kind of utilitarianism.

Our objection to utilitarianism does not imply, as Hardin seems to think it does, that the values of deliberative democracy "trump" the values of util-itarianism. To criticize deliberative democracy for trying to trump other values is to confuse two quite different kinds of political theory (what may be called first and second order theories).[1] First-order theories like utilitarianism seek to resolve moral disagreement by rejecting alternative theories or principles with which they conflict. They measure their success by whether they resolve the conflict consistently on their own terms. Second-order theories like delibera-tive democracy deal with disagreement by accommodating first-order theories like utilitarianism that conflict with one another. They measure their success by the extent to which they can justify their proposed resolution and the remaining disagreement to all who must live with them. They may be called second-order because they are *about* other theories in the sense that they refer to first-order principles without affirming or denying their ultimate validity, and they can be held consistently without rejecting any of a wide range of moral principles expressed by first-order theories.

This distinction is more fundamental than the distinction between policy and institutional levels of analysis, with which Hardin is preoccupied. Both policies and institutions can and should be assessed by second-order theories: part of their distinctive contribution is that they transcend the conventional distinctions between policy and institution, and their relatives, substance and process, outcomes and procedures. Hardin may not think that the contribution of second-order theories is so important because he is committed to a particular first-order theory, utilitarianism, which in his view provides the right answer to moral *and* political questions—if not of policy, then of institutional design. If one thinks that utilitarianism (or any other substantive moral theory) has the right answer or even the right method of reaching the answer, then one will not consider persistent moral disagreement a serious theoretical problem. What will count is designing the right institutions, the ones that best maximize the right policy outcomes. As Hardin writes: "First create institutions accord-ing to how they can accommodate whatever normative principle drives us. And then we let them run."

Hardin invokes Hobbes in support of this view, but Hobbes gave a sub-stantive argument for *his* normative principle, a logically brilliant but morally flawed argument that would authorize absolute power for the sovereign. On Hobbes's account, any policy endorsed by the sovereign turns out to be moral by definition because the sovereign defines morality. The justification for the sovereign's doing so is the overriding value of maintaining order. Hardin evidently does not accept all of Hobbes's premises or his conclusion, but he does not provide the substantive arguments that, within the formal structure of a Hobbesian argument, take us to democratic conclusions.

Hardin's view, in contrast to Hobbes's, begs the hard questions. How should policies and institutions be distinguished? If capital punishment is an institution (as Hardin suggests), then almost all the moral controversies we discuss in *Democracy and Disagreement*—such as those about health care, welfare, taxation, electoral districting, and education—should count as institutions. (They should therefore also be regarded, in the terms of Rawls's theory of justice, as part of the basic structure of society.) However the distinction is drawn, why should a political theory consider only institutions and not policies and decisions? If Hitler (Hardin's infelicitous example) had received a slightly larger proportion of the vote in Weimar Germany and therefore had won office without staging a coup, does Hardin really think a democratic political theory should criticize the result only if it could show that no other set of institutions would have prevented Hitler's rise to power? (This surely would be what Bernard Williams, in another context, calls having one thought too many.) Our theory, and we assume any adequate democratic theory, has the resources for criticizing the authority of a Hitler. Deliberative democracy is certainly not a mere method or procedure but includes explicit protections of basic liberties and opportunities. Deliberative democrats do not seek a sovereign, absolute or otherwise, and do not claim sovereignty for themselves, absolute or otherwise.

The Limits of Deliberation

The second group of commentators agrees that moral conflict in politics merits a moral response, and that deliberative democracy provides an appropriate one. In our own response, we develop and strengthen a conception of deliberative democracy that we hope these commentators can share. Some of them extend deliberation further than we think it can or should go. In exploring our differences, we expose the limits of deliberation.

The Economy of Moral Disagreement (Sunstein)

If citizens seek what we call an economy of moral disagreement, they will search for significant points of convergence between their own moral understandings and those of the citizens whose positions, taken in their more comprehensive forms, they reject. They will seek the rationale for a law or public policy that minimizes rejection of the position they oppose. Cass Sunstein, who has helped us appreciate the importance of this principle, has developed it further through his idea of "incompletely theorized agreements." These are agreements that result from convergence on specific analogies and particular rules rather than on any consensus on philosophical ideals or general principles. Such agreements are especially appropriate ways for courts to deal with disagreements, he believes, but may also be useful for many other multimember decision-making bodies.

Sunstein has almost completely theorized incompletely theorized agreement. We would add only two qualifications. The first is that there should not be any presumption in favor of seeking agreement at lower rather than higher levels of abstraction. An economy of moral disagreement can be sought and found at any level. The agreement on abstract principles is often not explicit but may nonetheless be essential. Judges and legislators conduct their arguments within a framework that presupposes certain abstract principles, such as equal protection under the law. These principles may not determine any particular result, but they can frame the debate and influence the outcome in significant ways. Focusing on agreement about particulars risks neglecting the value of this consensus on more general constitutional principles, which can help judges and legislators resolve their disagreements in particular cases or at least narrow the range of their disagreements.

The second qualification concerns what an economy of moral disagreement recommends. It should not be understood as precluding or even discouraging vigorous challenges to the strong convictions of one's fellow citizens when they are necessary to make a moral case for one's own position. Economizing on moral disagreement does not call on citizens to seek agreement per se, only agreement consistent with their own fundamental principles. Citizens should try to accommodate the moral convictions of their opponents to the greatest extent possible without compromising their own moral convictions. Martin Luther King Jr. certainly challenged the deepest convictions of committed racists, but he did so consistently with economizing on moral disagreement. In some cases, the economizing process may sharpen the disagreement that remains, but it will usually also narrow it. The remaining disagreement, thus narrowed, may then become easier to resolve in the future. But even if it becomes more intense, the agreement that the process produces on related issues provides a basis for future cooperation among citizens who would otherwise have stood in stable opposition.

Sunstein is no doubt right that citizens may reasonably disagree about what we call the content principles and what laws and policies they imply. The specific substance of the content principles is contestable. (In our reply to Wertheimer below, we consider the consequences of extending deliberation in this way.) But we also think that without content principles such as liberty and opportunity, a conception of deliberative democracy is morally incomplete. Its constitution could be reasonably rejected by the citizens who are bound by it.

Just Democracy? (Young)

Like Sunstein, Iris Marion Young wants to keep principles of justice (liberty and opportunity) outside a conception of deliberative democracy. She endorses our content principles (as may Sunstein) and would like to "persuade everyone" to accept all six of our principles. The substantive difference between her view, Sunstein's, and ours therefore seems slight. Deliberative democracy itself, we think, should include principles of liberty and opportunity in order to avoid its reasonable rejection by the people who are bound by its constitution. Basic liberty and opportunity cannot themselves be derived from other principles of deliberative democracy. It is true that the principles of liberty and opportunity specify only partially and provisionally in advance what justice requires of democracy. But this is not because deliberative democracy excludes general principles of justice but rather because in advance of actual deliberation, it cannot specify completely what they require.

Nonetheless, Young is right to warn about a potential danger of including liberty and opportunity as part of the conception of deliberative democracy: "We should not have to wait for a societywide commitment to basic opportunity in order to have a degree of deliberative democracy that can give moral legitimacy to many political outcomes." We agree. But we also think Young should agree with us that the circumstances under which deliberation takes place should make a moral difference in how one assesses the legitimacy of both deliberation and its outcomes. She presumably believes that at least some of the "unjust inequalities and wrongful socially caused constraints" to which she points diminish the legitimacy. No doubt she would agree that the only acceptable way to overcome these injustices is by "democratic means." Yet these democratic means are not sufficient for justifying legislative ends, in the absence of at least some minimal satisfaction of the claims of liberty and opportunity. Citizens can reasonably doubt whether laws aiming to reduce injustice actually do so if they are made under conditions in which personal integrity is systematically threatened, even if the process is otherwise properly deliberative.

Partly in response to the problem of inequality, Young proposes the addition of another principle—"inclusion"—which requires that "all interests, opinions and perspectives present in the polity are included in the deliberations." This principle responds to a problem that is created by separating justice from democracy. Our conception does not need an inclusion principle because it already incorporates the basic values of inclusion in the principles of reciprocity, liberty, and opportunity. This is why the practical implications of our theory, even without such a principle, coincide with hers, as do our assessments of the welfare reform debate.

Young argues that "a deliberative procedure is legitimate only if" it satisfies her inclusion principle. This way of conceiving deliberative democracy, though compatible with ours, is vulnerable, we suspect, to the same kind of danger she sees in constraining deliberative democracy by principles of liberty and opportunity. Turning her concern against her own principle of inclusion, we could say that we should not have to wait for a societywide commitment to complete inclusion in order to regard as justified some political outcomes produced by a deliberative process that is not adequately inclusive. Deliberative justification should be understood as a continuous rather than a threshold property. It is a matter of "more or less," not "all or nothing." Justifications of this kind are no more (or less) separable from considerations of liberty and opportunity than from considerations of reciprocity, accountability, and publicity.

The Priority of Deliberation (Knight)

Knight believes that deliberative democracy should include substantive principles such as liberty and opportunity, but he thinks it needs no other values beyond deliberation itself in order to justify these principles. He also believes that deliberation has absolute priority over these nonprocedural principles. Knight is right that a more purely procedural conception of deliberation than ours "can go a long way toward guaranteeing the substantive values of liberty and opportunity" that we seek. But it does so at the price of packing too much value into democratic procedures and taking too much independent value out of individual liberties and opportunities. Democratic procedures do not necessarily require, for example, the extent of religious freedom guaranteed by the Constitution. But (as Galston points out) there is a publicly defensible value of religious freedom, quite apart from its role as a precondition of procedural justice. Something similar can be said for other substantive values, such as the fair opportunity to compete for highly prized (but relatively low-paid) jobs in society. Many people reasonably care about such liberties and opportunities independently of whether they are the result of a fully deliberative democracy. Knight's more purely procedural conception does not respect the independent value that most citizens understandably attribute to liberty and opportunity.

But Knight asks: if we do not see the substantive constraints as "derivative of the procedural requirements" or as "implied by the procedural dictates of the democratic process," how can we justify them? We rely in large part on the principle of reciprocity, which is not a purely procedural value. Knight agrees that a reciprocal perspective for resolving moral conflicts must make room for moral judgments not only of procedures but also of outcomes, but he takes this idea to mean that the relevant substantive values must be derived only from procedural ones.

A reciprocal perspective is both procedural and substantive and therefore equally capable of comprehending the principled conditions (reciprocity, publicity, and accountability) and the principled content (basic liberty, basic opportunity, and fair opportunity) of deliberative democracy. When we argue that the content of the liberty and opportunity principles is *partly* determined by democratic deliberation itself, Knight interprets us as claiming that "the content of the liberty and opportunity constraints *is determined* by deliberation itself." When we say that deliberation is *a* source of the legitimacy of collective decisions, Knight takes us to be arguing that "deliberation is *the* source of the legitimacy of collective decisions." Because he is so committed to giving priority to the process of deliberation, he neglects the possibility of the dynamic interaction between the conditions and content that our theory emphasizes.

We justify basic liberty, basic opportunity, and fair opportunity, first and foremost, on their own terms by identifying core convictions illustrated by paradigmatic cases (for example, prohibiting forcible removal of organs) to which no one would reasonably object. Then, by analogy and other forms of reasoning, we try to thicken and extend the principles to apply to more controversial cases. This is also how much of actual political deliberation proceeds.

Deliberative democracy expresses a bootstrap conception of the political process: The conditions that define the process pull themselves up by means of the process itself, and the content that is partly determined by the process in turn constrains the process itself. This self-defining capacity is paradoxical only if one mistakenly assumes that all the conditions or all the content of deliberation are challenged at the same time or in the same way. At any particular time, some of the "constitution" of deliberative democracy remains fixed.

Knight denies that our "content constraints are a necessary feature of an adequate account of deliberation," because they might be (reasonably) rejected by "a functioning constitutional deliberative democracy." Certainly, what we take to be the correct understanding of the liberty and opportunity principles may be mistaken. We also take the results of a deliberative process to be relevant in deciding whether they are. But what Knight neglects is that a precisely parallel argument can be made about procedural principles. Procedural principles may also be rejected by a functioning constitutional deliberative democracy (and so may a purely procedural conception of deliberative democracy). Pure proceduralists do not have access to some moral basis, which our conception lacks, on which to claim that the procedural constraints they recommend for a constitutional deliberative democracy are correct or authoritative. Their rejection by a functioning deliberative democracy could also provide some reason to doubt their validity. But in both cases, rejection (or acceptance) in a deliberative process alone cannot suffice to show that the principles are morally wrong (or right).

The notion that deliberation alone determines the morality of its results comes perilously close to deliberative narcissism. It suggests that as far as independent or intrinsic moral value is concerned, democratic deliberation is ultimately about nothing but the value of deliberation itself. Our conception accords the principles of deliberative democracy value independent from deliberation itself, while also recognizing that well-conducted deliberation is necessary to help interpret and specify those principles so that they are sufficiently justifiable and therefore mutually acceptable to the people who are bound by them.

Deliberation All the Way Down (Wertheimer)

Alan Wertheimer asks: why should one "want to accommodate a position that strikes one as clearly wrong . . . even if it meets the standard of minimal plausibility . . . [and even if] one should want to accommodate the person who holds that view"? There is an important ambiguity in Wertheimer's premise that the position is "clearly wrong." We do not argue for accommodating a position that one thinks is clearly wrong if this means that one has good reason to think that it lacks any significant value. But many positions that citizens reasonably regard as wrong contain important values that they can promote without compromising their own moral position.

We should have distinguished more clearly between the positive case of finding grounds of moral accommodation with similarly motivated political adversaries and the negative case of reaching compromises that undermine one's fundamental principles. A positive example of moral accommodation would be an alliance of pro-choice and pro-life advocates to promote a program that supports poor teenage mothers who want to carry their fetuses to term. Neither side is compromising its basic moral principles, although pro-choice advocates may be giving this program higher priority than they would otherwise. A negative example of moral accommodation would be a compromise in which pro-choice advocates support the Hyde Amendment, which denies federal funds to poor women to have abortions (except in cases of rape or incest or to save the mother's life), while pro-life advocates accept the legalization of abortion. In such a compromise, both sides act in a selectively unfair way by the lights of their own convictions by making abortion legal but unfunded. Pro-choice advocates abandon poor women who cannot afford an abortion, and pro-life advocates advantage rich women who can.

To sustain the positive kind of moral accommodation, citizens on one side must recognize that the position of those on the other side cannot be reasonably rejected. But Wertheimer argues that citizens may reasonably disagree not only about the moral status but also about the plausibility of a position, such as the idea that the fetus is a human life and therefore has rights. Although the idea that the fetus is a person at the moment of conception or at very early stages may be moral, according to Wertheimer, it is not plausible.

This example does not help prove Wertheimer's point. Pro-life advocates do not mean to say that the fetus is a person who possesses prior sentience and consciousness. They generally hold only that even at very early stages the fetus is a human life, a position many people find plausible (and we suspect that Wertheimer does too). For pro-life advocates, this status (and its projected natural development into a person if it is not killed) is sufficient to establish its claim for some basic rights.

Deliberative democrats have no special access to moral truth and no special authority to impose their own judgments about moral truth on other people by means of laws and policies. Like everyone else, they have to offer reasons, which can be assessed by the citizens who are bound by them. When in *Democracy and Disagreement* we conclude that a certain policy or a certain interpretation of a basic principle is beyond deliberative disagreement, we accept that *this* conclusion is open to the same challenge. We arrive at these provisional judgments on the basis of our own reasoning, but we draw on arguments from actual political discourse and also acknowledge that our own arguments, suitably translated, would have to be tested in political forums.

A neutral position on the issues that give rise to disputes about deliberative disagreements is impossible. A defense of discrimination against African Americans either is or is not a matter of deliberative disagreement. We argue that it is not. We may be wrong, but it would take a substantive moral argument to demonstrate that we are wrong. Whether a position is a deliberative disagreement, furthermore, may be a matter of degree; or, more precisely, the confidence one should have in the conclusion may be a matter of degree.

Deliberation is no substitute for voting, and voting no substitute for deliberation. But together, as Wertheimer helpfully shows, they constitute a morally powerful combination for justifying laws and policies democratically. We should have devoted more attention to defending the moral power of this combination, but we accept Wertheimer's extension of the theory on this point. He adds importantly to our argument that a majority vote alone cannot justify a decision as being substantively correct: "If the majority vote comes on the heels of a deliberative discussion, it may do a lot to legitimate a decision—whether or not basic liberties or opportunities are at stake."

Wertheimer worries that "reasonable people can ... disagree about whether they have done enough deliberation and whether it has been done with appropriate attention to the relevant values." But claiming that there has not been enough deliberation should not be confused with challenging the legitimacy of deliberation. There is certainly broad scope for reasonable disagreement about how much deliberation is precisely enough and whether a particular instance of deliberation is as good as it can be. But "precisely enough" and "as good as it can be" are ideal standards, and failing to meet them does not render the results of a deliberative process illegitimate.

It is logically possible, as Wertheimer speculates, that "there may be reasonable disagreement all the way down." But until someone actually shows that a deliberative agreement or disagreement *at whatever level* is illegitimate, there is no reason to believe it to be so. This is because democratic decision-making includes actual arguments, not just hypothetical or logically possible arguments. It therefore takes actual arguments, not just possible arguments, to defeat the claim of legitimacy of an actual decision in a deliberative democracy.

Respecting Positions or Respecting Persons (George)

Robert George denies what Wertheimer affirms: citizens should respect some moral positions they reasonably find implausible. Both use the same example, but they arrive at opposite conclusions. The example, not surprisingly, is abortion. Whereas Wertheimer finds the pro-life position implausible but respects it as a moral position, George finds the pro-choice position implausible and does not respect it as a moral position. However, both agree with the implication of our reciprocity principle that citizens should respect reasonable people who hold an unreasonable position on a particular issue, even one as important as abortion.

Why does reciprocity call for respect of persons even in the face of unreasonable disagreement? George's answer is that reasonable people who are doing their best to think through a moral question deserve respect for their goodwill even when they are defending a view that is (as far as their political adversaries can discern) unreasonable: "This mutual respect among citizens has intrinsic as well as instrumental value." The intrinsic value is the expression of respect for your fellow citizens who are similarly motivated to find fair terms of social cooperation, even when their search leads them to defend a position that you find unreasonable. The instrumental value is that such expression not only generally helps maintain social peace but also encourages a productive search over time for fair terms of social cooperation. As George writes, reciprocity is "what might be called a 'common good' of the political community, a mutual moral benefit to all concerned, even (or perhaps especially) when people find themselves in irresolvable disagreement over fundamental moral issues."

We welcome George's elaboration of our general perspective on reciprocity and its requirements of mutual respect, but we have reservations about two specific parts of his argument. First, we are concerned that George leaves too little room for respecting moral positions with which one disagrees. His view seems not to allow for the possibility, familiar enough even in actual moral and political debate, that one may see some moral merit in a position with which one deeply disagrees. The bases on which citizens reject positions with which they disagree vary considerably, and the implications for how they regard the position should similarly vary. Varying degrees and kinds of respect or disrespect are due, depending on whether one is rejecting a position that is less morally justified than one's own, as well justified, or not morally justified at all.

Because he does not see any basis for reasonable disagreement about the core issues on the abortion question, the case that we take as a paradigm, George may be reluctant to accept our view that competing moral positions can merit respect. George believes not only that the pro-choice position is morally wrong but also that our position that the pro-choice position is reasonable is wrong. But our position is not that both sides in the dispute are "rationally deadlocked." It is that they both fall within the range of reasonable disagreement. This position is admittedly controversial. But it is not "just one controversial view among a range of controversial views about abortion." It stands on a different logical level than the pro-choice view, the pro-life view, and the view that the two sides are rationally deadlocked. The proof that it stands on a different level is that one can consistently hold the view that there is reasonable disagreement along with any one of the other views, but one cannot consistently hold any two of the other views.

As George recognizes, we take seriously the strongest arguments advanced by pro-life thinkers, including a version of some that George himself presents in his commentary. We would accept his view that the growth of the fetus to infant is "concretely . . . some being's natural development from the fetal stage of its life into its infancy." The "unitary substance" is a human being, and its development, if allowed to go forward, would be "the life of a particular human being." But all of this (and more) that George presents so well does not establish the basis for a knockdown argument against the strongest version of a pro-choice position. Pro-choice advocates do not need to dispute these claims. They need only question the extent to which constitutional rights should be granted to a human being that has no existing or prior sentience or consciousness and is dependent for developing sentience and consciousness on the continuing support of a pregnant woman, who is the subject of the full range of constitutional rights.

On many disagreements, especially reasonable ones, people will not change their minds, no matter how respectfully they deliberate with their opponents. If citizens still defend the same position with which they began, what difference does it make if they regard their opponents' positions as morally reasonable? This thicker kind of respect encourages citizens to consider their opponents' positions on their merits, rather than to try to explain them as products of unfavorable conditions such as impaired judgment, misguided motives, or cultural influences. Such an attitude is more conducive to appreciating that even benevolent and intelligent but fallible people are likely to disagree on such morally difficult matters as abortion, capital punishment, affirmative action, and health care reform. Moreover, considering positions on their merits generally provides a stronger basis for respect for *persons* than explaining positions as a product of unfavorable conditions. Certainly, some disagreements are the result of such conditions, and when a position can be shown to be justifiable mainly from a perspective that depends on such conditions, mutual respect (of both persons and positions) does not prevent, and may require, that the critics of the position point out its defective origins. But in the absence of a specific showing of this kind, the presumption of respectful deliberation is that positions should be challenged on their merits.

The second reservation we have about George's argument concerns the analogy he draws between defending a pro-choice view on abortion today and defending a proslavery view before abolition. He regards this as a test case for showing how and why it is possible to respect persons who hold a morally abhorrent position. Just as some proslavery advocates may have deserved respect in the past, he argues, so some pro-choice advocates may deserve respect now. We are not so confident as he seems to be that proslavery advocates should have been treated with respect at any time in history. But to maintain that they should have would surely require showing that, under the particular historical circumstances, they had reasonable grounds for holding the *position* they did. Perhaps that is what George also has in mind when he refers to the "prevalent cultural conditions" that kept reasonable persons from seeing that slavery was an intolerable evil. But if so, the analogy does not serve well to support George's view that pro-life advocates should respect their pro-choice opponents. The implication of the analogy in this case is that the judgment of pro-choice advocates is impaired, if not by "prejudice, self-interest, pseudoscience," then by some other serious defect of reason or will. This does not seem a very propitious basis for grounding mutual respect.

We doubt that the analogy with slavery will be helpful to either side in this (or similar) contemporary controversies. Pro-life advocates may well "hope and pray" that people "will look back on the era of abortion on demand the way we now look back on the era of chattel slavery." But so may pro-choice advocates hope (and some may even pray) that everyone eventually will come to see the moral similarities between denying women the right to an abortion and enslaving them. Imagining the time in the future when one's argument might win the day does not add anything to the strength of one's argument in the present.

Instituting Deliberative Democracy (Daniels)

In *Democracy and Disagreement*, we argue that the principles and practices of deliberative democracy should be extended broadly throughout what we call "middle democracy." Norman Daniels effectively pursues that project in one important area of social life by constructing, as he puts it, an addition to the house we built in *Democracy and Disagreement*. His application of the principles of deliberative democracy to managed care organizations shows how such principles may be used to evaluate the practices of other kinds of nongovernmental institutions. More specifically, he demonstrates how the principles of reciprocity and publicity apply to debates about health care, and he adapts the principle of accountability to a nongovernmental organization. These are useful additions.

But does our house have an adequate foundation? Daniels thinks Rawls's theory of justice provides a more solid foundation (although in his own analysis Daniels never invokes any claim specific to Rawls's theory). He argues that to support the principles of liberty and opportunity (which constitute the content of deliberative democracy), we need a theory of justice, and that we should and in fact do rely on Rawls's theory. As we indicated earlier in our replies to Young and Knight, the constitution of our deliberative democracy includes principles of justice. Furthermore, we assume that Rawls's moral arguments (along with others, including ours) support an overlapping consensus that helps justify deliberative democracy.

However, we criticize a more specific claim, often assumed to be implied by Rawls's earlier views, that constitutional principles should be immune from revision in the deliberative politics of "middle democracy." The deliberative process on the view we oppose is only a means for elaborating the implications of constitutional principles that result from a prior thought experiment, like that of the original position. Because the thought experiment is prior to actual democratic deliberation, the principles themselves—as distinct from their practical implications—are protected from political deliberations.

On our conception, the basic principles of justice should be subject to revision in the deliberative process. Even if the principles are regarded as part of the foundation of deliberative democracy, their basic content is still contestable. To try to define the constitution of deliberative democracy in terms of only one of several competing theories of justice is to evade a central problem of politics to which a democratic theory is supposed to supply an answer—how to secure morally justified decisions in the absence of agreement on foundational principles of the kind defended in most theories of justice. (That is why Rawls's later political liberalism is more consistent with our conception than his earlier comprehensive theory of justice.)

Does justifying laws to the citizens who are bound by them always require that one give only reasons that one's opponents can fully accept? To get a deliberative democracy going and keep it going, most citizens must accept both some general notion of reciprocity and some of its implications. They must accept that they owe one another reciprocally acceptable reasons and that those reasons create some obligations of the kind (not necessarily exactly the content) of our basic liberty principle. With respect to any particular law or policy, however, acceptance may be more attenuated. Indeed, attenuated acceptance is all that citizens should reasonably seek in the case of what we call deliberative disagreements. In these situations, citizens "share" reasons in the sense that the reasons are generally accessible, relevant to the issue in dispute, and defensible as moral considerations (not necessarily overriding ones) even to those who oppose the position in question. Citizens certainly do not have to agree on which reasons are the most important considerations, or how relevant reasons are to be weighed.

As Daniels recognizes, the requirements of reason-giving implied by our principles of reciprocity, publicity, and accountability have implications for the design of institutions. We agree with Daniels that more attention should be paid to "institutional function and design," and we think his commentary represents another step toward that end. Especially welcome is his analysis of four conditions (which roughly follow our condition principles) by which managed care organizations should be assessed. But he concentrates more on specifying those four conditions than on comparing how well they are satisfied by various alternative institutional designs.

Although in *Democracy and Disagreement* we do not ourselves provide such comparisons, we suggest both some criteria to guide the design of institutions and some proposals for institutional change. The most important criteria are based on the implications of the continuity of theory and practice we describe in the book's conclusion (358–60). The basic idea is to try to design institutions so that they all have adequate opportunities for deliberation. Since many of the nineteen specific proposals for realizing this idea are scattered throughout the book, it is worth mentioning some of the most important ones.

Legislative institutions should offer more opportunities, and establish more requirements, for providing reciprocal reasons for laws and policies. Although the reasons that individual legislators give may not constitute a coherent justification for the legislation, they could help citizens better understand its basis and enable them better to hold individual legislators accountable. On a quite different approach but with a similar aim, we suggest that a system of multimember districts could strengthen the inclination of legislators to give reciprocal reasons. Administrators too should give reasons (as administrative law already emphasizes), but we would extend this duty to requiring such officials to issue impact statements, similar to those required now of environmental agencies, on a wider variety of policies. More generally, institutions should encourage what we call "reiterative" deliberation: a sequential consideration of proposals in which citizens and officials have multiple opportunities for criticism, revision, and reconsideration.

Publicity also has institutional implications, and not always in favor of more openness, as one might expect. Because secrecy is required to protect the privacy or security of individuals, a publicity principle stipulates that information in some cases should be released in statistical rather than individual form and therefore implies, for example, that public affairs agencies should have the capacity for collecting and disseminating such information. For those institutions that cannot function without high degrees of secrecy, we suggest some institutional devices to secure either prior or retrospective accountability. Despite its evident defects, the process to develop health care priorities in Oregon was reiterative in this way.

Accountability has quite radical institutional implications. If representatives are accountable to their moral constituents as well as their electoral constituents, deliberative democracy should create forums in which representatives of citizens of foreign countries could present their claims and respond to the counterclaims of our legislators. Moral constituents include not only citizens of other countries but also unborn citizens. Changes in tax laws and lobbying requirements could increase the incentives for citizens to organize groups that speak for future generations. Institutions should also be designed in such a way that poor and otherwise disadvantaged citizens have an effective opportunity to be involved in those policymaking areas—such as welfare reform— that most directly affect their lives.

To promote an economy of moral disagreement, we suggest promoting broad-based political organizations that encourage citizens who hold different moral positions to work together on other causes whose goals they share. Public schools should be designed so that they develop students' capacities to understand different perspectives, communicate their understandings to other people, and engage in the give-and-take of moral argument with a view to making mutually acceptable decisions.

Everyday Talk (Mansbridge)

How far should deliberative values and principles extend beyond the political institutions that we discuss in *Democracy and Disagreement*? Jane Mansbridge argues that deliberative values apply well beyond what is ordinarily understood as political life, even beyond the institutions of the kind in which Daniels is interested. "Everyday talk," Mansbridge writes, is "a crucial part of the full deliberative system that democracies need if citizens are . . . to rule them-selves." She does not think all everyday talk is part of the deliberative system, only talk that is "political" in the sense of being intentionally directed to issues that the public should discuss and possibly act upon. And not all deliberative principles fully apply even to everyday talk that is political in this sense. The woman who calls her husband a male chauvinist is not to be judged by the standards of accountability or publicity.

But even if some everyday talk should be part of the deliberative system, we still need to know whether it should be judged by the same principles of deliberative democracy that govern the ordinary political forums. Mansbridge thinks that the principles should apply, though in a substantially modified form. The standard of reciprocity requires less modification than accounta-bility and publicity, "only a shift in emphasis" when applied to everyday talk. She does not actually say much about how the principles should be modified, but she does insist that their requirement of mutual justification should be retained.

"When a woman calls a man a 'male chauvinist,' " she writes, it is "a recognizable step in a process of mutual justification, a step in an ongoing dialogue over what should be considered just in the relations between men and women." This is a plausible interpretation of the specific example, but should we generalize it so that all everyday political talk is regarded as part of a process of mutual justification? Everyday talk of this sort often has many different purposes, only some of which are intended to influence political decisions that bind people with whom one does not have any other relation-ship. Other purposes, such as seeking to change the attitudes and conduct of one's spouse and children, may call for different standards, not necessarily less stringent but more specific to the individuals involved.

Nevertheless, everyday talk can serve two important political purposes. The first is to challenge conventional assumptions of everyday life, such as the subordinate role of women. Calling one's husband a male chauvinist can serve the initially quite local purpose of criticizing the traditional role that he has been socialized to play within the family. Mansbridge's examples tend to high-light this critical function of everyday talk. Including such talk in the delib-erative system expands the repertoire of resources for change in private life. The changes may of course eventually affect public life by enhancing the liberties and opportunities of citizens in all spheres of politics.

The second purpose is political in the familiar sense. Everyday talk can directly or indirectly contribute to conventional political deliberations. Social movements, such as feminism, encourage new kinds of everyday talk that challenge and thereby help change conventional politics. To the extent the ordinary talk transforms wider political talk, it can open the deliberative agenda up to issues such as gender relationships, issues that were once considered private. Mansbridge's examples (and some of her own previous work) point to this connection between social movements, everyday talk, and conventional politics.

Deliberative politics works best when it is not experienced as an alien world by ordinary citizens. Some substantial continuity between everyday talk and political talk is therefore desirable. While broadening the deliberative system, we should still distinguish between talk that is directed toward producing publicly binding decisions that claim authority (backed by force) over many people in whose name they are made and talk that is intended to influence private relationships. This distinction raises the stakes of justification in politics. Maintaining a distinction between these kinds of talk also enables one to see more clearly the interaction between public and private power. The self-identified conservative woman who calls her husband a male chauvinist in private benefits from debates about gender equality that have taken place in public. The private everyday talk of this woman (and many others like her) in turn expands the influence of feminism in the public sphere.

Another reason to maintain the distinction is to ensure that those officials and citizens who have power over other people with whom they have no other relationship are held to standards that are publicly and generally accessible. In more personal relationships, the individuals may legitimately prefer standards more closely tailored to their own character and circumstances and may allow for talk that serves a wider variety of purposes. More generally, the closer the aims of everyday talk coincide with the aims of ordinary politics, the more subject it should be to the full force of the principles of deliberative democracy.

Implications for Democratic Theory

Deliberative democracy supplements rather than supplants the procedural and constitutional values of conventional theories of democracy. Proceduralists assume that if citizens agree on some basic rules of the game, most of the moral disagreement can be removed from the political agenda, and what remains can be left to political bargaining. Constitutionalists assume that citizens agree on fundamental moral values, which can be insulated from the pressures of ordinary politics, and that democratic theory needs to say no more about the moral disagreement that remains. For both, the important moral questions are assumed to be settled at the borders of ordinary democratic politics. But as issues ranging from funding health care in Oregon to legalizing abortion in the United States show, the moral disagreement that remains is much more pervasive and persistent than these theories assume. There are reasonable moral disagreements about what procedures democracy requires, what fundamental values citizens hold, and how both should be interpreted. These disagreements cannot be settled once and for all at the beginning of the procedural game or at the sidelines by impartial constitutional referees.

Our theory of deliberative democracy takes this moral disagreement seriously and puts it back into the center of democratic theory. In the book, we present many specific implications of taking moral disagreement seriously for the principles and practices of democracy. Here we suggest three general implications that concern democratic theory itself—its broader scope, provisional status, and limited autonomy.

Broader Scope

One of the most important implications is that democratic theorists, whether deliberative or not, need to find better ways to deal with the reasonable disagreement that is more pervasive and persistent than democratic theory traditionally acknowledges. The moral conflicts that arise in society, as well as the means of dealing with them, affect and are in turn affected by politics. Democratic theory must concern itself with civil society, as many theorists now recognize, but even more with the interaction between civil society and democratic processes, as few emphasize. Theorists should examine such questions as how social institutions such as families, schools, and health care organizations can create the capacities for dealing with disagreements, and how governments can help or hinder such processes.

Because disagreement will persist, democratic theorists should examine more systematically the principles and practices that enable citizens to live with it on moral terms. The agenda of democratic theory should give more attention to a wide range of ordinary political phenomena that can contribute to creating an economy of moral disagreement, such as moral compromise, multi-issue cooperation, coalition-building, and political civility. In defending policies on moral grounds, citizens who economize on moral disagreement seek the moral reasons that minimize rejection of the position they oppose. In this way, citizens manifest mutual respect as they continue to disagree about morally important issues on which they need to reach collective decisions. This does not mean that theorists should give up abstract principles, but it does imply that theorists should make room for less comprehensive justifications for laws and policies.

Provisional Status

Deliberative democracy expresses a dynamic conception of politics. As a result of deliberation, the principles and practices that are justified at any particular time may be revised and replaced by different principles and practices over time. This is why we emphasized throughout the book the provisional nature of not only the conclusions of deliberative processes but also the conclusions of our own interpretations of deliberative democracy. The principles themselves are subject to deliberative challenges. One principle can be revised deliberatively while holding the others constant, or several of the principles can be reinterpreted by applying them in a different context or at different times. Oregon citizens could disagree about the precise content of basic opportunity (exactly which health care services it includes) while agreeing that the claim has some content and should take priority over claims to less basic goods. They could conduct their deliberation within a framework that assumed some basic opportunities, even while the complete content of that opportunity remained unspecified.

The capacity of deliberative democracy to encourage changes in its own meaning over time is one of its most important virtues. It supports a democratic process that is more likely to be self-correcting—open to changes in moral understanding and to new sources of moral conflict as well as new resources for dealing with such conflict. For all its imperfections, the reiterative process in Oregon produced more justifiable results than the judgment of expert decision-makers, in part because the conclusions at each stage of the more deliberative process were regarded as provisional. Moreover, this provisional status does not merely express some general sense of fallibility: it is specific to resolutions of deliberative disagreements in politics and carries implications for political practices and institutions.

Limited Autonomy

The distance between theory and practice is less in deliberative theories than in other theories of justice. Theory itself becomes subject to a practical test under certain conditions and, to this extent, is less autonomous than other theories are usually assumed to be. Recall our defense of basic opportunity as a deliberative principle and our argument that it requires funding more health care services for the poor than is provided by the Oregon Plan. Even if the principle and the conclusion we draw from it are correct, actual deliberation is still necessary.

How can we consistently insist that deliberation is necessary while affirming a conclusion that deliberation may not produce? After all, we reached the conclusion without engaging in much actual political deliberation. Simon sees a paradox here. On the one hand, if he accepts our arguments and conclusions, why should he bother calling for actual political deliberation? Just let Gutmann and Thompson decide. On the other hand, if he disagrees with our arguments and conclusions, then why accept the results of our simulated deliberations, which among other conclusions recommend more actual political deliberation?

We have not preempted deliberation by our substantive arguments, because we are not actually doing the deliberation (or even simulating it). Rather, we are drawing on deliberations that have taken place in politics, showing how they might be improved, suggesting how deliberation might be extended where it is now neglected, and identifying conditions under which deliberation might work better. We offer our arguments not as philosophical constraints on democratic politics but as moral contributions to democratic deliberation. They are based on actual claims already made in actual political debates and are rooted in principles of political morality and fragments of political theories implied by or contained in those debates.

Our substantive conclusions about principles and the policies they imply can be understood as normative hypotheses: given certain assumptions about reciprocity, citizens should accept certain principles and conclusions. The hypotheses are normative because they cannot be refuted simply by showing that someone (even a majority) in fact rejects our principles or conclusions. But they are still hypotheses because they may be refuted by showing that there are better arguments for competing principles or conclusions in the same context. Whether it be refutation or refinement, this kind of criticism can succeed only by subjecting rival arguments to the rigors of actual deliberation, allowing for the imperfections in the conditions of any actual deliberative process. (The more morally defensible the conditions, the better the deliberative test.)

Even under nonideal conditions, those who are convinced by our substantive conclusions about liberty and opportunity and the policies we recommend have the same reasons we have to favor deliberation to test the conclusions. And those who disagree with our conclusions must believe that they have better reasons and arguments on their side than we supply. They, too, should want to support deliberation in order to show that we are wrong.

Despite its expansive scope, its provisional conclusions, and its political dependency, deliberative theory is firmly committed to some central values. The idea of reciprocity, as we have emphasized, is fundamental to deliberative democracy and expresses a distinctive commitment. Affirming the value of reciprocity and related deliberative values is not simply asserting another morality. Deliberative democracy is offered as the morally best basis on which citizens who reasonably disagree *about* moralities can act collectively to make laws and policies. It provides a second-order moral perspective on first-order moral disagreements. The justification that deliberative principles need thus differs from the justifications typically offered for moral claims that do not take seriously the persistence of reasonable moral disagreement. Deliberative principles, which provide a basis on which those who morally disagree can cooperate, may be appropriately criticized only by proposing an alternative basis, not by simply reaffirming one of the moral claims that constitutes the reasonable disagreement.

Deliberative democracy is also committed to the possibility of moral justification in politics and therefore rejects approaches that base politics only on power. Some of these approaches are "closet" moral theories, because they assume that, substantively and procedurally, power-based politics is morally the best. Their assumptions can be assessed in moral terms, and in this respect (if not in their conclusions) these approaches may be reconciled with deliberative democracy. But those who reject any possibility of finding a common perspective for criticizing the distribution of power that happens to result from the play of politics are reduced to accepting the status quo, however unjust it may be, or to condemning it but in terms that (on their own view) their fellow citizens have no reason to accept. As we wrote in *Democracy and Disagreement*: "Those who would renounce moral reason are either trying to persuade the converted, or they are trying to reach the unreasonable. In the first case, their audience has no need, and in the second, no reason, to listen."

Like citizens in a deliberative democracy, deliberative theorists seek a common perspective by appealing to reasons that can be shared by their fellow theorists who are similarly motivated. Like citizens, theorists may fail either because their fellow theorists fail to appreciate their reasons, or because they fail themselves to present good reasons, or because a common perspective remains beyond the will or understanding anyone is capable of mustering at the present time. But by making democratic theory and practice more deliberative, all of us stand a better chance of resolving some of our theoretical and moral disagreements, and living with those that will inevitably persist, on terms that are as reciprocal as possible.

Note

1. See Amy Gutmann and Dennis Thompson, "Why Deliberative Democracy is Different," Social Philosophy & Policy (1999), v. 17, no. 1.

Index